Samuel Beckett's Wake
and Other Uncollected Prose

Also by Edward Dahlberg

Bottom Dogs

From Flushing to Calvary

Those Who Perish

Do These Bones Live (rev. *Can These Bones Live*)

The Flea of Sodom

The Sorrows of Priapus

Truth Is More Sacred (with Herbert Read)

Because I Was Flesh

Alms for Oblivion

Reasons of the Heart

Cipango's Hinder Door

The Leafless American

The Edward Dahlberg Reader (ed. Paul Carroll)

Epitaphs of Our Times

The Carnal Myth

The Confessions of Edward Dahlberg

The Olive of Minerva

Bottom Dogs, From Flushing to Calvary, Those Who Perish, and hitherto unpublished and uncollected works

*

The Gold of Ophir (ed. Edward Dahlberg)

Edward Dahlberg

Samuel Beckett's Wake
and Other Uncollected Prose

Edited with an Introduction by Steven Moore

Dalkey Archive Press

Library of Congress Cataloging in Publication Data
Dahlberg, Edward, 1900-1977.
  Samuel Beckett's wake and other uncollected prose / Edward Dahlberg;
  edited with an introduction by Steven Moore.
  Includes index.
  I. Moore, Steven, 1951-   . II. Title.
PS3507.A33S2 1989   818'.5209—dc20   89-7856
ISBN: 0-916583-42-2

First Edition

Partially funded by grants from The National Endowment for the Arts and
The Illinois Arts Council.

Dalkey Archive Press
1817 North 79th Avenue
Elmwood Park, IL 60635 USA

Contents

Introduction i

I *Essays and Longer Reviews*

Ariel in Caliban 3
Hunger on the March 9
Hitler's Power over Germany 16
Nightgown Riders of America 23
Waldo Frank and the Left. 29
Fascism and Writers 35
Randolph Bourne 44
Ford Madox Ford 56
Our Avant Garde Illiterates 67
Laurels for Borrowers. 75
Conrad Aiken. 84
Herbert Read 93
The Classics and the Man of Letters 100
Majorca. 108
Hart Crane 122
Beautiful Failures. 134
Return to Kansas City. 149
A Letter to *Prose*. 160
Old Masters 170
Ignorance and Malice at the *New*. 176
The Gold of Ophir 181

II *Shorter Reviews and Prefaces*

Roman Literature 201
Robert Cantwell 206
Erskine Caldwell 208
Lincoln Kirstein. 213
Down from the Ivory Tower. 215

James T. Farrell 217
From Flushing to Calvary 222
Kenneth Fearing: A Poet for Workers 226
Robert Smith 231
Giuseppe Berto 232
Charles Baudelaire 234
Algernon Blackwood 237
Mary McCarthy 239
Sören Kierkegaard 241
Fyodor Dostoevsky 243
Colonial Writers 246
John Donne 250
Ezra Pound 251
Tradition of Opulence 254
Paul Verlaine 257
Log Cabin Art 259
The Healing Word 261
Four Harvests 264
William Carlos Williams 276
D. H. Lawrence 279
Leo Tolstoy 284
Lewis Mumford 287
Henry James 290
George Ross Ridge 293

III *Fiction*

The Dream Life of Mary Moody 297
Graphophone Nickelodeon Days 306
Samuel Beckett's Wake 320

Index 325

Introduction

Steven Moore

The modern reaction against the impressionistic criticism of the Victorian era has escalated recently into an attempt to turn literary criticism into a science, appropriating a scientific objectivity and a critical vocabulary only a technician could love. At its worst, impressionistic criticism amounted to little more than the feelings that a work aroused in a critic; at its best, however, such criticism had force, personality, color, and the courage of its convictions—qualities lacking in most academic criticism today. One such impressionistic critic, the folklorist Gershon Legman, once declared, "I believe in a personal and intense style, and in making *value judgments.* This is unfashionable now, but it is the only responsible position."

Edward Dahlberg staked out just such a position in his critical essays, expressed in a personal, intense style modeled (in later years) after the exuberant prose styles of Elizabethan writers and seventeenth-century bibliomaniacs like Burton and Browne. A self-proclaimed Ishmael wandering the deserts outside the walls of academe, Dahlberg was neglected by critics most of his life. But during his (and the century's) sixties, he began receiving the appreciation so long overdue, beginning with a steady stream of appreciative reviews of the many books he published in that decade, and continuing with several book-length critical studies: Harold Billings edited a collection of appreciative essays on Dahlberg's work in 1968, Jonathan Williams followed with a festschrift in 1970, Fred Moramarco revised his dissertation as a Twayne book that came out in 1972, and Charles DeFanti published his biography of Dahlberg in 1978, the year after his subject's death. But since then,

Dahlberg has slipped back into neglect; aside from the occasional article in a scholarly journal, critical attention has wandered. This may be due partly to the backlash often visited upon writers once they die, consigning them to a purgatory until they are revived by a new generation of critics. It may also be due to a feeling that Dahlberg is not "politically correct," that he is too autocratic, phallocentric, sexist, reactionary, too insensitive for these sensitive times. Or the neglect may be due to a continued confusion as to what exactly to make of this outlandish writer with that extraordinary style and those genre-defying works. Add to this the sad fact that only a few of his many books remain in print and the case for neglect seems closed.

This collection seeks to reopen the case by displaying the full range of Dahlberg's literary abilities in shorter forms, from skillful reportage to imaginative essays, from proletarian fiction to inspired parody, from travel pieces and personal memoirs to historical studies, along with some of the most cantankerous book reviews ever published. The purpose here is to gather all of the shorter pieces that were left out of (or written after) his two earlier collections of essays, *Alms for Oblivion* (1964) and *The Leafless American* (1967, recently reissued by McPherson & Co.). These writings span Dahlberg's entire writing life. After publishing two immature pieces in the college magazine of the University of California at Berkeley (not reprinted here), Dahlberg amassed a great deal of manuscript material which he took with him when he left for Europe in 1926. There he found a sympathetic editor in Ethel Moorhead, as he recounts in "Beautiful Failures," who accepted enough of his material to fill nearly a fourth of the spring 1929 issue of her magazine *This Quarter.* Along with a few poems and the opening chapter of his first novel, *Bottom Dogs,* this issue contains the two earliest pieces in the present collection: "Ariel in Caliban," an aesthetic statement that would govern his writing style for a decade, and "The Dream Life of Mary

Moody," a story in his early naturalistic mode that was reprinted shortly after in the *Fortnightly Review*. Following Joyce's lead for reasons outlined in "Ariel in Caliban," Dahlberg soon produced the impressionistic collage "Graphophone Nickelodeon Days," intended for his second novel, *From Flushing to Calvary*, but never used after its 1931 appearance in *Pagany*.

On the strength of his first novel, Dahlberg found the pages of several political magazines open to him upon returning to America in 1929. During the next half-dozen years, he published a number of essays and reviews in the *New Republic*, the *Nation*, and the *New Masses*. Many of these dealt with proletarian writers, but in his essay on his own second novel (included herein) he disassociated himself from them, anticipating his later renunciation of his own work in that genre.

His reporting of the 1932 Washington hunger march, Hitler's growing power for the *New York Times* in 1933, and the fascist movements in America for the *New Masses* in 1934 give some indication of Dahlberg's political commitment in those years, culminating in 1935 with his role in organizing the Marxist American Writers' Congress, where he delivered his provocative paper "Fascism and Writers." But some measure of his growing disenchantment with the Marxist approach to literature is indicated by a dispute that occurred in 1934 at the founding of the *Partisan Review*. According to the account he wrote for his *Confessions* but later omitted—it was published in *Prose* instead and appears here as "Ignorance and Malice at the *New*"—Dahlberg and "Saul Hobinol" (Saul Funaroff, a communist writer) were selected as cofounders of the magazine, but he resigned after the editorial appointments of "Lob Miching and Cog Murrain" (Philip Rahv and William Phillips). Dahlberg was writing his anti-fascist novel *Those Who Perish* at that time, but within a few years he quit both the political and the publishing scenes in order to continue educating himself, to revise his aesthetic, and to forge a new style.

Aside from his early masterpiece *Do These Bones Live*

(1941), Dahlberg published no criticism in the fifteen years from 1935 to 1950, with two exceptions: in 1937 he published the first of many essays on Randolph Bourne, and in 1942 he contributed to a symposium in the *New Directions Annual* honoring Ford Madox Ford. In 1950, however, he returned to the literary world in a flurry of activity. In addition to publishing his enigmatic book of parables *The Flea of Sodom* that year, he began turning out reviews in rapid succession for *Tomorrow,* the *New York Times Book Review,* but mostly for John Chamberlain's ultraconservative periodical the *Freeman,* where Dahlberg had a regular column called "Second Harvest" until 1953. From that time on, he had little difficulty finding outlets for his essays, publishing in a variety of magazines and journals, and becoming a regular contributor in the 1970s to Coburn Britton's elegant but short-lived magazine *Prose.*

In the literary criticism that makes up the bulk of this collection, Dahlberg makes clear that he is less interested in form and technique than in an affirmative moral tone. He went to a book "looking for maxims and parables of benefit to our lives," for something "of fundamental importance to the spirit," but finds these qualities lacking in most modern fiction. "There is neither health nor sun in Faulkner," he complains, "and his readers are compelled to witness the spectacle of fetid, dying people who are dour and wicked. There is no wit, or good ripe bawd, in him as ease or balm for the suffering, ailing mind." Again and again in his reviews, Dahlberg asks "Is there no balm in Gilead?" as he surveys the works of writers who fail to provide any nurturing or wisdom for their readers. Instead, writers like "Frank Norris's successors, Faulkner, Hemingway, Caldwell, for all their avowed social purposes, are vandals who pour bile upon nature, the human seed, women." Although he shows grudging respect for Pound in his review of Pound's *Letters,* Dahlberg later wrote: "Pound's shibboleth, Make it New, is for the sham Gideon; I say, Make it Human."

Dahlberg ransacked world literature in search of "the healing word" which would ease "the suffering, ailing mind," and the fact that he found such words more often in myth and ancient literature than in modern fiction accounts for the learned, allusive style of his later essays. In the best of them he achieves the ideal set in his tribute to his friend Herbert Read: "The essay is an epistolary art, full of maxims and wise sayings, which, when well done, lead us to believe that we possess all the knowledge of great men, but none of their defects." Dahlberg had his share of defects, of course, and his work is "full of invectives, metropolitan irritations and heated diatribes" (as he said of Catullus), intent as he was on "sweep[ing] the dung out of the Augean stables of literature." Nor has he had many followers; among contemporary writers, only Alexander Theroux works successfully in Dahlberg's manner. Few readers today would affirm Dahlberg's radical vision of the literary canon, perhaps, but few readers will emerge from this ordeal of fire with their former views unsinged by the heat of his moral fervor.

*

These pieces were published in a variety of magazines with a variety of house styles. I have not hesitated to bring Dahlberg's punctuation into conformity with the *Chicago Manual of Style,* but I have hesitated to alter his own words. I have corrected a few slips—*The* to *An American Tragedy, Solitaria* for the Rozanov book Dahlberg consistently misspelled *Solitario* —but only such items that his original copyeditors should have caught. I've not corrected more idiosyncratic errors. For example, near the end of his essay on Kansas City, he characterizes his home town with Milton's "bokeless and museless," but near the beginning of the next essay he reverses it to "museless and bokeless." Actually, Milton wrote "museless and unbookish" (in the *Areopagitica*), but I've limited myself to using "bokeless" for both quotations since Dahlberg uses "boke" elsewhere. In the Pound review I've changed his "pinchback" to "pinchbeck" since that seems to be the word he intended (it's used in the Aiken review), but I've not tampered further with Dahlberg's splendidly archaic vocabulary. A few of the titles are my own: "Four Harvests" gathers four of his "Second Harvest" columns; "Old Masters" originally appeared simply as "Dahlberg on Dreiser, Anderson and Dahlberg"; and "Ignorance and Malice at the *New*" originally appeared as "Two Diatribes: The Second." ("The First" went into Dahlberg's *Confessions;* the essay entitled "Beautiful Failures" was also revised for inclusion into the *Confessions,* but this earlier version is fuller and interesting enough to warrant inclusion here as well.) Dahlberg always gave his editors a remarkably free rein when preparing his books for publication, so I trust he'll overlook these small liberties from whatever shade he now inhabits. Among the living, I would like to acknowledge the assistance and advice of Mr. Coburn Britton, Dahlberg's literary executor, and Mr. Harold Billings, without whose bibliography of Dahlberg's work this volume could not have been assembled.

I

Essays and Longer Reviews

Ariel in Caliban

Flaubert once said that an artist should look long and intently at an object until he could discover some shadow or line in it that had not been seen by any other one before reproducing it. Flaubert was possibly the first conscious poet of analogies. He deliberately set out to find curious juxtapositions and new color schemes. His aesthetic adventures were in some measure wider than those of Oscar Wilde. The latter, though extraordinarily elastic in his appreciation for form, was still a little too eclectic. Too many things disgusted him. He, who lived so fully in his dream world, did not realize the lyric possibilities of the commonplace. Only at moments did he sense the unreality of a wet street or a city gas lamp. In one of his light, intuitive moments he said that it had become quite middle class to admire a sunset. Mid-Victorians and badly dressed people did such things. He felt that the influence of modern painting, the poetry of planes and surfaces had made us less naïve in such matters. Too, perhaps other things have been happening that have put us on guard. We watch ourselves more closely than ever. No one now would write a pastoral. It would be ridiculous and seem very much affected. Mary Antoinette was quite right in conventionalizing Rousseau's return to nature. Life on a dairy farm whose settings and design had not been deliberate and which had not been contrived to create an effect would have been very sentimental and insincere. Here we find some of the first traces of the mechanical note in nature. Baudelaire understood this and with good reason preferred rouged women and metal trees. He realized that we had to have new scenic effects and more diabolical impressions. Nothing has contributed so much to this aesthetic of diablerie as modern industrialism.

The German UFA cinema productions are exploiting in full measure modern decorative art and cubistic architecture both of which have arisen out of the social and economic conditions of a life and nature thoroughly mechanized. In *Backstairs,* a film shown at the intimate Fifth Avenue Playhouse, the twisted stairway, the miniature windows, the misshapen, monastic walls, suggested a thwarted and warped soul. Had the settings been less restrained and subdued melodramatic sentimentality would have followed and the effect would have been spoiled. Whenever the thing or object reveals the symbol, drama follows, but when the symbol is made to personalize or isolate an emotion, sentimentality is the result. UFA's *Faust* was a dismal failure, because Mephistopheles was too obviously the biblical allegory of fire and brimstone and left the same unsatisfactory impression upon the audience as any colonnade which too manifestly incarnated carnality. In *Tillers of the Soil,* the protagonist, a young sculptor, was constantly actualizing in clay his ideas and, alas, exhibiting them to the cinematic spectators! Only an actor who was also a Brancusi could do such an audacious thing with impunity. The gestures of Henny Porten, the Anne Boleyn of *Henry the Eighth* and the maidservant in *Backstairs,* suggest a puppet—but a puppet bent and gnarled by suffering. Here, tragedy, in its true Greek sense has transmuted the face into a mask and the body, its twists and contortions, into a marionette—here, without directorial intervention, God, happily, no longer interferes without our dramas, tragedy becomes one of the Fates, standing apart from the actor whom he afflicts. Harry Langdon, in another way, has without conscious design rivalled the marionettes of the Grand Guignol in the Tuileries. His face, faunlike, his long swallow tail coat, his inelastic jerks and movements have bodied forth Bergson's theory of the comic. Too, there is another element upon which Bergson has not touched and that is the tragic suggested by the mechanical.

When Don Quixote sees the basin as a helmet, his perception

4

like the prismatic colors which a refraction of light produces, is born not of volition but of a cerebral illusion. Sancho Panza, like the American naïve realists of today, always perceives the barber's basin as a basin. James Joyce, unlike either Sancho Panza or Don Quixote, whose personality so impinges upon the object as to detect its sensuous relations to other experiences, views the barber's basin, without necessarily perverting its optical value, as an impression not separable from other fluid impressions. Such an expressionistic cosmos, perhaps paradoxically enough, is more in keeping with things as they really are.

James Joyce has done with ordinary Dublin what no artist has with the subway and surface cars of New York. He has found Ariel in Caliban. Joyce is the poet of smell, color and sound. He has a better stomach than Zola and a finer feeling for subtle analogies than Flaubert had. He has mingled perception and audition more sensuously than any of his Parisian predecessors. He is the most virile of all the neurotics. In his *Portrait of the Artist As a Young Man* a direct appeal is made to the olfactory sense which has long been neglected. Stephen Dedalus, a shadowy Joyce, tells us that no smell was repugnant to him. With him odors are always intensely suggestive and stirring. The smell of cedar wood, moist ashes, and the decomposed dampness of graveclothes cause the nerves to tremble. A mauve train of ideas and fugitive portraits arise from them and delicately etch themselves upon the brain. Dung, if not lovelier than the namby-pamby scent of lilac and acacia blossoms, has a more reminiscent appeal to modern experience. Joyce's writings are inferential and highly sensory. He excludes no phase of experience, and just because it is experience, it has an artistic value. Through Joyce we have possibly learned that in the end the Kubs of Paris will be more useful to life and letters than the French Academy.

Ulysses is not, as some one said, a satirization but an intense personalization of Dublin life. Like Coney Island where the scenic railway, the waxen figures lying in state, the merry-go-round which seems to move in a void and whose jangling music creates the illusion of a vacuum, like Noah's Ark in which the tragedy of machinery is bodied forth by an ingenious materialization of biblical symbols—like Hubert's Museum whose freaks and hermaphrodites by virtue of their unquestionable reality shadow forth an imaginary world, *Ulysses* with its pubs, brazen and golden barmaids, hoofbeats, the barang of the auctioneer's hammer, the rich Gaelic prose out of which arises Bloom's thoughts, Dublin becomes a mechanized and diabolical cosmos. Such an effort could never have been born of a satirical intent which only requires the employment of the dry intellect.

No one up to the present time has given us an impressionistic study of misshapen American cities. Sherwood Anderson, who understands in a sort of vague and unreflecting way the ugly power of death, knows nothing of its aesthetic relations to things. He does not personalize or diabolize them. His nature is too reportorial and has nothing of the grotesque that arises from artistic monism. The emotions and the objects upon which it impinges are too separable. Even in "Hands," an interesting flash from *Winesburg, Ohio* in which the schoolmaster no longer able to affectionately touch the little boys must beat his fists against fences and signboards in order to retain his entity and egotism as a person, he never enters into the life of these inanimate things. They never become an essential part of his own emotions. The conflict is purely psychological and social and never aesthetic or diabolical. Objects have no pictorial value for Sherwood Anderson and other American writers. They have not gone one step beyond the Russian novelists and in most instances they have neither their penetration nor their facility. There are no aesthetes in America. Poe was possibly the only one, but like the small literary group among whom is Paul Rosenfeld, they are entirely too provincial. They look toward the Midwest and not to the city for their

American novel. That is artistic myopia. Mr. Rosenfeld still writes English with a flourish and has an indefinite, optimistic idea that American art should be more social and standardized. Optimism in art is certainly a fault, for instead of expressing life in the States, it merely imitates it. Van Wyck Brooks's dejection though not essentially creative is more vital. But Mr. Brooks has not forged out of the fires of his sullenness or from his biographical studies a newer criticism of ugliness or form. He leaves us to despair with the dead. Let the dead take care of themselves. They are better fitted for it than we are. There are other things for us to do. Spingarn's *Creative Criticism,* a fine bit of Croceanism, does not solve our problems . . .

By some intrusive allusion, a dissonance, Dreiser destroys the illusion of impersonality he has created—the walks along Madison Avenue, the office buildings, Mr. Haymaker's veiled vagaries, like the pensive mist of Central Park West—this mood is gone. His repetitions, unlike Joyce's, are discords, not poetic motives. Sherwood Anderson is quite right. Dreiser never resorts to tricks or effects. His figures by the necessity of their own characters have in themselves the drama of inevitability. That which must be follows without any interference on the part of the writer. However, unlike the philosophic fatalism in *Jude the Obscure,* which is contrived, the sustained mood which arises out of it is not implicit in the unfolding of Dreiser's Americans. His characters are always breaking off with "and yet"—"or only"—this is highly suggestive if used with economy; but this psychological motive, not without the poetry of doubt and vacillation, is used excessively.

Colorless America has its own discords, tones and poetic possibilities. Chicago, Cleveland and San Francisco are lyric fragments. The lake air of Michigan Avenue, the Hydraulic Pressed Steel, the painted Chinese dolls in black silk pantaloons noiseless rustling through the throngs of Market Street—these are articulate ink stains on soft lemon-colored parchment paper. They are as fugitive impressions of the rue de Boetie.

7

The barber shop, with its odor of soap and hair tonics, the Paramount Building on Times Square with its tawdry lighting effects at night, the offices and hotels along Broadway, a cheap yellow and red symphonic surge in brick are just as artistically suggestive as the Chartres Cathedral or the cafés along the walk of the Montmartre.

The skyscraper has given us more shadows and a longer twilight. The light would no longer interest us if it did not streak the buildings and stain the pavements violet and blue. The city sidewalk, the glare of the taxi, its rhythmic glide, the desolation of an iron train shed, the dun smoke of Pittsburgh are more genuine poetic motives than poppies, oaks and blades of grass. For the artist in quest of moods, for the speculative mind interested in the comedy and mechanics of gestures the American Vaudeville Theater is a rich library. There, watching the puppet-like movements of the jiggers or contemplating the purple and green shadows cast on the curtains and settings by lighting reflectors, one may feel the unreality of New York life or sense the metaphysical pathos of color.

Everything is artifice and machinery. Below art you may find it, says Bergson. The city trees, become gaunt, have a mechanical aspect, and their leaves, appearing artificial, like the crystal flowers of Chanel, underneath the flare of the electric lamp, are made more miniature by smoke and the blue fumes of gasoline. The Chinese had a true philosophical understanding of nature when they conventionalized its objects. They are the forerunners of Baudelairean prose. The metaphysics which arise from machinery and mechanism has more aesthetic value than one which has its roots in naïve phenomena. Philosophy and art, like all physical processes, are ever becoming, and must of necessity move toward a nature with mechanical and industrial encrustations than return to one with a pastoral decor. These no longer have any decorative value either in prose or painting.

This Quarter, 1929

Hunger on the March

The Washington hunger march, though it produced no sensational results, was nevertheless significant as another example of the growing use in America of the hunger march as a vehicle for mass protest. It was no sporadic spectacle. To be understood it must be viewed in relation to two other demonstrations—the march on Washington last spring of the bonus army, composed of the homeless and uprooted, and the recent Farmers' National Relief Conference, which was the culmination of riots, evictions, mortgages, and starvation. Both were essentially hunger marches.

Of the three groups the bonus army was the largest, numbering 45,000 at its peak. It was also the least organized and politically the least aware. Perhaps one of the major reasons for this is that most of the veterans were caught up in the amorphous, floating population of déclassé workers. Economically unconnected and having no impetus toward collective protest except recurrent joblessness and social spleen, their understanding of the forces that had deracinated them was very befuddled.

The farmers, on the other hand, despite hunger and taxes which have reduced many of them to serfdom, still have their roots in the soil. As producers they are fully conscious of their position in relation to non-producers—the bankers and the middlemen. As a result, they have come to realize the interdependence of the farmer and the city worker. At the farmers' conference in Washington the repeated slogan was that if the farmer and the city worker do not stand and fight together, they will starve together.

Taken as a whole, these organized units of unemployed, including steel workers, miners, farmers, the war veterans, and city proletarians, are rapidly developing the political art of permanent and cyclical mass protest. Following close in the wake of the three thousand hunger marchers who descended on Washington in the first week of December and who promise to return in greatly increased numbers this spring, came the farmers. The leaders of the farmers' conference demanded a half-billion dollars for immediate relief. If they gain this objective, which, in the words of one farmer, "to the United States isn't equal to a raindrop off a waterspout," they will come back with other demands. And now a new bonus army, which has risen out of the dust of the militia that evicted them with gas and bayonets last July, is straggling back to the capital.

No realistic appraisal of the Washington hunger march is possible without some picture of its organization and at least a brief mention of strategy and police tactics. Each of the three thousand men and women was directly delegated to represent from one to two hundred jobless, underfed Americans who could not come themselves, either because of their families or because they no longer had the physical stamina for a cross-country truck-march. With dimes, nickels, and quarters, those who stayed at home had created an authorized delegation to go to Washington to demand unemployment insurance, a cash payment of $50 for winter relief, and $10 additional for each dependent.

Cumulative evidence from the very outset seems to point to official sanction of provocative acts by the police. The Wilmington episode was the inevitable result of what appeared to be a tacit agreement between the authorities and the police. In Wilmington, Delaware, men and women were indiscriminately clubbed and beaten because they had attempted to assemble and speak; they were, besides, tear-gassed inside the church which they had rented. Moreover, all along the line repeated attempts were made to discourage and dispirit the marchers. Difficulties were raised so that they could not obtain sleeping quarters, hold demonstrations, or even communicate with hundreds of thousands of other hungry Americans.

Having failed to split up the marchers and to turn them back, the authorities then proceeded to terrorize them. Accordingly, on Sunday, December 4, the hunger marchers were met in Washington by a large police escort and shunted into an isolated street, which was immediately sealed by heavy cordons of police at both ends. Twelve hundred policemen, seven hundred deputized firemen equipped with tear gas, sawed-off rifles, and submachine guns, in addition to the militia which was held in readiness in the barracks, were prepared to meet three thousand unarmed, weary, worn, and undernourished men and women.

The street in which the marchers were imprisoned for nearly three days lies between a railroad yard and a treeless hill on the outskirts of town. The yard, glutted with empty Pullman cars that could have housed from ten to fifteen thousand homeless people, was covered by plainclothes men to cut off any escape that way. On top of the hill were machine guns, which at first, and to an unprepared observer, looked like a battery of cameras. The tear-gas squad was stationed on the bluff. The photographer from the *Washington Herald,* who was standing on the roof of a truck, was carrying a gas mask. One of the officers of the tear-gas squad said to a reporter: "The trouble with the Ford job was that they only had $1,000 worth of gas." He went on to explain that $10,000 had been spent on gas for the present "hunger marchers' job." Four trucks were filled with it. In each policeman's kit there were two lots of tear gas to one of sickening or D. N. gas.

On Sunday the marchers were held virtually incommunicado. Besides, there was no water, no hydrant on the street. Not until evening was a truck permitted to leave to bring back cans of water. Many of the men and women went to bed without it. On December 5, while Congress on the floor of the House was arguing for and against beer, there was not enough water to drink and none to wash with in the hunger camp.

11

There were no sanitary arrangements either, and the men and women were harassed and chased from one place to another by jeering policemen. The second day the marchers were given permission to build a toilet. Four different times the men had gone ahead with this, in each instance having received the approval of the police inspector, and each time the police doctor had informed them that they would have to construct it elsewhere in order to comply with sanitary regulations! In the face of this, and notwithstanding the fact that the police had violated the most fundamental health rules provided by law and medicine, the marchers maintained unbroken discipline and order. They carefully refrained from offering the police the slightest provocation.

There were no cots or beds in the camp. Although "sympathizers," among whom were Quakers, radicals, workingmen, and humanitarian citizens of Washington, had offered accommodations sufficient to house a thousand hunger delegates, the police would not release them for the night. Some slept in the trucks. Others, ill with fever and exposure, old and young, men and women, fatigued and with nothing in their stomachs but a cup of coffee and a sandwich, lay down on the cold asphalt. For pillows they used ragged bundles or shoes.

Sick men and women could not get hospital attention without the approval of the police doctor. When a feverish marcher was taken out, it was feet first. As one was being carried out to the ambulance, a policeman said: "Well, I guess it would be inhuman to let him die!" At the same time it was apparent that the police were dominated by a determination which one officer expressed when he said: "Let him die here. We don't want him to die in Washington." It would not do to allow a hungry American to die of starvation on the streets of the capital. The hunger marchers were political prisoners and were accorded the treatment meted out to criminals, with the difference that even in the most backward jails convicts are at least provided with food and water.

The next day the hunger camp hummed with cameramen, detectives, reporters, stool pigeons. The citizens of Washington were still sanctimoniously isolated from the marchers. In accordance with this policy, Major Brown, the Police Commissioner, who wanted to perform his duties with more competence than General Glassford, his predecessor, who had been "too easy" with the BFF, issued a Foch-like pronouncement: "They will not parade."

Congress had opened its session. Members of the League of Professional Groups and the National Committee for the Defense of Political Prisoners were knocking at the door of every Senator and Representative who, they thought, might evince some interest in the constitutional rights of American citizens. Legal machinery was set in operation by liberals in an attempt to obtain an injunction restraining the police from holding the marchers.

The police, having failed to incite the hunger marchers to riot, started a campaign of more pernicious provocations and red-baiting. The tear-gas squad on the hill began to "test" the bombs by throwing them into a bonfire. As the bombs exploded, the wind, which was blowing in the direction of the delegates below, carried the sickening fumes into the trucks where men and women were sitting and standing, causing them much discomfort. Committees of citizens passing back and forth were spat upon and jeered at. Whenever a marcher came near, one policeman would leer at another with "Hello, Comrade."

Doubtless the press played a large role in all this. In order to give their stories a sexy and gamy flavor some papers stated that men and women were sleeping standing up locked in each other's arms. The newspapers had previously run column articles declaring that each hunger marcher was receiving five dollars a day from Moscow. Sensation rather than fact was the dominant feature, and the following kind of reporting was typical. A headline ran: "Rumor, Dynamite in Communists'

Trucks." Below, in small letters, was "Rumor Unfounded." This must have helped to inflame the police force. As a matter of fact, one police officer said that he knew there was a nest of machine guns in one of the marchers' trucks. However, no investigation was ever made. And even when articles, representing the opinions of individual reporters who had actually witnessed the scene, were sympathetic to the hunger marchers, the headlines, expressing the editorial policies of the paper, were more often than not at complete variance with the stories.

Toward five that afternoon the marchers fell into ranks. Two columns, each four abreast, extended down the street for more than half a mile. It was a dress rehearsal for the parade the following day. Since no permit had been granted, the police inspector took the demonstration for a threat and put in a riot call. A siren rang out over the hill. Motorcycle cops bounded over the bluff, buses of policemen were unloaded. The police with clubs in their hands dared the marchers to cross the line where the rope was stretched across the width of the street.

Banners were hoisted by the marchers: "We Demand Shelter for the Homeless," "We Demand Unemployment Insurance," "Fight Against Starvation." The red-front band started to play the "Internationale" as the ranks came nearer and nearer the rope. As the tear-gas squad stood in readiness, bombs poised in their hands, one yelled: "The yellow rats, why don't they do something? I'm rarin' to go!" Then, when it seemed as if the bombs were about to descend, a plainclothes man turned his head the other way saying, "I'm not going to look at this." At that moment the writer, who was also standing on the bluff next to the tear-gas squad, felt as if he had been turned over in an automobile accident and had lost consciousness for several seconds. In geometric formation and with the clicking precision of typewriter keys the marchers made a left-squad turn. The police jeered hysterically and the hunger marchers booed.

Later, Senator Costigan came out and was indignant at what he saw. La Guardia was there and equally aroused. Congressmen Swing and Amlie visited the camp, among others. Howard Williams of the LIPA said that if there were no police, there would be no trouble. That night about four hundred men and women were allowed to leave the camp and sleep in lodgings in Washington. The police, many of whom were drunk, broke loose and slashed the tires of seventeen trucks.

The permit to parade the next day was granted, but the guard surrounding the marchers was so thick that some of the unsuspecting spectators in the throngs must have thought it was a police and firemen's parade on the way to a ball and that the hunger marchers were a crowd of curious civilians following it. The crowds neither booed nor cheered. There was in Washington that morning all the semblance and surcharged atmosphere of martial law. The citizens were explosively timorous. Perhaps something of the tense and electric silence with which they watched the hunger marchers may be explained in terms of Mark Twain's *The Mysterious Stranger,* in which but one man of all those who threw stones at a beautiful witch really had a grudge against her. The others threw stones because each one was afraid that the man standing next to him was antagonistic.

It seems that the significance of the hunger march, which must include the bonus army and the farmer's conference, and its place in the political history of the United States will depend not so much upon the present, tentative reactions of public opinion as upon the kind of organizing and mass maneuvering it may release in the near future. Prognostications will be much more in order by the end of 1933, the year of our lord Franklin Delano Roosevelt.

The Nation, 1932

15

Hitler's Power over Germany: The Nazi Strength Analyzed

How strongly entrenched are the Hitler forces? What is the opposition and what are its possibilities of making itself felt? These are the questions which the world is asking while anxiously awaiting the outcome of events in Germany.

At the present moment the Brown Shirts, completely at the beck and call of Hitler, and numbering perhaps 1,500,000 men, have absolute military and political control of the Reich. However, there is an undercurrent of dissension between the Steel Helmets and the Nazis; and although conflict between the two would be very unequal, if no other forces joined the Steel Helmets, a general mass strike as well as civil war might follow, should the workers also rebel.

It is possible that a general strike of the working classes in Germany may occur, but at present it seems remote. For the large cities and the provinces are under martial law and the mildest sort of opposition is ruthlessly crushed.

A short time after the elections which gave him undisputed power Hitler announced that the Nazi enrollment books would have to be closed and that no more enlistments could be accepted. This strategic move no doubt kept out of the party the subversive influences of refugees and counter-revolutionaries. The requirements for volunteers who wish to join the army of Brown Shirts have been very stringent. In order to keep the ranks "pure," each applicant had to present his birth certificate, besides swearing under oath that as far as he knew neither of his parents, grandparents nor great-grandparents were Jews. The political affiliations of an applicant were also meticulously investigated.

As a result of this selectivity, Hitler has a highly disciplined and strongly organized army of more than 1,000,000 Brown Shirts, which has the civilian population of Germany completely under surveillance. These Nazi storm troops have subjugated Bavaria, always jealous of its independence, quelled dissension and opposition in Munich, Dresden, Frankfort and all the provinces, and engulfed Berlin. Today the police and the small regular army are timorously performing their routine duties in the background. The only mobilized army is the Brown Shirts, and they take their orders from Adolf Hitler.

The Brown Shirts are made up of boys ranging in ages from 15 to 21. Déclassé workers, the unemployed, peasants, the petit bourgeoisie and the students, these are the real buttresses of Hitler's Brown Shirts.

Supporting this army is a legion of war veterans, older men, from 35 to 50. They are the Stahlheim, the Steel Helmets, the soldiery of the Nationalist party led by Alfred Hugenberg, who is at present in the Hitler cabinet. With much less revolutionary zeal than the Nazis, the Steel Helmets are not as passionately united an organization as the Brown Shirts. The Steel Helmets' support of the Nazis is to a certain extent fear-strength. Not strong enough to oppose by force the Brown Shirts, they are, on the other hand, too large a unit not to be reckoned with by Hitler.

There are already certain disruptive influences at work inside the allied ranks. In the eyes of the young Nazis, the Steel Helmets are suspect. Having been through the war, the older men are looked upon as defeatists and as being somehow or other tainted by Marxism. This psychological reaction of the aggressively militaristic youth in Germany toward those who returned to their fatherland weary, crushed and vanquished, is penetratingly set forth in Remarque's *The Road Back*.

The Junkers, who have always insisted that the Germans did not lose the World War, are also giving support—but not an undivided support—to the Brown Shirts. The Junkers hope

17

that they will get back their places in a restored empire. Many of the Junkers have, however, joined the Hitlerites, not because of mystical and galvanized zealousness but through fear of a return of Communists and Social Democrats. This anxiety has other facets also. The Junkers are afraid of the armed Nazis, and they do not want to find themselves in the position of émigrés in their own country. This is a psychological dilemma that has fallen upon large segments of the population.

Allied also with the Hitler government, though the connection is at present peripheral, is the "heavy industry." The industrial titans expect to come into the foreground again, and here political sentiment is inextricably bound up with coal, chemical, steel and armament contracts.

In face of any uprising within the country Hitler could count upon the students of Germany in almost a solid block. Eighty per cent of the students today are Nazis. With little sympathy for the workers, with whom they feel they have had to compete since the overthrow of the monarchy, they want to win back class distinction, economic preferment, all the prerogatives of caste that the Hohenzollern empire had previously given them.

Never having spilled their blood for the republic, they are still strongly monarchistic in their leanings. Intellectually, too, they despise internationalism and the brotherhood of the nations. They would remove from German life and culture once and for all the Heinesque touch, which was formerly all the mode.

Expressing the views of this bloc of the students, Baron Börries von Münchausen of the University of Göttingen said:

"The difficult economic situation has compelled many of them [the students] to work together with factory workers, miners and farmhands and their experiences have shown them plainly how unclear and impractical the ideals of the workers are."

With the Brown Shirts, like a German Pretorian Guard, in control of the large cities, the provinces and the capital, the opposition to Hitler cannot muster its forces. The Social Democrats are either in jails, concentration camps, or *en marché*. The Communist party has been driven far underground. Although radical papers are beginning to have a sub rosa circulation again, Communist activities are badly shattered for the moment. Hitler proposes to keep the Communists and Social Democrats in concentration camps "for the duration of the war," as it were; he recently stated that he would not release them, for once they were free they would immediately start agitating.

The workers' press has been abolished by decree and often by violence; in several instances their buildings were demolished. Alexanderplatz, the nerve center of radical activity, is today completely quelled. Visitors and foreigners are warned to give Alexanderplatz a wide berth at night. The swastika has replaced the red flag on every house.

Trade unionism in Germany has been disorganized and crippled. Workers' organizations and labor centers are today beset from without by heavy cordons of Nazis and sabotaged from within by Nazis. Thus labor organizations have been rendered as ineffective as company unions. Labor legislation, which was put through by the Communists and Social Democrats, has either become a dead letter or been nullified. Consequently, wages have dropped considerably and the working hours have been increased. With long hours and low wages the worker has little energy at present for militancy or counterrevolution. Besides, the ubiquitous Brown Shirts are so watchful that there is little opportunity.

However, sentiment among the laboring classes in Germany may be deduced from the vote in the last election. In a typical workers' district, Professor Sigmund Schultz stated, two-fifths of the population voted the Communist ticket, two-fifths the Social Democratic, and the remaining fifth that voted for Hitler

19

was made up of Communists and Social Democrats. The Centrists received only one-third of the support of the Catholic workers in the March elections, the remaining two-thirds going over almost en bloc to the two Leftist parties.

The schools for children have been taken over by the Hitlerites in much the same way as the trade unions. Radical teachers have been replaced and the student body is surrounded from within and without by young Nazi students. The feeling among the children is very high. Before the elections they were organized into military divisions and units. For the most part they are either Brown Shirts or social revolutionaries. Highly political-minded, the young students follow the news of the day with impassioned feeling.

The Nazis have left no stone unturned to suppress opposition. Even five or six people on their way to the theater do not dare to stop at corners for a moment's conversation. The Brown Shirts see to it that the cafés are not used for meeting places either, bearing down in large numbers upon the coffee houses and places where radicals, bohemians and the literati gather. People are even afraid to have parties in their own apartments, for raids and searches are made every day without a warrant. Late at night or early in the morning people are awakened by processions of Nazis loudly chanting or by scattered shots. Berlin nights are punctuated by pistol shots.

The Nazis have developed a technique of boycotting restaurants and cafés owned by Jews or frequented by anti-Hitlerites. As soon as the clients are persuaded that they must go elsewhere, the Nazis desert the places, which are thus left empty for weeks.

The average German citizen has developed a Nazi obsession. He feels very uncomfortable whenever he passes a Brown Shirt in the street. Every one is on guard. After the elections people found it necessary to have their telephones disconnected, for conversations were intercepted and people were followed and watched. Politics is taboo. The German will tell you, if he has known you for a long time, that he has no way of knowing whether the next man is a Nazi or an agent provocateur.

There is very little and only the most subterranean criticism of the present régime by word of mouth. Germans, in a large measure, are being held incommunicado in their own country, and this applies to practically all classes. Dr. Curtius, a conservative and a member of the Brüning cabinet, sent a statement to the press that he could grant no interviews. And Social Democrats, especially the leaders who had enormous influence and prestige before the Hitler dictatorship, if they are not in jail, keep moving from house to house so as to avoid any sort of attention.

The censorship of the press is so close that the average American reader of the newspapers knows more about conditions in Germany than the majority of German people do. In the main, the German population may be compared with civilians behind the lines who have no way of ascertaining what is happening at the front.

To say that the press is muzzled is inaccurate. There is no opposition press. Catholic, Jewish, Liberal, Social Democratic and Communist newspapers (with the exception of two or three underground papers which must necessarily have an extremely restricted circulation at the moment) no longer exist. Hitler either owns outright, or has completely under his thumb, the German press today.

The publishing houses have been seriously damaged by the ambiguities which surround the censorship. The establishments which made a specialty of proletarian literature are out of existence. Apart from the publication of Nazi romances, novels whose purpose it is to increase the nationalistic sentiment of the youth, German publishers do not know what the government will permit them to print. Literature with liberal social and political implications is not only not in demand today but extremely hazardous to publish. Germany, which once afforded to American novelists like Dreiser, Lewis and

21

Anderson a tremendous public, is no longer interested in the translation of books from foreign countries. The government is discouraging the taste for cosmopolitan ideas.

Although there is widespread sentiment in Germany against Hitlerism, the Brown Shirts give it no opportunity to express itself. With the opposition leaders either in hiding or out of the country, in Prague, Paris, Vienna and Switzerland (never has Swiss air been so exhilarating), there is no opportunity for even a cultural protest at present.

Social Democrats and Communists who were fighting one another tooth and nail less than six weeks ago, instead of combining their forces to combat the Nazis, are now sitting together in the cafés of Vienna, lamenting their political astigmatism and making plans for a united front against Hitler. However, Hitler is not waiting, and already deep incursions have been made into Austria, so that Vienna is no longer especially healthful for radicals.

The Steel Helmets may yet bolt, for there is dissension between Hugenberg and Hitler. If so, they might join forces with the workers, who are also biding their time. It is also possible, though not probable, that Hindenburg might attempt to exhume the Weimar Constitution and dismiss his Chancellor. But as long as Hitler has the support of the Brown Shirts it is unlikely that the octogenarian President can do much.

Workers in the suburbs of Berlin have already once successfully gone on strike against Hitlerite tactics; if there is a counter-revolution it may come from that quarter.

New York Times, 1933

Nightgown Riders of America

(Although the comic opera insurrectionists behind the various revamped Ku Klux Klan shirts are inconsequential in themselves, they are significant as political trends. Even the smallest, doggerel Napoleon, like a Hitler, can rise to leadership. And in rapidly reviewing the fatuities and illiterate inanities of a Pelley or an Art Smith, there is no attempt to belittle the seriousness of these sporadic, mushroom movements. The role of the Social Democrats, and the silly beer putsch staged by the slapstick insurgent, Adolf Hitler, in Munich, 1923, have been too instructive.)

William Dudley Pelley, seer of the Silver Shirts, and a kind of outhouse, picaresque Rabindranath Tagore, has had a career worthy of a column in the Americana of the *Mercury.* Erstwhile treasurer of a toilet paper company in Springfield, Mass., 1909-1912 (see *Who's Who*), and at one time a secretary with the International YMCA (during American intervention in Siberia, 1918-1919), then a scenario writer in Hollywood, he is today one of the venal harbingers of reaction and fascism in America. Founder of Galahad College (for Aryans only) which was created for the purpose of training American storm troopers in graduate courses in anti-Semitism, fascism and red-baiting, he is also an editor and a soothsayer. Pelley has had astral communion with the disincarnated shade of Adolf Hitler from whom he received instructions and subsidies of a much less otherworldly sort.

The Silver Shirts of America, started less than a year ago, has a culture and a philosophy behind it. An admixture of fake cosmology and postcard evolution, after the manner of, "If I were a tadpole, and you were a fish, in the Paleozoic times," it served Pelley first as spiritualist and then as functionary for Nazi agents. Pelley lives in Asheville, North Carolina, a pleasant, resortish town whose bland climate attracts tuberculars and the leisure class—arable ground for theosophical speculation.

Incidentally when Pelley goes to his office, he removes his good clothes and puts on an old pair of trousers and shoes in order to give the appearance of austerity and frugality. Pelley has received money from wealthy widows who wished to communicate with their dead husbands. The Seer almost succeeded in marrying off his nephew to a relative of Senator Reynolds, a widow, who wanted to make clairvoyant cable connections with her dead husband. Pelley promised to put through this message provided she would become the wife of his nephew; but she declined.

However, as spiritualism did not prove lucrative enough, and as a Nazi official was looking about for an alert American propagandist, William Dudley Pelley shifted his interests to anti-Semitism and organized the Silver Shirts. He showed no intention of burying his mystagogical gifts which he immediately brought to this new movement; but proceeded to develop a philosophy for the Silver Shirts based on the knowledge of Sanskrit, pituitary glands and God. Briefly, his thesis reads as follows: the Nordic's evolutionary metamorphosis is traced from the lizard. The most highly developed Nordics, who come from lizards, have pituitary glands at the end of which is the Radio Eye, which can see into the Realms of Higher Frequency, that is, the Styxian regions of the dead. William Dudley is a highly developed Nordic and has at the nethermost end of his pituitary gland such a Radio Eye.

Pelley, an apostle of Nazi Gleichschaltung, has coordinated bookkeeping, spiritualism and Hitlerism in the following way: In May, he had collecting agents at work in California, Ohio, Pennsylvania, Maryland, Utah, Nebraska and the South. These agents were employed on a commission basis and received half of each ten dollar membership fee, and twenty-five percent on all money paid for dues, tax, literature and general contributions. Silver Shirt subsidiaries for raising funds were established: The League for the Liberation, The Foundation for Christian Economics, The Galahad Press, and The Galahad Fellowship Extension. It goes without saying that, like the Galahad College, which actually does not exist except on papers, these Silver Shirted auxiliaries are theosophical fictions somewhere at the end of Pelley's pituitary gland.

A few excerpts from Pelley's sleazy sheet, *Liberation,* indicating their similarity in tone, temper and contents to the Nazi organs, are in place here. In short, only a few weeks ago, there appeared in *Das Neue Deutschland* a verbatim transcript of Pelley's article in *Liberation.* Simultaneously, Grissible, acting Nazi leader, announced that the Friends of the New Germany and the Silver Shirts are on the most amicable terms and "welcome wholeheartedly the wonderful understanding which the Silver Shirts have for the Nazis."

Liberation says that Dawes, Young, the Van Sweringen brothers of Cleveland and Lenin are Jews. Further: "In America there are hundreds of men who saw nothing extraordinary that Senator Morrow 'happened' to be stricken fatally the day after his attendance at a Jewish banquet." And elsewhere (July 15, 1933, vol. 4, no. 13): "speaking of applause [reference to President Roosevelt's yachting costume alias Rosenfeld], have you noticed how thin and spasmodic it is of late, when the sport shirt, the ice cream pants and the old hat are paraded for our aforesaid weekly edification." Also: "Mutilated bodies of women hostages, and S. Ivanovna, owner of a drapery business, and Mme. Khlopova, a property owner, had their breasts slit open and emptied. It is all but impossible to enumerate the forms of savagery which the Jewish Chekka employed. A volume would not contain them" (*Liberation,* vol. 5, no. 1, August 26, 1933).

This same pseudo-proletarian appeal to the masses is also found in Goebbels' early writings. Note the descriptive cartoonist's epithets and the orientation to workers in the *Nazi-Sozi,* a pamphlet by Goebbels: "There can surely be nothing more hypocritical than a fat, well-fed capitalist who protests against the proletarian idea of class struggle."

The aforementioned quote is typical of the disingenuous and fake proletarian political vocabulary adopted by the National Socialists who have bilked and betrayed the workers more shamelessly than any party in the history of Europe—the Nazis who have abolished collective bargaining, dissolved all organizations of "Marxist class warfare," and decreed in their stead that the wages of employees shall rest upon the "social honor" of employers. That is, upon Fritz Thyssen, the coal and steel king of the Ruhr, one of the principal instigators of the World War, and today an archetype "labor trustee" of the Third Reich.

Among other mushroom fascist organizations that have sprung up in North America are the Blue Shirts in Quebec, the Crusader White Shirts in Chattanooga, Tennessee, and "General" Art Smith's Khaki Shirts in Philadelphia. A brief case history of Art Smith should be recorded: At the age of eight he was committed to the County House for stealing a horse, a pistol and for attempting to shoot the sheriff. Later, but still a minor, he was about to be indicted for the murder of a drunken lumberjack whom he had "rolled," taking his watch and ninety cents, and then burying him underneath a dungheap; but the man recovered.

Approximately illiterate, he had no difficulty in enlisting in his ranks the Philadelphia police. His men carried clubs, "loaded" riding crops and guns, and like all the vigilantes in the history of America, who have murdered and brutally beaten workers, they were abetted and aided by the forces of reaction. The papier-mâché "general" rode about in swanky automobile with two armed guards standing on the running board.

Smith had a large store of Lee-Enfield rifles, which can only be obtained by order of the U. S. War Department, and he challenged the government to find them, but the Department of Justice, dealing with a useful strike-breaker and a thug, did nothing.

The Khaki Shirts have since fallen into obscurity; but white-haired boys like Seward Collins and Lawrence Dennis have come to take their place. The *American Review,* the literary trade journal of fascism in the United States, has become a fustian *Liberation,* on a slightly higher level.

Collins, like Lawrence Dennis, editor of the *Awakener,* has joined ranks with Pelley, buffoon meglomaniac; Art Smith, pathological criminal type; Rosenberg, sadist; Göring, dangerous paranoiac and morphine addict, who was committed to an asylum in Stockholm in 1925; and Captain Röhm, notorious pervert who created a scandal in Berlin a few years ago—a delectable coterie to whom the masses of unemployed and starving should turn as their political leaders.

In the meantime, Adolf Hitler is enjoying the claque of the American press in the novel and unpredictable role of good Samaritan and connoisseur of music. Hitler is shown in a photograph on the front page suavely bowing in dinner jacket to Gigli, Italian opera singer, which makes him a lover of the fine arts. Through the Radio Eye and the pituitary gland of Ivy Lee, Hitler is so emotionally affected by the plight of a hitchhiker crossing the American continent that he sends him money. Unsuspecting readers who may not know that Hitler is doing nothing to feed German workers who have been reduced to a pellagra diet of potatoes, and that every first-rate composer, writer and artist has been compelled to fly for his life from the terroristic storm troopers in Germany, are offered this mendacious fare by American newspapers.

Each week at Turner Hall some agent provocateur from Germany speaks to large audiences of German-Americans. Last Tuesday there was a lecture announced on "Children's Institutions and Homes in the Ruhr," but not a word was mentioned on this topic, the platform agent confining himself to—"Awaken

27

German!" Parents are asked to enroll their children in private Nazi schools. Under the heading University of the State of New York, State Education Department, they are offered *Freie Kurse für Erwachsene.*

Hitler's *Mein Kampf* is the bible for Deutschen Rings in America, German concert, dancing and singing groups. These are the new little innocent clubs behind which the political tactics of Hitlerism are masked. In an unbowdlerized edition of *Mein Kampf,* there appears the following, which might have been written in collaboration with Judge Callahan who has condemned the Scottsboro boys to die: "The black-haired Jewish youth lies for hours in ambush, a satanic joy in his face for the unsuspecting girl whom he pollutes with his blood. . . . It was, and is, the Jew who brought Negroes to the Rhine, brought them with the same aim and with deliberate intent to destroy the white race. . . ."

In both Hitler's swastika regime and in the moldering plant-ocratic and industrial south, it is the Jew and the Negro who are pilloried as the classical ravishers and rapists. The political observer, however, is compelled to look to the harrowing decline in the world markets, to starvation and unemployment, and not to race, color or creed for the real reasons.

The nightgown ghost riders are spreading fascist terror in Mexico and South America. And in this country, it is the American Legion, the Patriotic Coalition Societies, A. F. of L. officials and Congressmen who are giving the illiterate Pelleys and Art Smiths their support.

New Masses, 1934

Waldo Frank and the Left

It becomes increasingly doubtful whether it is possible to have a major school of writers without the aid and lenses of the critics. Both from the Right as well as from the Left there is today a Babel of criteria that makes for the interment of works of art rather than for their creation. "The education of a people with a view to culture," said Nietzsche, "is essentially a matter of good models."

The *Saturday Review of Literature* used to be afflicted with that peculiarly Jamesian malady known as gigantism. Every three months it used to discover an enormous genius and every fourth month it bewailed the fact that there were no great novels being published. The progression of this "will to believe" in literary criticism has since then been consistent, linear and downwards. And the true opponents of this gigantism have either vanished or withdrawn. Louis Vernon Parrington, a critic of scope and ample understanding, is dead; Van Wyck Brooks, the most impassioned and despairing man of American letters, has retired from the contemporary field; and Edmund Wilson, highly gifted, and author of that remarkable study in imaginative literature, *Axel's Castle,* has gone into retreat.

In such a period of chaos when graduated distinctions between books seem of marginal importance, Waldo Frank's *The Death and Birth of David Markand* has appeared.

The Death and Birth of David Markand is a swan song of the American bourgeoisie and Waldo Frank's farewell to that class. For a just perspective of the book something of a restatement of its contents is in place here: David Markand, a stockholder in the United Tobacco Industries, is deracinated, twisted, and wishes to escape from the death and moldering around him. His wife seeks surcease in cloistered Catholicism, but Markand, altogether alien to such fraudulent nostrums, wants to get out into the world of production and labor, among the oppressed farmers and proletariat to learn and to unknow. His relentless peregrinations, industrial, social, erotic, are continental. Markand, tortured, mazed, starves, works as itinerant laborer in the Chicago stockyards, as coal stoker and as bartender in New Orleans. He meets up with Georgia crackers, Negro sharecroppers, chambermaids, Wobblies and Marxists. Each panel of city, street and incident is a torturously heightened experience for him, a "transvaluation of values."

The depiction, all too brief, of John Byrne, a working-class leader, and Jane Priest, who has evolved from a poor white to a class-conscious organizer, and of the knavery and stark wickedness of the coal operators, is one of the most authentic pieces of labor narrative in the American novel. It is doubtless a transcript of the reign of terror in Harlan, Kentucky, where Waldo Frank, a member of a writers' investigation committee, was blackjacked. The prose here has impact and political pungency:

The four men rose. Lowrie, the greatest local operator and the richest man in Howton, was short with a frog-like body and a flushed face in which the little eyes shone green and the mouth set like a trap. Beside him was Judge Freeter, incumbent of the local United States District Court, a huge man with lofty, gray locks, aquiline nose and fierce small eyes. On the other side of Lowrie was County Prosecutor Lincoln, a trim youth with a low brow, who kept twiddling the Phi Beta Kappa key on his vest; and on the other side of the Judge was a man with a full-moon face, eyes watery blue, a pug-nose and pudgy hands— Governor Garent of the state. They shook hands with the miners, and said over and over: "Mighty glad, suh, to meet you." The miners carefully laid their guns under the table. . . . In this instant, the truth between them lived on the table. The Governor opened his mouth to dispel it; his voice issuing from the moon visage was a reverberant tenor, velvet to the closest ear, yet audible, one felt, to the farthest Appalachian slope. He said: . . . "For I'm here, I tell you, as Gov'nor of your state to say to you that if you've a right to what you want, a right as Americans, by God, sirs! you're going to get it."

30

And twenty-four hours later, John Byrne and Jane Priest, strike leaders, lie buried underneath a fresh foot-stamped mound of wet earth, murdered by the Governor's deputized thugs. For firm and gainly chronicling, the following is typical of one cross-section of the book:

He traveled to Minneapolis and marveled at its difference from St. Paul. A smooth, blond town, closer in color to wheat, and yet it had a tidy hardness that made Markand understand the farmers' hate of middlemen. Middleman town it was. Abolish the middleman would mean to abolish Minneapolis—its haughty houses, swanking boulevards. St. Paul was darker and lustier.

The novel is varied in tone and texture; there are passages of erotica which rival those of John Donne, and there are other sexual episodes which discomfit the reader in much the same way that D. H. Lawrence's often do.

For picture, pigment and social insight compressed into violent and fragile imagery the reader should note the following:

The red-clay road gashed into banks, high or low: the young corn and cane racing with the breeze; the already sturdy cotton, and always the red road . . . cabins standing on stilts, so sudden rains could sweep under and leave them alone: cabins rhythmic in shape and weather-hued like the reflection of dappled flowers upon water. Sparse farms of white folk, larger, stiffer, with more rubbish in the yards; always the red road. Black folk on foot, faintly emergent from the red earth and the blue-gold sky, like their red duroc hogs; sparse white men, splinters from an alien world of coolness and of angles. . . .

Compare the above passage with the bass drum profundities of Thomas Wolfe, selected by Burton Rascoe in the *Herald Tribune* as a specimen of profoundly imagined prose: "After all the blind, tormented wonderings of youth, that woman would become his heart's center and the target of his life, the image of immortal one-ness . . . the immortal governance and unity of life." Thomas Wolfe is the most recent bourgeois hero of gigantism.

31

One or two critics of *The Death and Birth of David Markand* have assailed Waldo Frank as a mystagogue and have said that his approach here to communism is special, tinctured with the religiosity of a convert. There is, of course, no one way, or any one hundred ways of perceiving or arriving at a new social and class outlook. In this book the fault is not Frank's. It lies in the electric fusion of images and sensations, in his quickened and, as it were, stratosphere prose-responses and antennae, which have been mistaken for transcendentalism or what Lenin called God-creating or God-building. Whatever Frank was in the past, he is not a mystic in this novel. The deity, whenever alluded to by the author, is altogether a literary and social device, as, "It is easy to see which of these two classes of men the Lord has smiled upon."

However, Waldo Frank's book raises several very significant aesthetic problems for the American Writers' Congress. Revolutionary novels about the middle class in which the proletariat has no dominant role, or only an incidental part, have received a rather tepid reception. The technic of indirection, strikes, class-war murders, hunger, used as a dramatic cyclorama to heighten the torture and the awareness of the protagonist, the more peripheral and roundabout approaches to communism in fiction, have been summarily dismissed or ineptly considered. Vacillation, conflict, anguish have been viewed as unrepresentative sick emotions of a sepulchral figure or milieu. This attitude is not without a touch of babbitry and a not too dim echo of the slogan: nothing succeeds like success. In short, is it essential that a character in a revolutionary novel walk out of the book or off the stage like a Marchbanks? Is it necessary that the David Markands or the Studs Lonigans beset by the present-day Furies know all that the readers know? The poignant dilemma of poor Ernest in *The Way of All Flesh* is a case in point. Ernest, to the very end, jots down abstruse metaphysical insights and axioms; he never emerges triumphant from the clerical haze and aura of the

32

church—but the reader does.

This brings us to another point: the introspective psychical man. Jung, dealing with psychological types, has written that the extroverted person has "an element of caricaturing depreciation" and is more easily describable than the introvert. But the contemporary author, whose novel, torsoed like its heroes, with realistically-drawn legs, arms, bodies but no hearts or intellects, has excised sensibilities and introversions. "Layers and layers of sensation and no heart in it" characterizes the truncated protagonist of modern American fiction, bourgeois or communist. Parrington has stated the problem in his addenda on Sinclair Lewis: "These brisk pages are filled with astonishing verisimilitude, speaking an amazingly realistic language, professing a surprising lifelikeness—yet nevertheless only shells from which the life has departed. . . ." And it is these "shells" that we have learned to pity, and even despise, not because they are tortured and harried but for the very opposite reasons, because they are so miserably supine. Almost every character in American fiction today, Clyde Griffiths of *An American Tragedy,* the Jeeters in *Tobacco Road,* Conroy's itinerant semi-proletarians, Dos Passos's men and women (who always go from place to place but never evolve), are from the point of view of creative energy and will, horizontal.

What has happened, among other things, is that reporting, a doggerel, slangy prose, has taken the place of a literary vocabulary. As a method of chronicling and as a stenographic record of surface relations and tabloid events, the use of the Americanese is often highly effective. But it imposes definitive limitations upon the writer, so much that a conscientious critic must constantly remind the reader that the prose, and the cerebral processes projected, are not the author's mind. Consequently, insights, nuances, graduated perceptions cannot be gotten even out of a very highly formalized journalese. Nor a whole man. In fact too often when an American novelist who is Left or liberal tries to suggest a mood of sadness or some emotion, he writes that his character felt "kinda goofy or queer." However, it is not entirely surprising that the novelist who has given us the most complete character, the living, vibrating man, David Markand, in the class-conscious American novel, has been given short shrift by some reviewers.

The Death and Birth of David Markand is a major novel of our times. Waldo Frank has been a voice of the middle class, the intelligentsia, the students, the teachers, for a decade or more. The frustrations, the chaos and anguish of Markand is, one might say, *ipso facto,* the representative fluxional emotions and doubts of the social conscience of an entire class and era.

New Masses, 1935

Fascism and Writers

Abraham Cowley, the seventeenth-century English poet, said that a tragic age is the most interesting to live in but the most difficult to write in. Contemporary writers who have gone through the horrors of the World War, Italian fascism in 1922, the world crisis in 1929, and Hitlerism in 1933, know this perhaps more poignantly than the English poet did. One can say that while Clemenceau was writing to Woodrow Wilson during the World War "a drop of oil is worth a drop of blood," and Sir Henri Deterding, the British oil magnate, was subsidizing the Wrangels and Kolchaks to gain possession of the Baku wells, a great many writers were intoning, "A rose is a rose is a rose is a rose." H. G. Wells, addressing a labor congress, mind you, said that the horrors of the World War were only a darkness of the mind. And what darkness, we might add. The statements of the fastidious Henry James about the Huns in the World War read like a tabloid account. Kipling, who has been a consistent imperialist and jingoist, naturally was for war. Anatole France was willing to shoulder arms for *la belle* France. Among our own American writers who went to war "to make the world safe for democracy" are Edmund Wilson, John Dos Passos, E. E. Cummings, Malcolm Cowley, Ernest Hemingway. Many of us remember the impassioned letters of Romain Rolland to Gerhardt Hauptmann, importuning him as an artist, as a voice, not to be deceived by warmongers. With the exception of writers like Maxim Gorki, Romain Rolland, Shaw, B. Russell, it seems that the only realists during that period were the capitalists on the one hand and the revolutionaries on the other. Not the author of *The Weavers,* but the heroic Karl Liebknecht and the Junkers like Krupp, saw where history was going.

However, most of these writers were profoundly disillusioned—and out of their bitterness came the following books against war: Barbusse's *Under Fire,* Ludwig Renn's *After War,* Plievier's *The Kaiser's Coolies,* E. E. Cummings's *The Enormous Room,* Dos Passos's *Three Soldiers,* and so on. Some, however, were so shaken by this horrendous experience that they viewed the whole heritage of humanity as something that was near an end. T. S. Eliot's:

> We are the hollow men
> We are the stuffed men
> Leaning together
> Headpiece filled with straw. Alas!

and Proust's *Remembrance of Things Past,* which Edmund Wilson in *Axel's Castle* calls "the Heartbreak House of capitalist culture," illustrate this complete hopelessness.

The next test, so to speak, came with Italian fascism in 1922, with Mussolini's "legendary march" on Rome in a luxurious sleeping car. There were philosophers like Croce who protested at first. Even Giovanni Gentile, I believe, was not for this barbarous state. However, since then, Croce has become acquiescent, and Gentile has become the fascist Minister of Education in Italy. Marinetti, the Futurist, adopted fascism and publicly stated that "war is the hygiene of the youth." I think all of us here can tell Mr. Marinetti to take the hygiene. We may divide the aforementioned writers in accordance with their attitude toward war and fascism as follows: First, jingoists like Kipling, Marinetti and D'Annunzio; those who wavered or were confused, like Hauptmann, H. G. Wells, Ludwig Renn, Neukrantz (author of *Barricades in Berlin*); those who were permanently disillusioned, like E. E. Cummings, T. S. Eliot, and Ernest Hemingway, the last having found some kind of surcease or anodyne in Catholicism (note in *Death in the Afternoon* the implications of Mithraism and the entire ritual of the bull, which later became the wine and wafer ceremony in the Catholic Church).

By 1929 writers had begun to take a different view of things. Hoover had made the following pronouncement, "The worst will be over in sixty days," after which the patient died. But the writers were already making violently incisive comments upon the crisis and were organizing to cast their votes for Foster and Ford. A new *Weltanschauung* had taken the place of despair. A number of noted novelists went to the Soviet Union. Among them were Theodore Dreiser, Waldo Frank, Josephine Herbst. The latter had enormous misgivings about communism. To know where she stands today just read her profoundly compelling articles on Cuban oppression in the *New Masses*. Or examine Waldo Frank's *The Death and Birth of David Markand*, a novel of finely-wrought art and propaganda for a workers' and farmers' government.

In 1933 Hitlerism came to Germany. Here we must pause to take a closer view of fascism, its philosophy and its outlook on education and culture. To begin with, we recall that when fascism came to Italy, a secondary capitalist state, the petty-bourgeois columnists referred to it as a peculiarly Latin and Mediterranean outburst. Today, many Americans speak of the Nazi menace as a direct result of the highly regimented German temperament. Anna O'Hara McCormack, writing an article on fascism, said that Hitlerism is medieval whereas Mussolini's fascism is baroque. If we wished to carry this absurdity to the nth degree we could employ a musical instead of an architectural vocabulary and say that Pilsudski's fascist dictatorship is mezzo-soprano.

Mussolini wrote in 1921: "Italian fascism now requires, under pain of death, or worse, of suicide, to provide itself with a body of doctrines. . . ." This new "philosophy," writes R. Palme Dutt in his remarkable book, *Fascism and Social Revolution*, was ordered as simply as a wagonload of blacksticks. And in two months' time. Two years ago an essay written by Mussolini appeared in an English periodical, and among those listed as the founders of a fascist culture were Renan, Claudel

37

and Péguy. There is no theory then. The best that the Nazis in Germany could offer to the people were points. This barrenness was totally illustrated in Father Coughlin's address in Detroit recently. The philosophy he offered his audience of sixteen thousand was: "United we stand and divided we fall." Who can deny it.

All this is exceedingly important for American writers to consider. For fascist governments cannot continue without a mass base; and in order to hold the workers, farmers and middle classes whom they have deceived, they must gain the support of the writers. That the most telling line of the Nazi playwright Hanns Johst is, "When I hear the word culture, I cock my revolver," and that Goebbels' play, *Destiny,* has such a refreshing call to humanity, "Perish Carrion. I trample upon your brains," does not matter. The fascists who cannot give the millions of unemployed bread and butter and work must give them hope. So the most belligerent enemies of culture are the first to take over any statement made by a poet or a novelist or a dramatist that will help rally forces around them. The fascists employ every technique to ensnare the oppressed. So that the fascists who pursued capitalist exploitation to its fiendish limits today pose as anti-capitalists. The Thyssens and the Krupps, through their mouthpieces, Hitler and Goebbels, who are attempting to destroy humanity by the profit and war uses of the machine, have become, in a word, the machine-wreckers, the romantic modern Luddites. The capitalists, our saviors, are today in revolt against the machine! And against science too! Joseph Caillaux, "progressive" financier and politician, baldly stated in 1932 that "science must be hamstrung"; otherwise it would upset production, for profit, naturally. How enormously helpful then is the spinning wheel of Gandhi to the British imperialists; how useful to the Nazis are Bertrand Russell's apotheosis of a decaying pre-capitalist Chinese civilization and Spengler's lachrymose hatred of the machine age, "primitive man roosting solitary as a vulture, without any communal

38

feeling." It goes without saying that the fascists and the indus-trialists have encouraged an anti-rationalist approach; they have had most to gain by questioning science, disvaluing the intellect. Setting up in its stead, blood-thinking, along with Aryan grandmothers, swastikas, anti-Semitism, race theories, brutal sterilization of the Negro. But those writers who have found primitivism, a return to medieval culture, most appeal-ing should know that this fraudulent revolt against the machines has been inspired from above, by the industrialists. In precisely the same way Nazi theorists are creating a meta-physic of torture: pain becomes a medium for heightened experience and clairvoyant insights. So the masses are being told to scrap the machines that they have invented and built for lessening the burden and toil of humanity, and to restore the long, wearying hours of a handicraft society. Similarly, they are told that torture and maceration of the flesh are a good in them-selves, that hunger *per se* is almost a goal, since it, like war, evokes the noblest in mankind: sacrifice. But communists in Germany tell workers how to combat torture, and they will show them how to use the machine when fascism is overthrown.

Unfortunately, the cult of primitivism and medievalism has made a favorable impression upon various writers, much more so than the hollow twenty-five points in the National-Socialist program. Not the silly embarrassing cult of Wotan or the he-man Siegfried, but the agrarian anti-machine commune has captured the imagination of a Miguel de Unamuno. And the fascist governments have not been slow in realizing the appeal this will make to poets and artists and novelists who are waver-ing or unclear.

What place has literature and culture in a fascist country? This of course is of the utmost importance to us. What Dimitrov said at the Leipzig Trial, "Tell me in what country is not fascism wild and barbarous," applies specifically to the few fascist books that have been published throughout the world. Note the sadism, which has the smell of the concentration camp, of

39

the following *canaille*-fictioneers in Great Britain: "I readily admit that war is the supreme tragedy . . .," writes Margrie in *A Cockney's Pilgrimage,* "But even a great war has one or two advantages. It unites a nation as nothing else can do. It stimulates people to do their best. It makes us forget our small personal troubles." This reads all too familiarly like the doggerel postcard verse and Uncle Sam billboard posters of the last World War. Unmindful of collectivization among workers in the Soviet Union, there are certain writers, sincere but confused, who arrive by some process of psychological prestidigitation at war-wishing, pointing out that soldiers in the trenches knew greater love and humanity and sacrifices than in peace times. If this is true of our present society, what a commentary it is upon decaying capitalism. The fascist Margrie has also some cliché insights into pictorial poverty which should be quoted here: "It is a mistake to suppose that people who live in slums are unhappy. They are the happiest people in London. It is all a question of freedom. The worse the slums the greater the freedom."

Another sleazy fascist novel, *Blue Shirts,* published under a pseudonym in London, shows how to take care of a militant worker struggling for more civilized living conditions: " 'I've pulled the two ears off him and left them hanging down his neck,' said Jerry cheerfully."

The attitude toward women is not less barbarous. Women in Germany have been given a medieval handicraft point of view and a program: *Kinder, Kirche, und Küche.* It is significant how similar the three K's are in any part of the world where there is oppression and fascist backwardness. Göring has told the women of Germany to bear children for the state, for war, till they are exhausted. How then was it possible for the writers, the builders of culture, to adopt an attitude of forbearance toward an anti-cultural fascist government? The Hitler technique was bold, fantastically demagogic. There were National-Socialism, the attack against the bankers, Junkers, industrialists,

40

promises to divide the estates, the anti-machine theories for intellectual medievalists and agrarians. Most important of all there was vast misery and unemployment, which explains why 80 per cent of the students in Germany went Nazi. In Social-Democratic Germany in 1931-32, of 22,000 teachers who completed their training, only 999 found posts. Conditions such as these made for the social basis of the desperate armies of fascism.

In the light of such fascist political methods, the silly public statement of a Feuchtwanger fleeing for his life from Germany with only a knapsack and his manuscript is understandable. At that time Feuchtwanger said that the atrocities that were being perpetrated in Germany were unknown to Hindenburg, who had buried the Weimar Constitution, had called in Hitler, and had sold out Germany in order to escape the inheritance tax, and for a nasty swamp in Neudeck given him by the swindling Junkers.

At this stage of Nazism H. G. Wells actually spoke at Oxford for a liberal fascism, and George Bernard Shaw said: "Give Hitler a chance." The *Fascist Week* wrote: "G.B.S. On the Brink. Will he ever wear a Black Shirt?" Klaus Mann, a refugee and certainly a sincere opponent of fascism, desired to overcome fascism with "intellectual manifestations." This is somewhat vague, and it leads us to believe that we can combat a storm-trooper by reading Anatole France or Proust to him. Of course, since then, both Wells and Shaw look toward the Soviet Union and not Nazi Germany for the hope of humanity.

Other writers have gone to the extreme right. But they are comparatively few in number. Wyndham Lewis, Vorticist painter, pamphleteer and novelist, wrote a book called *Hitler*; and he is today one of Sir Oswald Mosley's sponsors. It is interesting to note here that he at one time was a most astringent opponent of everything that was German. But he was anti-philistine and not anti-bourgeois. Plekhanov in the past has in essays on Flaubert and Zola remarked upon these very things. Only recently Joshua Kunitz in the *New Masses* has made a special point of this in his appraisal of Soviet and fellow-traveler writers. T. S. Eliot from the start hailed Sir Oswald Mosley's fascist sheet. About a year ago Eliot wrote for the *American Review,* which has marked fascist tendencies, that we must strive for homogeneity in America, and that Jews are disruptive and we must not be too tolerant. Dorothea Brande, an American writer with lean gifts, attacked Ludwig Lewisohn's recent critical work solely on racial grounds. This is not very clever of Miss Brande; for she must have been intellectually hard put, if she would attack Lewisohn as a Jew when it is so easy to destroy him as a writer.

Anti-Semitism is a key question today; wherever you find Jew-baiting you will not have to dig far to uncover a brown-shirt mentality. A writer who cannot completely embrace the cause of the oppressed racial minorities, Negro and Jew and others, will never be able to fight for or enter the new socialist order for which every civilized human being must contend. We have tried to understand and to sympathize with the confusions and dilemmas of writers; to point out that some were unclear, some wavered, but that with few exceptions they were sincere. But the times now are too urgent, and as Lenin put it concerning Turati, the Socialist, who had betrayed the working class in Italy, we cannot go around sticking sincere-ometers in people's sides. We must close our ranks and get rooted. And we should note that those writers, like Plievier, Neukrantz, Marchwitza, the murdered Mühsam, Johannes Becher, Heinrich Mann, Brecht, who were either with the proletariat or sympathetic with it, never wavered and were never confused.

We cannot wait. The fascists Huey Long and Father Coughlin are not waiting. We must take history in our hands and help write it from the creative point of view of those who labor and produce. Otherwise the Attilas will mangle it, and there will be nothing left of civilization.

The late Lord Balfour wailed over the fact that some day the earth would be destroyed, would be absorbed into the sun, and all consciousness and the heritage of awareness would be forever lost. In the meantime, as a man of contemplation as well as action, he had invested his money very heavily in the Vickers-Armstrong Munition Works. Well, we propose to be men and women of contemplation and action too, and invest what we have as writers in the working class of America and the world.

American Writers' Congress, 1935

Randolph Bourne

To Alfred Stieglitz: A Living Intransigent

To reëssay Randolph Bourne is to exhume a past, so immediate, and yet as forlornly lost as Atlantis. This fragment of our tradition has not yet found a ranking historian. Randolph Bourne, dead at thirty-two, in New York City, 1918, does not belong to us because we have not yet discovered him—because we have not disinterred ourselves.

Randolph Bourne's principal legacy to the present times is enveloped in two slight volumes, both regrettably out of print, *The History of a Literary Radical* and *Untimely Papers.* There were three other books anterior to these, *Youth and Life, Education and Living,* and *The Gary Schools,* which attest to his range and culture. A regular contributor to the *New Republic,* Bourne was also one of the "inner circle" of the *Seven Arts* magazine, founded by Waldo Frank and James Oppenheim, and defunct since October 1917. Here were first published the clairvoyant war essays, which, once set in motion, formed *Untimely Papers.*

The most interesting and poignant of his early writings is a "Philosophy of Handicap." The emotional energy which supplanted the low vitality flows into us and then back to him who needed it so sorely. We read with spasms of hurt "his failure" at sports, which he had as a boy attributed to "moral weakness" because of a "rigid Calvinistic bringing-up."

This self-portrait becomes acutely sculpted in our minds when we pause to consider the flesh-and-bone man, five feet high, with malformed back and chest, with stump of ear on left side of face, with twist to corner of mouth, an inward slope to the jaw. But the large gray eyes held the listener, and the speaking voice, despite the difficulty of muffled utterance, was sensuously pleasant. The spidery fingers, according to a classmate, could span two notes above an octave. When Bourne was travelling in the hill-towns of Italy, the native women and children crossed themselves in superstitious awe.

More telling, perhaps, than these physiognomic recollections, is the drawing of Arthur G. Dove from the death-mask by James Earle Fraser: the drama of the broad planes of the head and the face and the mouth are powerfully informed by an almost physical and mass-like intellect that deeply stays in the memory.

At Columbia University he had sat at the feet of Professor John Dewey, knelt there, and in 1913-14 as a holder of the Gilder Fellowship from that same institution he had received his baptism in those electric pre-war days in Europe. It was a violent farrago of impressions: the bitter Dublin strike, meetings in London halls of the early-martyr-suffragettes whose roar of "Shame!" at the "mention of wrongs done to women" was like a congregational Negro shout; there were the student demonstrations in Paris yelling: "Cail-laux As-sas-sin!" Florentine Futurism, the General Strike, a protest against the shooting of two workers in Ancona, and in Denmark "flaxen-haired boys, mobilizing along the country roads." Opposites were juxtaposed, social revolutionaries living side by side with the Church midst the superlative oxymoronic shibboleth that then prevailed in imperialist Europe, "armed peace."

With this preparation he returned to America, and to Romain Rolland's brave but ineffective "Above the Battle" Randolph Bourne rejoined with "Below the Battle" published in July 1917. We have but to recapture the aura of befogged intellectualism in the oceanic ambiguities in the April *Seven Arts* supplement on the war, or witness the amorphous flaccidness of Walter Lippmann's pages, or plough through Herbert Croly's *The Promise of American Life* to comprehend Bourne's isolation.

II

Bourne's problem was how to remain uninvaded by the war; and here we must remember that there was no defined precedent whatever for such action. For a moment, he believed that an intellectual sabotage, an anti-toxin seepage, already at work upon the youth of America, would effect a nation-wide breakdown. He hoped for a General Strike of the American Mind and Spirit against Woodrow Wilson's war conscription. Like the younger intelligentsia to whom Bourne had always addressed himself, he awaited word, the "papal blessing" of John Dewey. But Dewey had already gotten "into satisfactory relations with the other parts of our experience." The "slightly pedestrian gait into which the war had brought pragmatism," Bourne wrote, had also brought Dewey alongside of Spargo, Gompers, A. M. Simons and the vigilantes. So Pragmatism made the supreme sacrifice in 1917, and in the name of John Dewey, became the Unknown Soldier of Philosophy.

In the meantime, the intellectuals were caught up in a white-heat drama of nerve-vibrations, in the lust for motor rejuvenescence that only the orgasmic state of the "peacefulness of being at war" could bring. The war was a felicitous detour from drab everyday motor-control. On the extreme right the poet Donald Evans, whose letter in the *Sonnets from the Patagonian* reads like the Psychological Attack of the White Guards in the Soviet film *Chapayev,* had written: "Could I enlist a Battalion of Irreproachables, whose uniforms should be walking suit, top hat and pumps, and their only weapon an ebony stick, and sail tomorrow, we would march down Unter den Linden in a month, provided in our kerchiefs we carried the Gospel of Beauty, and a nonchalance in the knot of our cravats."

Randolph Bourne, who was deemed malicious by some critics—and how often is passionate accuracy, which foreshadows and challenges, mistaken for doggerel spite?—knew as Nietzsche had said, that we have to destroy one sanctuary in order to create another. And so he denounced John Dewey and the adjusters in "Twilight of Idols." He plainly saw that the instrumentalist technique of a bright and vivid cooperation with reality must accommodate itself to all levels as any literature of philosophy must that *cooperates* instead of violently colliding with things, incidents and their movable relations. A philosophy of reaction rather than action, pragmatism wholly lacked that "robust desperation" that Bourne demanded and which man must have in times of travail.

Bourne's remarkable polemic on John Dewey not only charts the casuistries of the liberal defensists on an "antiseptic war," but it also searchingly fluoroscopes the immediate and imminent behavior of a succeeding generation in another war period soon to come. Considerable proof of this lies in Dewey's *Human Nature and Conduct,* published in 1922, after the event. The Philosopher draws up such a super-subtle balance-sheet of opposing class thought-processes and counter-morals that the result is not an increased pragmatic understanding of bourgeois democracy but a political *tabula rasa.* The failure to recognize where the authority of morals must give way to the hegemony of economics leads the University Professor right back to zero. Yet the thinker who said, " 'I own, therefore I am,' expresses a truer psychology than the Cartesian 'I think, therefore I am' " can scarcely be maligned as an innocent.

III

There is a remorseless progression from "Below the Battle" to the "Unfinished Fragment on the State," and the hiatus in time between the appearance of the two essays is but six months. The mocking analysis of the Heraclitean myth that war is the father of all progress, the study of the intellectual stripped of the "psychic burden of adulthood" by complete absorption into the Motherhood of State, are in themselves searching studies in irony and paradox. When the herd-mind was at highest rage for conformity, believing in the "pure filial mysticism" behind Fatherland, Bourne was impelled toward logic. "But the war, which drove all the world including Dewey mad, drove Bourne sane," wrote Waldo Frank in *Our America* in 1919.

The art and ritual of the state sacrament, the metaphysics of the toy flag, permeate our fairy-tale histories. With the outbreak of war, we have a recrudescence of child fetishes of the flag, the army and navy, and other taboos of draft-evaders, Wobblies, and pacifists. We see the *toy* stars and lovers of the screen arousing the pen pusher to the most infantile religious and economic piety of the state by the sale of baby bonds!

The History of a Literary Radical reveals the blander tissues of Randolph Bourne's temperament. In a sense, the book is the obverse side of the black polemist in *Untimely Papers*.

Miro, the young idealist American prototype, in the *Literary Radical,* is a finely-wrought chalice for Bourne's aesthetic and psychological observations. We see Miro soon after matriculation submerged in the pallid ghost background of American university life; he is seeped in the phantom academic fluid translations of "Gallic battles and Anabatic frosts" subtly rendered less abstruse and otherworldly by fiscal commencement orations delivered annually by the college president. Only after the first crack in the "Ptolemaic system of reverences" does Miro emerge into the secular world of *Anna Karenina, Smoke,* and Thomas Hardy.

Bourne's reëssaying of Stuart Sherman's pathology of "the sanely and wholesomely American," his compressed analysis of the "pachydermatous vulgarisms" of Mencken's highbrow Bronx cheers at Philistia and Meredith Nicholson's "folksiness," still current in present-day confectionery agrarian novels, his neat placing of the Arnoldian quantitative ideal of culture, were an anachronism in 1917.

48

A Danish thinker has said that we live forwards and understand backwards. However, the tragic fissure between retrospection and the present in the poet was almost preternaturally absent in Raldoph Bourne. The demonic insights and leviathan revelations, which we associate with poetry and the novel, with William Blake or *Moby-Dick,* make us forget that criticism has been, and can be, a preterhuman madness in art. *America's Coming of Age,* published in 1915 by Van Wyck Brooks, is a literary anachronism because criticism in America has not yet caught up to it; and Randolph Bourne's *Untimely Papers* and *The History of a Literary Radical* also had that sense of the archaic about it because he was years in advance of the "old orthodoxies of the classics and the new orthodoxies of propaganda."

The inclusion of the "Portraits," in the *Literary Radical,* posthumously published, six small ironies on advance-guard feminism in essayistic short story form, is no cemetery garland bequeathed *con amore* by a few friends. These studies in the "tissue of personal relations," in which the unpredictable quirks and reactions of the feminine mind are allocated and examined with a mathematic tenderness, are wholly without the pedestrian sensationalism of more recent examples in literature. "Karen," who sought a "smooth and silky rapport," just this side of those "naïve collisions between men and women" in her finely-spun fabrics of friendship, "Sophronisba," M.A. at an American college "invented for slender and thin-lipped New England maidens," "Fergus," a "princely connoisseur" who walked "through his own historic galleries"—these and the others are engraved pragmatic theories, "unstiffened" into narrative incidents.

His sitters are professors, feminists and a university president, Alexander Mackintosh Butcher, alias for the monetary educator, Dr. Butler, who draws "analogies between the immutability of Anglo-Saxon political institutions and the multiplication tables."

"The Professor," very recognizable, is a hagiographic study in life and letters of a university career. "Shuddering pensively on the brink of declining faith," the Professor writes "Ganymede," the prose-poem, and at the age of twenty-three does his masterly thesis of "The Anonymous Lyrics of the Fourteenth Century." Further absorbing himself into the "Circumambient life" of the college, we capture the quiet meditative poesy of the tread leading to the Chairmanship of English Literature. But one of the most memorable moments is the Professor's poem of himself emerging from the "Dim organ-haunted shadows" of the chapel into the sunlight where "careless athletes" run "bare-leggedly past him, unmindful of the eternal things."

Bourne's essay on Newman's *Apologia* is now so apposite. How fit are these phrasings of Bourne's, the "Sin of schism," "the precious milk of doctrine." To what uses might not the Marxian critics of literature put Cardinal Newman's passionate quest for the Holy Grail of infallibility and for Dogma, "the bony structure and life blood" of Experience, as a safety-valve against ecclesiastical communism?

When we pause to consider Randolph Bourne's own youth and remember what Amiel had said, that only at fifty could a critic hope to "have made the rounds of all the modes of being," we are astonished at his scope and manifold interests in philosophy, literature, sociology, politics. His "Ernest: or Parent for a Day" is a charming excursus, a realistic phantasy on child education. The reciprocal pleasure and ease between Bourne and the child make us aware of the magic effect of the plangent voice and the large gray eyes which so effortlessly rearranged the body dwarfed "by the fumbling hand of nature." We, too, are completely changed and our senses cleansed and sunned by the pagan pleasure Bourne took in the sensitive plant life of childhood: "He would look so calmly and yet so eagerly, and give you a pleasant satisfaction that just your mere presence, your form, your movement, were etching new little lines on his cortex, sending little shoots of feeling through his nerves."

In America, where the soil is so hospitable to the rankest stalks of compromise, Randolph Bourne was that rare impossibilist he had set out to be—an intransigent in Letters, Politics and War. For our own *Democratic Vistas* we must go not to Whitman but to *Untimely Papers* and to the *Literary Radical.*

As a figure Randolph Bourne was perhaps the noblest of our young century: and as a writer he bears a certain special comparison to Stephen Crane. Both Bourne and Crane were minor poets, one in imaginative criticism and the other in verse and the short story, minor, because their lives were too brief to bring them the fullest fruition of their extraordinary temperaments—minor, but perdurable.

Randolph Bourne wished to rescue Thoreau, Emerson and Whitman for our literature and life, and now Bourne, who belongs with them, must in turn, the sad grim truism of the repetitious history of American Culture, be salvaged and brought back to us.

American Spectator, 1937

*

The History of a Literary Radical and Other Papers, by Randolph Bourne, introduction by Van Wyck Brooks.

Many books have been canonized by the dullards of the press and the American academies. We are still piling up mediocre books in our charnel-house of literature in order to give us a false, big Parnassus. Who but a gray-haired boy of an English department can still prate about William Dunlap or Charles

51

Brockden Brown, or intone Emerson's "Oversoul," or Freneau's "A Fly Drowned in a Glass of Water," which are elocution exercises for a crepuscular doctor of letters waiting for the cemetery laurels of the emeritus professor.

Randolph Bourne is a minor figure, but not a niggard one. Now that he is venerable ashes, it is with great reluctance that I relegate this dear nature to a region of half-limbo in our literature. Bourne was a monumental experience of mine, and if I may be allowed to say it, is the literature of my juvenilia. Just as I admire Bourne, I still give homage to Tolstoy's *Letters* and his *Patriotism and Slavery,* and George Gissing's *By the Ionian Sea,* but I cannot reread them or no longer have any artistic need of them.

Randolph Bourne, dead at thirty-two, was a humpback, not more than five feet tall, with the head of a savant and the body of a crippled child. He was more flawed by nature than Pope or Kierkegaard. Theodore Dreiser, once strolling in the evening along the walk by the old courthouse at the corner of Eighth and Greenwich Streets, saw a gnome pass him and stepped back to brace himself against the brick wall. The poor dwarf was wearing a black wide brimmed hat, and a cape, resembling the mourning weeds of a witch in a Walpurgisnacht. Bourne was a disciple of John Dewey, and belonged to that castaway sodality of Grub Street, earning his indigence as an illuminated hack book reviewer.

He was a gentle nature, that is high-spirited, as Edmund Spenser would use these words, and had no intention of being the mellow or decayed gentleman of belles lettres. He was too audacious for the canting literati of his day and ours, or for the pragmatic priest of philosophy, John Dewey.

Nothing has changed since the time of Bourne. In his endeavor to rouse the lotophagi from their long pragmatic sleep, he earned their malignity. After he rebuked Dewey, in his essay "Twilight of Idols," for inveighing against the conscientious objector, the professor demanded that the *Dial* shut its literary columns to him. The *New Republic,* unable to tolerate one helpless dissident who could not envisage an "antiseptic war," banished him, refusing to let him earn that pauper's locusts and honey for writing literary reviews. The American cannot digest one negation. The mildest iconoclasms are a threat to the national homogeneity, fostered by trade, avarice, and unimaginable sloth. Had not Van Wyck Brooks in his younger days when he was not venal declared that American literature had never had the least effect upon the United States. This gendarmerie of the press and the periodicals inter books that are not in agreement with their visionary democratic programs in a literary necropolis known as the book reviewing supplement.

Charles Beard called him a guttersnipe. Amy Lowell, whom he admired, detested this political mystagogue and his opposition to war. Bloat with elephantiasis herself, Amy Lowell called the humpbacked Bourne diseased. The woman who provided the money for the *Seven Arts* withdrew her support because she could not abide Bourne's distrust of a war waged abroad for democracy, while at home there was suppression of every kind of freedom in thought and feeling. The Justice Department had confiscated his trunk filled with papers which they thought contained secret ciphers of espionage, but they were only his unpublished verse.

It is a somber irony that the two burghers of our pecuniary Olympus, Van Wyck Brooks and Lewis Mumford, are his advocates. It has become the custom to hire men who cannot write to write about those who can. Unless the reader is made familiar with Bourne's sufferings and his devout loneliness during this Stygian period, he will be revivified by those who buried him. For it is the foxes who spoil the grapes who feign to dress the vines of Jericho.

What were Randolph Bourne's ideas which were regarded as some fungus in Tartarus growing upon the tender fabric of the libertarian American commonwealth?

He had little faith in our colleges of lower learning. Had not Erasmus said that wherever there is popular education there is no higher learning. His essay on Miro's education should be read by every professor and student. Those who are graduates of the gigantic cartels of arts and letters still cringe when recollecting those lectures on Anaxagoras, Anaximenes, and the *Iliads*. The pre-Socratic philosophers and Homer were crepuscular and congealed algebra, and never the sorrow and the intellectual laughter of human bowels. How long it took a student accustomed to the etiolated ambiguities of a secular friar in the English department to discover one viable man. With a delicacy too difficult for the nervous system the student had to eschew the exquisite vocalisms of the otherworldy professor as well as the popular boyisms of the academic vulgarian.

Bourne saw that there was no difference between the "cultivated herd and the rabble," but he was more of an instrumentalist than an icon-breaker, for he imagined that we had traveled farther in learning than the great medieval Abelard. He had in mind a university which was a kind of trans-figured vocational guidance school. As a young man he had done a callow volume, with another, on the Gary schools.

He had that faded, period belief in cooperatives, in a radical, robustious equality, in workingman's suburbs, and in socialist "model garbage-disposal," which have been woefully realized. No earthquake, hurricane, or bomb could make of our cities and streets such a wreck and shambles as these functional Marxist slums, all brand new, and of such an insane similarity that the soberest person is no better than the drunkard when looking for his own apartment at night. As a "moral equivalent for war," a shabby phrase he borrowed from William James, he suggested that American boys and girls, somewhat after the manner of the traveling Miracle Players, should go from town to hamlet, mending "slovenly fences and outhouses."

I mention these flaws in Bourne, but I do not hesitate to

declare that he is of more worth to the young, purblind pilgrim in the universal dunghill of nations than Farquhar and Vanbrugh, and most of the writers of the Restoration. I couple his name with theirs because they were all dead around thirty and had not time to come to know that it is ritual and fable that are the groundwork of a true commonwealth. It is better to be Musaeus—though he wrote nothing except the "Hymn to Demeter"—than to be a rag-raker in politics. Whether Bourne would have relinquished those Utopias, which are Gorgons in our bowels, and returned to Hellas, no one can know.

Randolph Bourne wrote five books, but three are dross. Most of the essays in this volume have been culled from his two best books, both posthumously published, *The History of a Literary Radical* and *Untimely Papers*. May Pan and Aesculapius guard his name and works so that they will not be the loot and the plagiarized fame of the modern illiterati. Fame is always a bawd who leers at the living as well as the dead.

New Mexico Quarterly, 1957

Ford Madox Ford

Several years ago Ford Madox Ford had a small apartment above a French restaurant, on lower Fifth Avenue. He spoke and breathed with much labor so that his words were hardly audible, and he was very fat. He is such an obese, porcine Falstaff, I thought. A little later, I met at Stieglitz's American Place Sherwood Anderson, who also had a fleshy face. I began to change my mind about what a writer should look like, turning less to the famished, crucifixed Savonarola, the St. John of locusts and honey, for wisdom, than to your heavy, jovial knights, with beer and sausage in their cheeks. Recall what a lean silhouette Don Quixote on the modern French canvas is; how elliptic and halved he is without the mutton in Sancho's belly. I began to believe, particularly in a coarse, macadam land, where Baal and Dagon are the Philistine automobile and the villainous garage, and where all grassy, rural crafts are almost extinct, that a writer ought to live near Italian olive oil, table wines, fine citrons, and that he ought to have some human, mother's touch of the trade in his countenance, the shoemaker, the baker, the miller. I do not know why we look to the gaunt wolvish eye, for goodness. Does not Isaiah say that only the skin that is seasoned with butter and honey can discern good and evil.

Ford had a large, loafy face, and a titan's head, in which were set vast blue orbs, really two sea coves. This is not just a literary mannerism for creating a dimensional effect. He really had girth to his features, which I remember furtively doting upon at one of his Thursday afternoon teas at 10 Fifth Avenue. He was wholly your fat, fecund nature. Sherwood Anderson once said to me when we were speaking of Ford, "Ford used to invite friends, or anybody that came along, to a mansion, or manor in the south, that he never had." Of course, only a Quixote gives what he does not possess, because of a goodly, savory, free nature. And he takes, too, in the same manner, or else how can we know what a forlorn disenchantment there is in the gallant Don Quixote's heart when he says to the varlet innkeeper who demands money, "This is an inn; I have then lived in error."

He used to make those same ample, preposterous, and bellied remarks about literature, either out of mirth, or because his globular head rotated so fast, that in a man of less books, ay, real ones, a meaner palate, or taste, would have made me decry him as a pickpocket, a Pharisee, a Barabbas. I could not understand his sympathies for regionalism, which to me is just the apotheosis of yokelism. Once, over a pair of fried eggs, and some cheese, and while he sat with me, his suspenders down, because it must have been easier for his asthma that way, he said, "Everything that Shakespeare wrote, except *The Tempest, Timon,* was hack-work; *Hamlet* was a potboiler." From a lesser soul this would have been an obscene, a churl's observation. But such perverseness is the privilege of oracles; if a ninny or a Pilate makes the same statement, even if it be true, it is a lie!

And, of course, according to Ford, America had a drove of geniuses. He had that feeling for the writer that a medieval guildsman had, that heart's breeding of the European spirit, which the American author rarely shows. Like Maxim Gorki, Ford must have wept over so many geniuses he had helped, that a museum could have been established just for the vests his tears had fallen on, as one Russian had said. But then had not Ford discovered that witch with the russet beard, D. H. Lawrence, and that Empedoclean imposter, Ezra Pound. He got publication for how many talents and drones! He kept his door open to everybody. You could go to the apartment at 10 Fifth Avenue, of three or four secondhand Quatorze chairs, a poor spindly table, the scantest number of books, a jetty sphynxed cat, several of his wife Biala's paintings of Paris rains, or murmurously lighted artichoke-colored buildings along quays or the Seine, all of which was served to you with tea and Sutter's cakes, and not feel like the miserable Onan of the street the American has become. It was the only literary salon I know that was not a carrion sty and humbug; there was, surely, that "caitiff choir" of fops, panders, lady poetasters, literary agents, an illegitimate juxtaposition of words, and sprawling Lucifers of splinter political movements who had been hurled out of the communist planetary regions, that inevitably surround a man of letters. But you could see about him also a gifted face, the poet William Carlos Williams, the rare painter Marsden Hartley, the original puritan artist Elizabeth Sparhawk-Jones, or capture the flittering image of the gentle Brancusi. Ford had a relish for the gallant dimension. He told me once after reading passages out of Izaak Walton and Sir Thomas Browne, that he had not consulted a single book, or reference, for that Elysium of knowledge, *The March of Literature.* I do not know whether he was the picaro, the enchanted liar, that Richard Aldington has depicted him in his memoirs. My own doubts, I am sure, are the mean, pismire issue of a base, homunculus generation. Then does not Schiller say that a lie that elevates us is often better than the truth?

To say that Ford Madox Ford, expired at sixty-six, died at the right time, before the carnage of the man-eating cannibals, is to beg a widow's alms and heritage. It is to ask the gods, and the darkling devils, for compounded holocausts. Who can say how much alchemic dust, wilily sieved and shaped, over how many centuries and aeons, it takes to mould a Ford Madox Ford, or a Sherwood Anderson. As long as Ford Madox Ford and Sherwood Anderson were alive, was not the heart, that is exhausted long before the carnivore's rational brain, still jetting that wild asses' milk of vision and mirth, without which life eats us.

New Directions Annual, 1942

"OLD MAN MAD ABOUT WRITING"

The Life and Work of Ford Madox Ford, by Frank MacShane, and *Letters of Ford Madox Ford,* edited by Richard M. Ludwig

In the last few years it has been the custom of Yahoo biographers to vilify the heroes of literature. Hardly one nineteenth-century author has been spared by the Cerberuses who bay the moon and bark at the shades they pretend to commemorate. This screed of vulgarity has dominated the English reviewers who lick up the dregs of man's worst traits while neglecting his contribution to the commonwealth. We are told that Coleridge was inert and lumpish and hated to write, but the same was true of Dr. Johnson, who was a far better talker than an author. That Walter Savage Landor threw his cook out of the window because he fried a Hecate's supper, and not that he wrote the *Imaginary Conversations,* is important. We are advised that Oliver Goldsmith was a scantling for not supporting his nephew, and that Ruskin was immoral because he was impotent. Recently Mr. Swanberg has disclosed that Theodore Dreiser was a swindler and an implacable philanderer, and he has given us such a repulsive portrait that he has very likely buried Dreiser's works for a half century.

Frank MacShane in his *Life and Work of Ford Madox Ford,* however, has shown us a Quixote of letters whose kindness to obscure or apprentice writers was a visionary madness. His book is a festival of Ford's life. MacShane's memoir is a Herculean labor; he is more familiar with Ford than any of that author's friends. This life is a parcel of literary history few of the elders of letters know, and it is almost entirely obscure to the weanlings of our century.

It was said that Ford was the last of the Pre-Raphaelites, but

Ford denied this, claiming that Joseph Conrad and he were the first Impressionists. Dante Gabriel and Christina expected every Rossetti and Hueffer to be bred up as an artist. It might appear marvelous to have had such savants as relations, but since everyone's childhood is his nemesis, Ford was most anxious to get out of the museum of geniuses his family had created. Ford wrote: "To me life was simply not worth living because of the existence of Carlyle, of Mr. Ruskin, of Mr. Holman Hunt, of Mr. Browning . . ."

Early in his career he had to change his Teutonic surname of Hueffer to Ford. Though his tradition and sympathies were devoutly English—when he had a seizure of despondency George Herbert was his only balm—the scavengers of the patriotic Philistia were at his heels because he had a Germanic name. Ford enlisted in the army, was wounded on the Somme, gassed at Armentières, and was to be plagued for the rest of his life by the damage done him in the first World War.

As a callow author he had been the friend of Henry James, whose bourgeois high tea style of prose haunted many of his novels. Ford, as Merton Densher in *Wings of the Dove,* is "longish, leanish and fairish." As MacShane observes, Ford wrote a number of pseudo-Jamesian novels.

In 1894 Ford married the seventeen-year-old Elsa Martindale and tried the cloistered rural life as an impecunious gentleman of literature. In spite of visits with the Garnetts, Stephen Crane, and Joseph Conrad—himself a solitary—and epistolary friendships with H. G. Wells, Galsworthy, and W. H. Hudson, he grew weary of kitchen gardening, the mire and rural rain while diagramming fiction. Ben Jonson in sixteenth-century London might pretend "I'll purchase Devonshire and Cornwall and make them perfect Indies," but Ford could not. Already tired of planting potatoes in the English marshes he wanted to be a Cadmus who sowed letters in the bohemian quarters of great cities. His life was in all respects a paradox. When he dwelt in a literary metropolis he pined to be a novelist-farmer in

Provence or to be with the Tates in Tennessee. As MacShane has it: "In his *Women and Men* . . . as in *Provence* and *Great Trade Route* . . . he pitted the natural goodness of the simple agricultural class against the avarice and inhumanity of the financiers of Birmingham and London."

Although he saw that "gas and water socialism" was pseudo-utopianism, he founded the *English Review* which he regarded as a socialist undertaking. Above all he loathed what was mediocre—the Meynell family of poetasters, and Tennyson Victorianism. This was, in great measure, the reason for the existence of his *English Review*.

The august headquarters of this international periodical was a cock-loft above a fishmonger's shop; there he discovered and published Thomas Hardy, Joseph Conrad, H. G. Wells, D. H. Lawrence, Wyndham Lewis, and Norman Douglas. Many of those he befriended have left us rancid gammons of words about the young Ford. Garnett remembered him as having skin "the color of raw veal" and "rabbit teeth." Wyndham Lewis called him a "flabby lemon," and Richard Aldington who vilified everybody he knew, said Ford spoke under his breath to compel his word-apprentices to listen to him. As I knew him many years later he was a pink Nordic, with a steep, sloping forehead, tender azury eyes, and the sagging nether lip of a Silenus.

Ford published his first book at eighteen and by the time he had arrived, and experimentalist that he was he was always arriving, he knew the full, heady ripeness of disappointment. Of his trade he said it was "*un métier de chien,*" and added in a letter: "And all the time you will know fasting and cold nights for lack of covers, bitter viands and sleep tormented by regrets."

Pound claimed that Ford had "wasted forty novels in which there are excellent parts merely buried in writing done at his second best." Then who has forty immortal books in his shoaly soul? Having said farewell to the Elizabethans, what else was left but a perverse credo which has to be the Mosaic law for later writers. Ford had expunged more than a moiety of English poetry and suggested that modern slang was the manna of literature. As a result of his influence upon bookish men one is now considered an antiquarian if one mentions any writer who lived before the time of Henry James. Pound, his acolyte, had a craw for all the gravely dicta Ford could pour down it. Pound dismissed "The old crusted lice and advocates of corpse language."

According to Ford the Elizabethans were, with the exception of Shakespeare, a gaggle of turgid poeticules. "O, Lord! What a single one of them, except Shakespeare, cd. express a clear thought clearly?" When I knew Ford in 1937 or '38 he informed me that aside from *Timon of Athens* and *Lear* all of Shakespeare's plays were potboilers. *Hamlet* was just a piece of jobbing. Ford could say, forget the old diction, never mind your precedessors—and at the same time have his hero, Christopher Tietjens, in his novel *Some Do Not,* state that all that was good in English literature ended with the seventeenth century. But since life is senseless, and art is supposed to have the logic it lacks, I felt Ford had a monarch's privilege to behead what he believed was the flummery of the great poets. Besides, it does not matter what the writer says but what his books are that counts.

I can make nothing of his bizarre dogma: "*Education Sentimentale* is Stonehenge; but *What Maisie Knew* is certainly Stratford-on-Avon," and I allege that jargon, the howl of Lucifer, cannot quicken the pulses as Gavin Douglas, Ben Jonson, and Webster do—but take or leave it. All creeds are hemlock to the author, and any canon narrowly followed is likely to result in trumpery verse.

The *mot juste,* which Ford took from Flaubert as the magic and receipt for any good book, is often an accident. Ford exchanged one shibboleth for another, which did not bother the bourgeoisie who seldom read him. However, he also began to change women, and that was quite another matter. After Ford divorced his wife, Henry James, who relished a cuckold or adultery on his own pages but who could neither be the one nor commit the other, viewed Ford's misdemeanor with very English bowler and umbrella hauteur. Ford wrote to the young Herbert Read warning him about his own native Yorkshiremen who "conceal the Venus of Milo, as she used to be concealed in Leeds Art Gallery, behind Aspidistras!" By 1911, as MacShane tells us, "his reputation was ruined." Except for sporadic successes, he was a congenital failure.

But Ford knew how to come out of the dumps; again he leaned upon Flaubert's counsel, which Ford passed on to me: "After all work is still the best means of getting the better of life." He created another *belles-lettres* magazine, *Transatlantic Review,* and issued his usual manifestos from Bedlam grounded upon the vernacular, and bade farewell to the demigods of the past. But, of course, after twelve issues, including the works of Joyce, Gertrude Stein, Hemingway, Paul Valéry, Djuna Barnes and William Carlos Williams, the *Transatlantic* expired.

Meantime he had composed verses, as Frank MacShane divulges, which were loosely based on Pope's *Dunciad.* Although Ford claimed he detested rhymed verse, offering as an example *Greenwich* and *spinach,* this did not prevent him from ending one line of a poem with *drain* and the next *cellophane.* Always a droll, Christopher Tietjens makes sonnets.

By 1930 Ford was once more a celebrated obscurian. When I had the honor of knowing him it seemed to me he was writing posthumously. He felt that the greatest portion of his sublunar existence was spent "in a dismal world of falling leaves."

Ford's last five books, according to his biographer, had disappointing sales, and no publisher was eager to buy another. By the time he began *The March of Literature,* his ultimate book, he had scrabbled off well over seventy volumes. This is a tome of more than eight hundred huffing, wheezy pages, one half of which is eccentric and iconoclastic and the other part bread and butter gossip. MacShane says: "Ford's work was uneven and his conception of his subject rarely lived up to the technical brilliance of his writing." But Ford, to use his own phrase, was a "professional prosateur": he was sure to offer enough rashers of edible ideas to gratify a reader hungry for literature. The book will vex you, raise your curiosity, and never wholly appease your intellect, but one can cite many sound and absolutely right judgments that should placate the avenging Muses.

Ford was good and also froward to the end. Anti-academic, he took the position of the pedantic philister maintaining that most of Shakespeare's plays were written for money. Of course, he employed all the draff of Shakespearean apocrypha to prove his point; nevertheless, what Ford said makes the mob elocutions Shakespeare composed for the pit clearer.

How much Ford read to garner up all these bibliographical sources for his *March of Literature* would be hard to guess. His scanty remarks about Langland's *Piers Plowman* he could have gotten from an easy perusal of Skeat's Introduction and the Prologue to the *Vision*. Often Ford rants like Pound dismissing Virgil as "the good, upper middle class townsman." Again he is the mediocre textbook pedagogue in his description of Tacitus who "marshals his facts" in an "impeccable manner." And then who wants his maudlin trash about Heine's "Du bist wie eine Blume"? But rail at him as much as you like, call his work a jumble of antique curios, you are certain to come upon a truth you will always hoard.

Ford asked: "Where would English prose be without Walton's *Compleat Angler*, White's *Natural History of Selborne*." I suppose it is of niggling consequence to remind his hearers of the stale sophisms of his earlier days by quoting the following: "Without any Shakespeare at all, Elizabethan-Jacobean England would still have a great literature." Since everybody is unreasonable, including a great man like Ford, it would be cant to expect him to be other than he was.

64

After struggling for decades to bring the poems and novels of obscure practitioners of letters to the attention of the public Ford hardly notices them at all in this prodigious volume. There is no mention of D. H. Lawrence's *Studies in Classical American Literature,* which had been graved for seventeen years, or of William Carlos Williams's *In the American Grain,* also cast into limbo since 1925. In an epistle which I have taken from the *Letters* edited by Richard M. Ludwig, he spoke of "The Mediterranean," and several other poems Tate had sent him, as having a "lapidary sureness and hardness that puts you . . . alone among the poets." But Allen Tate too is omitted. There is not even a fugaceous allusion to Herbert Read's almost faultless pastoral *Annals of Innocence,* to Robert Lowell, or Josephine Herbst, one of whose novels he had gotten published.

Was Ford crafty, a clandestine admirer of literary goods for which there were then no customers? He had said nearly all writers from the eighteenth century to our own times were Lilliputian hacks. Was he larding the oblivion of writers he had so furiously defended? After *The March of Literature* appeared, Ford and I organized the Society of Friends of William Carlos Williams. A moribund "old man mad about writing," he secured publication of Williams's *The White Mule* in England, and hardly able to breathe he read my ms., *Can These Bones Live,* and offered to write the Introduction to it, but he died in Deauville.

Ford Madox Ford was the ridiculous man of passion whom Stendhal thought could not exist in the northern countries. An elegant, impecunious gourmet of letters and cuisine who but Ford, as E. E. Cummings remarked, could "find an urinoir in a bank on Fifth Avenue and have the courage to use it without having an account there." In another epistle culled from Ludwig's volume, Ford, quoting a Chinese proverb, wrote, "It is hypocritical to seek for the person of the Sacred Emperor in a low tea-house." I respect everything about Ford Madox Ford, for all his days he browsed among the asphodels looking for a novelist or a poet, a legend or a book, that would increase the republic of literature.

The *Letters of Ford Madox Ford* reveal his nature and also show that he was not just another proser of our century. Nobody can understand our age without a knowledge of Ford Madox Ford. Moreover I think *Joseph Conrad: A Personal Remembrance, Portraits from Life,* and even *Return to Yesterday,* amorphous reminiscences about Oscar Wilde and Stephen Crane, are enchanting. I can think of no remarkable memorabilia of a noble figure so faithful to its hero as Gilchrist's book on William Blake, and now Frank MacShane's *The Life and Work of Ford Madox Ford.*

New York Review, 1965

Our Avant Garde Illiterates

There is no more unlettered writer than the naturalistic novelist; in the name of bread, reason and enlightenment he has created a humdrum cage for simians. Garnett, the critic, once said that the Oscar Wilde trial had set English poetry back fifty years; the retarding influence of Zola's *La Terre* and *Germinal* on American literature has been even more disastrous.

The American naturalist, whose fount is Zola, is prurient, and his *homo economicus* is inert and without will; his anti-hero is a mediocre, fatalistic Colossus governed by the dreary wage god of economic determinism. This god employs the shears of Atropos, Greek Necessity, with the same sadistic violence that Popeye uses to cut up kittens in Faulkner's *Sanctuary*. Environment, poverty and wanton, wart-like illiteracy are the nemesis and the fate of the Popeye anti-hero. In the Faulkner and Caldwell fiction there is no difference between the sick stupidity of the protagoanist and that of the author. It was Gauguin who said that when the washerwoman in a Zola novel spoke, Zola wrote as she talked, and that when she ceased speaking, Zola still wrote like the washerwoman.

The American Popeye-hero is impotent, and the Popeye Faulkner novelist is a medieval corncob poet of everyday banalities that have a Rasputin odor. The product of the Popeye school of writing is a black, corrupt sacrament of bread and violence, a decayed, sham saviorism. Faulkner, the Nobel Prize winner, gives us a diseased world, a moldy poor white class—and all in the name of truth and humanity. His idols recall the dog-relics which, according to Gorki, the Russian monks used to sell to ignorant peasants as the sacred remains of a saint. There is neither health nor sun in Faulkner, and his readers are compelled to witness the spectacle of fetid, dying

67

people who are dour and wicked. There is no wit, or good ripe bawd, in him as ease or balm for the suffering, ailing mind. The ear is never quieted by the "faint sound of the trumpet of justice" coming from a Georgia cracker's ram's horn. Horus is the Egyptian god of writing and of the moon, but Faulkner's novels are moon-madness unworthy of Horus, and his language is a ruined and half-lost speech like the abc divisions of "she," "he," and "I," the characters in *The Sound and the Fury.*

Faulkner never bothered to learn how to write, as is evident in his amateur child-cult primitivism—"Twilight ran in like a violet dog"—or in that guttering infantile anthropomorphism in the "bearded watching trees" or the "sourceless . . . suspurant . . . moon." The baby cult speech quickly passes over into nausea and the impotency obsession. Faulkner's desiccated Taliafferro in *Mosquitoes* looks like an "extracted tooth," Jennie has "soft, wormlike fingers," and Cecily Saunders an "epicene chin and sexless knees." Faulkner's Januarius Jones contemplates his beloved with "yellow eyes, warm and clear as urine."

There is that nihilistic, ungovernable nausea in all the naturalistic or Marxist novelists who write with a pen that is a muckrake. Frank Norris's intellectual retching is plagiarized from Dr. Swift. The rodents in *Gulliver's Travels* are the results of hopeless, cruel revulsion against human flesh. When Gulliver returns home he faints when his wife kisses him, and he reels with queasiness as his son touches the bread on the table with his fingers. Swift regarded sex as abominable, and Norris in *McTeague* had the same misogynistic qualms; for when that ugly bulk of stupor, the quack dentist McTeague, looks at the young, delicate Trina Sieppe, her hair reminds him of ordure. After Trina has left his ursine, suety arms, she goes home, opening the door just as her mother is setting the mouse traps. Dr. Swift was at least a man of honest letters and recognized his malady no less than Thoreau, who did not even like the sex habits of cabbages. But Norris and the other American naturalistic novelists have no comparable self-knowledge.

Dostoevsky was very troubled about human odors: In *The Brothers Karamazov,* Christian Alyosha has real atheistical misgivings when he confronts Father Zossima's corpse. The odor of decay is hard evidence to refute, and those who depend entirely upon the evidence of their noses are likely to lose their reason, for as Thoreau (whose Puritan olfactories were much too agile and precise) said, "The imagination is wounded long before the conscience." Poor Alyosha Karamazov, who tries desperately to heal the injury done to his spirit, sits on the tomb of a saint whose body was said to have given off the remarkably good fragrance of a budding lemon branch.

There is no budding lemon-branch fragrance in the American naturalistic novelists; sadism and revulsion and communism have one miserable, cankered skin. Erskine Caldwell was a gifted, picaresque necrophile in his first book, *American Earth.* This early Caldwell book is a Georgia cracker prose-poem on fungused trees, an infected, pucc-colored evening sky, a dissevered hand, an amputated leg. Later on Caldwell made a Marxist proletarian rite of his corpse-lust, trying to palm off as communistic compassion a scene in which hogs devour an oppressed Negro sharecropper's throat. Miss Josephine Herbst, a sensitive author, writes of the sickness in the novel "where the worms are stroked with loving."

Hemingway, too, has always been swinging a sacramental gore-censer in such books as *Death in the Afternoon, Green Hills of Africa* and *A Farewell to Arms.* The constant Hemingway quest has been for horror, crime, war and cataclysm; whether he is shooting a doe or acting as a spectator of the Spanish civil war, he always stresses his fierce martial olfactories. Hemingway betrays the exquisite, murdering scent of the animal pursuing prey. His passion is best characterized by a Mexican insurrectionist in Azuela's *Underdogs* who shouts, "Villa, Carranza, Obregon! What do I care, so long as it is the revolution!" Or by Herzen, the Russian revolutionary who cries, "Long live destruction!"

Hemingway cannot write sharply unless a man is shooting an elephant or performing a caesarian operation with a jackknife. He has no intellectual virility and is a slack gawk in an amorous scene, of which there are many to attest to this debility in *A Farewell to Arms* and in his most recent book, *Across the River and into the Trees.* But Hemingway can break the slim flowing neck of a kudu in a firm, thrusting sentence, or cause an Indian to slash his throat with a razor in a remorseless, compressed phrase. He can paint the willowy quiver of a deer, or the Goya-like wound of a gored horse with Caligulan art. He is the most artistic assassin in the literature business.

Frank Norris's successors, Faulkner, Hemingway, Caldwell, for all their avowed social purposes, are vandals who pour bile upon nature, the human seed, women. Hatred of women is dominant in Faulkner; this is wantonly revealed in *Sanctuary* by Popeye, who ravishes Temple Drake with a corncob. The Faulkner males are traumatic impotents who commit violence for erotic shock, very similar to Poe's wan Roderick Usher, the ancestor of the Satanic ballerina male of today. Practically every Poe tale is about a feminine male who fears the "gigantic volition" of a Ligeia, a Madeleine Usher, or a Berenice. Every marriage bed in Poe is a catafalque. Baudelaire, who prayed to Edgar Poe before beginning to write, thought of sexuality as the lyricism of the masses—a revealing commentary on both Poe and Baudelaire.

Underneath the naturalistic novelist's text is the beast: Norris, Faulkner, Caldwell, Hemingway, have the same brute undercrust. The main fault with these writers is not a lack of talent; it is niggard character. Nietzsche said that creating is self-willing. Faulkner is a willless artist whose words are made up of the paste and blood out of which the Aztec god of war was composed. Faulkner, like the others, has never had enough volition to educate his gift; he is an unlettered monk with the most sadistic medieval superstitions. The Faulkner Gothic shocker is set for a Faustian drama, but across the stage stalks not Mephisto but Mickey Mouse—the "Colossus of the little," to use Wyndham Lewis's phrase.

Another in the brute tradition is James T. Farrell. Farrell's Studs Lonigan has the same sickness as Popeye, for how can Lonigan be a real stud in Farrell's unpigmented prose? As for Farrell's later books, the reader is tempted to ask: Why is it that when an author writes the same book often he acquires a reputation? Maybe, as Samuel Butler once surmised, dullness is so much further advanced than genius because it is so much better organized.

The mediocrity fetish was also strong in Dreiser, the erotica business writer whose books remind one of the Mt. Kisco mansion he built to look like a Log Cabin Syrup can. It was Dreiser who, after visiting the Tolstoy home at Yasnaya Polyana and seeing nothing on the shelves but almanacs, said that even he had read more than Tolstoy.

Faulkner and Hemingway are disciples of Sherwood Anderson, who on alternate days worshipped the literary baby prose of Gertrude Stein's "Melanctha." The primer grammar sentences of Anderson and Hemingway (born of a mixture of the McGuffey readers and Stein) are the signs of infantile pre-occupations. A poet does not have to write his confessions; his style betrays him. Kierkegaard once said that genius is sin; if so, then our American naturalistic novelists don't know how to commit it. In the Aztec religion the goddess of justice is a woman and a serpent, but there is no serpent knowledge of women in the American artist. The lack of such knowledge is traditional; it dates back to Melville, Poe and Whitman. Whitman's *Leaves of Grass,* a remarkable manifesto on physiology, is an erotic Shaker poem composed by a celibate. When Mrs. Gilchrist, widow of the celebrated William Blake biographer, suggested coming to America to be near the good, gray poet, he *shook* with fear!

Melville's *Moby-Dick* is Satanism washed in the innocent blood of the lamb. Ahab is not wicked; he is fissured, lonely, like the whole *Pequod* crew crying out for the marriage-pillows that were never to be theirs. The only hymeneal in *Moby-Dick* is the "wedlock" friendship between Queequeg and Ishmael, and though this reminds us of the love Hamlet has for Horatio, Queequeg is such a virgin cannibal that he has to crawl under the bed to put on his shoes because Ishmael is present. *Billy Budd,* Melville's last work, is as epicene as the name suggests. Indeed, an almost exclusive male friendship was dominant in nineteenth-century America; it was not Melville's Plymouth Rock marriage to Elizabeth Shaw but his affection for Hawthorne that mattered; Whitman's circle were men, and though Henry Adams went to Samoa for the "mulatto lily," his real affinity was for John Hay and Clarence King.

In the Old Testament Jehovah is Father, male morals and anger, but our authors believe in the feminine ethics of "smite me on the other cheek!" Sherwood Anderson is the apostle of Whitman's semi-female conception of Christ. In *Many Marriages* there is no difference between Christ and Mary, and John Webster stands nude before the two images, Jesus and the Virgin. Anderson brooded a good deal over his masculine nature, and Wyndham Lewis once assured him that he was as manly as anybody else. Anderson must have had a deep fear of his own nature, as the story "Hands" in *Winesburg, Ohio* shows. In "Hands" Wing Biddlebaum, a school teacher, is driven out of an Ohio town because his affection for the little boys in his class is misunderstood. Wing's hands had to be hidden from himself because they reminded him of that dark Bible sin of Ham. This is a very teachable American fable, for now that most of the manual arts are extinct, what will the American do with his hands?

The image of Christ as a meek and maidenly milksop is

72

dominant in Anderson and in other Americans who followed after him. For example, Nathanael West in *Miss Lonelyhearts* writes that Jesus is a maiden, and the boys in a mock Catholic sacrament buy a lamb and torture the poor bleating thing to death. Skipping to England for the moment, we notice that the same maiden-Christ image is in the D. H. Lawrence novels; in Lawrence masculine art decays considerably. It is true that Lawrence introduces into his tales a rooster, a fine and dandy coxcomb whose phallical crowing leaves no doubt as to his gender. But only the rooster crows in Lawrence; the human males make no such virile celebration.

Ezra Pound demanded a male art, the male verb, which Huysmans had asserted was the central force of the sentence. There is much to be said for a hard, stratified, exterior sentence. The greatest enemy of the Imagist poet was the adjective which so mothers the noun as to emasculate it. There is that kind of mothering adjective in Hart Crane, and in the early books of Waldo Frank, *City Block* and *Rehab*. The Objectivists, begun by Louis Zukofsky, the learned poet, demanded the craggy, obsidian line, which should have been the paradigm for such wanton satyrs as Dreiser, Crane, Frank and Rosenfeld.

Don't be duped by the national plaint that the American people is a new people. We are an old race, with seasoned vices more antique than the Pharoahs' or the Amorites'. The American is more concerned with time and space than with man; he finds the European man-tragedy archaic. In Poe locality takes the place of being; and Melville is a geographer. "We are the 'first' last people," writes Charles Olson in *Call Me Ishmael*.

The old parent orthodoxy is abhorrent to the Atlantic mind. Pound, detesting the Judaic-Christian "Thou shalt not," which is Father-Fear, broke the Mosaic tablets for American poetry. It is this "fear," writes William Carlos Williams, "that drives us to the homosexual out of dread of our fathers." This fear has corroded and ruined the American novel; our novelists cannot write of passion, only of the senses. To make the difference clear, let us recall that Herbert Read makes a lucid distinction (*Phases of English Poetry*) between passion and the senses. Lawrence, a poet of the senses, weighs sensation like a shrewd exacting hedonist belonging to the school of Wilde, Pater, Gide, the Greek votaries of male love.

How different from this sort of epicureanism is Chaucer's verse: "Her mouth was sweet as bragot." (Bragot was a beverage made of honey and ale.) It is this direct male spirit of Chaucer that the artist must recover; if he does not, we are doomed to a continuing succession of novels for the bored city Gothics and the pretty he-darlings of Gomorrah.

The Freeman, 1951

Laurels for Borrowers

The story of Herman Melville is the fable of the living American writer. Let no one assume that the disinterment of nineteenth-century genius means that the living are not entombed. Nothing has changed, and besides there is more profit in canonized dust than in living flesh. Those who praise Whitman, Poe, Melville, James and Emily Dickinson are promoting the same oblivion for the writer today that the author in the nineteenth century had.

One of the grim ironies of American literature is that people who cannot write are almost invariably chosen to do books on those who can. The shrewd batten on our memorial dust. Poets are nowhere near as astute as critics, for who but a fool would write *Moby-Dick* or be Edgar Poe simply to be reviled and go naked of love and friends. A fool writes a masterpiece, but the pickpocket sometimes called a critic gets the cash. For a poet good writing is often an accident; for a critic it is generally impossible.

Now that fruitful learning has declined, knowledge has become an abstruse fact about Petrarch or Dante. But wisdom, which has deteriorated along with true learning, has little to do with isolated facts. A good book, says the poet Louis Zukofsky, is a form of love and trust. Melville's *Moby-Dick* is a novel about blubber, sperm oil and candles, which are facts. It is also a novel about human faith. Our critics, with notable exceptions, have dealt with this faith in a most dismaying manner.

Let us look at the Herman Melville story. Today the reading of Melville is commonplace; there is a market for Melville's notes, diaries and letters as collected by Jay Leyda in *The Melville Log* and an audience for a theatrical work made out of

75

Billy Budd. But when Raymond Weaver in 1921 published *Herman Melville, Mariner and Mystic,* Melville was no more than a name or epitaph in American literature. Academicians like Woodberry dismissed our greatest writer in a line or two. John Macy in *The Spirit of American Literature* gave the author of *Moby-Dick* an italicized mention in his preface. Though Constable in London had done the complete works of Melville in 1922, his books were very difficult to obtain in this country. Melville books were sold along with volumes on yachts at a salt water bookshop in New York City.

In 1922 a small and useful collection of Melville letters, edited by Meade Minnegerode, was brought out by the gifted Byrne Hackett of the Brick Row Bookshop. Then, in 1923, D. H. Lawrence's *Studies in Classical American Literature* appeared. This sibylline work was scorned by the academic Philistines like Fred Lewis Pattee who made a handsome living out of textbooks (the most menial adversary of a book is a textbook). The Lawrence study was also ignored by the college hacks who are now writing for the American Letters Series, for Lawrence had no trade value then. The Lawrence volume was so neglected that Alfred Stieglitz gave dozens of copies away to people who came to his gallery at 291 Fifth Avenue just to get it read.

In 1928 Lewis Mumford, making an honest and cavalier acknowledgment to Raymond Weaver, published a book on Melville. Despite its flaws, Mumford's book was pioneer work, and it is not the purpose of this piece to diminish the chivalric labors of the pioneer Melville men. A tribute should also be given to Wilbert Snow, former Lieutenant Governor of Connecticut and the first Melville enthusiast in America.

In 1938 Charles Olson's rare and lovely essay, "Lear and Moby-Dick," appeared in *Twice a Year.* If I may say it, I fathered Olson's work; his *Call Me Ishmael* (Melville criticism) had come out of my own book, *Do These Bones Live,* published in 1941. Lest there be misunderstanding, let it be said that one good book begets another, as Abraham begat Isaac and Isaac, Jacob. Nobody but a churl or a plagiarist tries to hide his obligation to another writer, and Olson has paid whatever debt he owes to me in a prodigal tribute in *Call Me Ishmael*. Besides, there are passages in the Olson *Ishmael* volume which the sea oracles whispered to him and him alone and which I never heard or dreamed of—and, should a reader take it that I am trumpeting a friend, let it be known that Olson and I are strangered.

I have only two purposes here: one, to tell the truth, and, two, to expose those who would take undue credit for what other men have done. The care of American literature has been preempted by the grammar beadles of criticism, and no poet or novelist who is not a part of this cabal against American literature has a chance of being heard or reviewed. The college Polonius is omnipresent; he laurels dust and corpses. But he doesn't bring the corpses to life. He is a death merchant of letters, he controls awards—and he behaves toward living talent as though it did not exist. This takes us up to the present and to the American Letters Series volume *Herman Melville* by Newton Arvin, professor of English at Smith College and recent winner of a book industry award for his biographical study.

It is easier for a camel to pass through the eye of a needle than for an original writer to get into the Institute of Arts and Letters or be chosen to write for the American Letters Series. It is also better that it should be this way, for it is nobler to be a poet than to be shrewd. Poe so hated the Brahmins of his own time that he would not admit that he was born in Boston. One of his angers against the arts-and-letters boors he called "The Quacks of Helicon," and another and rougher piece he titled, "Mr. Longfellow and Other Plagiarists." If Poe were alive today he would obviously be sued for libel. But it is the verdict of time that Poe spoke the truth.

When Olson's "Lear and Moby-Dick" appeared, the title itself was a revelation. Unlike the torpid pedagogues, Charles Olson was able to pluck from the page the pith of a man. The pedagogues had not been able to discern the real portent of such Old Testament names in Melville as Ishmael, Ahab, Bildad. Despite *Clarel,* a long two-volume poem based on Melville's experience in the Holy Land, the pedagogues failed to appreciate the importance of the Bible in Melville. They also missed the influence of Shakespeare on our greatest writer. The pedagogues were too busy with such wights as Freneau, Brockden Brown, William Dunlap and the Peabody sisters to pay heed to Emily Dickinson, Melville or Poe. It would have taken the bold simplicity of a Goya kitchen trollop to sweep out such gnomes as Freneau and Brockden Brown. Even today it is scarcely understood that Emily Dickinson is a bride of St. Paul, or that her letters are epistles to the Ephesians and the Corinthians. The Hebraic names of New Englanders should have been sufficient to induce the academic to revalue American Puritan scripture.

When *Das Kapital* became the testament of the literati, the old moral orthodoxies were replaced by cant, a feminine male, and plagiarism; the perverse is now so dominant that evil is often called good. Our Institute priests have become Goya foxes with pens in their hands. They praise the ancients for wrong reasons and neglect to look for live geniuses who may be living in Texas, the Dakota Black Hills or on Avenue A. I want to see a little band of rough, honest poets who would be willing to go out, like Sancho on his wizened ass Dapple, to fight liars, coxcombs, plagiarists, imitators and the writing monks of the academy and the modern literary bourse.

The academic is a bibliographer and not an interpreter of books. Learning has palpably decayed; compare the frontier hardihood of a Francis Parkman, who pierced the Oregon wilderness to study the primitive Indian, with the modern academic historian whose name appears in a Chesterfield cigarette program blatantly disguised as patriotism. Everything now seems to be for sale; the modern stage is set for Professor Mickey Mouse of history, philosophy, and American literature. Instead of erudition and human wisdom, we have books like Newton Arvin's on Melville.

Arvin set himself the hard task of rewriting other men's books. Whenever he writes about space, myth, the Pacific world, the sea-prairies, or *Moby-Dick* as Christian Scripture, or the feminine in the Melville characters, he is treading the ground that Olson trod in *Call Me Ishmael*. Arvin does not trouble to say that Olson was the first to publish the story of the *Essex* disaster, which Melville used in the *Moby-Dick* narrative, or to allude to Olson's original reading of Melville's annotated and heavily marked Shakespeare. But it is obvious enough that Arvin adopts Olson's viewpoint.

Eleven years ago the Olson view of Melville was regarded as the worst heterodoxy. Our early New England Puritan books were read by the yokel literati as though no Bible had gone before them. The literati were such dull readers that they could not see that Whitman, Melville, Dickinson, are Nazarene writers.

When Mumford observed that woman was excluded from *Moby-Dick*, it scarcely occurred to him to look at *Pierre*, *White-Jacket*, or *Billy Budd*, to comprehend how close Melville came to that sin for which Sodom and Gomorrah were destroyed. But Mumford's work was generous and original compared to the later Melville essays of the academics. To prove that I am not afflicted with myopia or actuated by malice, I offer a comparison of significant items from Olson and Arvin:

From Charles Olson's *Call Me Ishmael*	From Newton Arvin's *Herman Melville*
"*Stage directions* appear throughout. *Soliloquies,* too. There is a significant use of the special	"Everyone is struck at once, of course, by the stage directions that accompany some of the

79

Olson	Arvin
Elizabethan soliloquy to the skull in Ahab's mutterings to the sperm whale's head in 'The Sphinx' (chp. LXX). One of the subtlest *supernatural effects,* the 'low laugh from the hold' in the quarterdeck scene, echoes Shakespeare's use of the Ghost below ground in *Hamlet.*" p. 68	chapters ('*Enter Ahab: Then, all*'); by the soliloquies . . ." pp. 154-55.
"*Structure,* likewise. *Moby-Dick* has a rise and fall like the movement of an Elizabethan tragedy." p. 66	". . . the book has a structural rise and fall like that of Elizabethan tragedy . . ." p. 155
"The first act ends in the Quarter-Deck chapter . . ." p. 66	". . . a movement that is marked thus by the great scene on the quarterdeck . . ." p. 155
". . . the book then moves up to the meeting with the *Jeroboam* . . ." pp. 66-67	So-called second act: ". . . the meeting with the *Jeroboam* . . ." p. 155
". . . and, after that, in a third swell, into the visit of Ahab to the *Samuel Enderby* . . ." p. 67	So-called third act: ". . . the meeting with *Samuel Enderby* . . ." p. 155
"The pitch of the action is the storm scene, 'The Candles.' " p. 67	". . . the 'fourth-act' climax of 'The Candles' . . ." p. 155
"From that point on Ahab comes to repose, fifth act, in his fate." p. 67	". . . and lastly the catastrophe itself." p. 155
". . . the final chase of Moby Dick precipitously following upon 'The Symphony.' " p. 69	"The fourth movement naturally begins with 'The Symphony' and comes to a close with the catastrophe itself . . ." p. 158

Olson	Arvin

"Melville was agonized over paternity . . . he demanded to know the father . . . Kronos . . . armed himself with a sickle and castrated his father Uranus." p. 82

"Ahab's rage and hate is scaled like Satan's, the largest enemy of the father man has imagined." p. 84

". . . what, then, does Moby Dick himself . . . shadow forth? It would be easiest to say simply the father . . . who imposes constraint upon the most powerful instincts, both egoistic and sexual . . . who threatens even to destroy the latter by castration . . ." p. 172

"There is a way to disclose paternity, declare yourself the rival of earth, air, fire and water." p. 85

"Moby Dick is thus the archetypal Parent . . ." p. 173

Olson expresses the whole conflict between fathers and sons as "Kronos and Saturn . . . were overthrown by their sons . . . The new gods of Jupiter were, in their turn, attacked by other sons." p. 82

"And the emotions Moby Dick evokes in us are the violently contradictory emotions that prevail between parent and child." p. 173

(Arvin speaks of Titanism here and Olson writes of Enceladus, one of the Titans. Arvin refers to the phallic serpent-god of the Ophites, and Olson to Osiris whose phallus is eaten by the fish of the Nile. Olson writes that Prometheus fathered man.)

"Melville's books batten on other men's books." p. 86

"Few books of its dimensions have owed so much to books that have preceded them . . ." p. 151

"Stubb's jollity and Flask's clodlike stupidity blunt the spiritual." p. 56. Both Stubb and Flask are clods.

". . . the jolly, unimaginative Stubb and the satanic Fedallah . . ." p. 154

The "compact" between Ahab and Fedallah "is as binding as Faust's with Mephistopheles."

". . . the diabolic Fedallah, to whom Ahab has surrendered his moral freedom, and whom Stubb

Olson	Arvin
Faust surrenders his moral freedom to Mephistopheles. p. 56	quite properly identifies as the devil in disguise." pp. 191-92
Melville studies Shakespeare's craft ". . . for characterization." p. 66	"[It was] Shakespeare, the creator of character, who acted on Melville's own creativeness." p. 151
". . . to understand the Pacific as part of our geography, another West, prefigured in the Plains, antithetical." p. 13 ". . . earth-seas." p. 11	(Galena) "Images of the inland landscape, of farms, of prairies, of rivers, lakes, and forests, were to recur throughout Melville's work as a counterpoint to the dominant imagery of the sea . . ." p. 46
"The fulcrum of America is the Plains, half sea half land . . ." p. 12 "The Pacific is, for an American, the Plain repeated . . ." p. 114	"Yet it was not the lakes and the forests of the great west that sank deepest into his memory but the prairies and the Mississippi River." p. 47 "As for the Mississippi, . . . it cast a less profound spell over Melville than the prairie did . . ." p. 47
". . . lowest wages and miserable working conditions—vide *Typee,* early chps., and *Omoo,* same." p. 21	"At its worst, says E. P. Hohman in *The American Whaleman,* the life of a whaling seaman represented 'perhaps the lowest condition to which free American labor has ever fallen' . . . he remarks elsewhere that American whaling 'had all the essential
"The Pacific as sweatshop." p. 23	characteristics of a sweated industry.' " p. 51
"Melville makes little of the love of man and woman . . . Melville had the Greek sense of men's love." p. 45	". . . Melville, implied inevitably a Greek-like cult of physical love . . . the beauty, . . . of the men especially . . ." p. 56

Olson	Arvin
"Melville likens the effect to 'that which in Genesis attends upon the beginning of things.' " p. 66	". . . a primordial fable, the fable of the Fall of Man . . . vibrations in it of the book of Genesis." p. 294
"Melville's ethic is mythic." p. 83	". . . serious as are the moral meanings of *Moby-Dick* . . . in the end . . . one is aware . . . that [the book] can only be called mythic." p. 182

In 1938, when Olson did the "Lear" essay, the influence of Shakespeare on Melville had only been hinted. There are only two or three references to Shakespeare in Raymond Weaver's book. But in time the pioneers are honored by those who can repeat without offering proper homage. Here, for example, is Arvin's implied tribute to D. H. Lawrence:

From D. H. Lawrence, *Studies in Classical American Literature*	From Newton Arvin, *Herman Melville*
"South Sea Islanders belong to the Stone Age . . . The Heart of the Pacific is still the Stone Age . . . vast vacuum . . . the life of myriads of ages back . . . phantom, illusion-like track of reality." p. 1035 "This is a bit of birth-myth, or rebirth myth . . ." p. 1034	". . . but from the world of enlightened rationality . . . and cultural complexity backward . . . to the primordial world that was before metals, before the alphabet, before cities; . . . the pre-rational myth." p. 87

When the works of the pioneers in criticism come to be echoed in derivative books written for wider circles of readers, it might be said that education is improving. But why should the derivative books be honored while the pioneers go unsung?

The Freeman, 1951

Conrad Aiken

Ushant: An Autobiographical Narrative, by Conrad Aiken

When a man ceases to strive for his fate, he grows homesick for his past. *Ushant* is the aerial, illimitable isle where the mind, no longer heroic, meanders and sleeps, and supinely remembers. It is a homesick, water book. Mnemosyne, which is memory, the mother of the Muses, is intellectual force, but nostalgia is the soft, mulled lees of recollection. This lotus-stupor is in every Odysseus. Odysseus weeps for Ithaca, for the bed of Penelope, his swine and for Telemachus, but the sea is his dominant deity. Man's destiny is his nemesis for which he must struggle to give himself a just fate; Heraclitus says that the Erinyes are the handmaidens of justice.

Ushant is a long lotus sleep, and as the title suggests, it is not only anti-epical, but a florid, comic pun. "To utter a mere jest ornately is like beautifying an ape," one ancient rhetor remarked. When the life is finished, and the work for one's bourne is over, the poet grows garrulous and tired. Great autobiography has a conscience that is so gifted that it drops its blood continually. It is wise analects, the confession of one's ideas, impenitence and perversities; but *Ushant* is an archive of piddling obscenities, and is a loose-anecdotal recollection of puerile eroticisms.

Conrad Aiken has selected Henry James as his master. As he himself is a residual, Jamesian hyphenate, what he requires are not the panicky, indecisive velleities of the old master, but a stable, and more roughly-hewn tripod. James is altogether anti-epical, and his irresolute style is canonical gabble. Virgil took as his guide Homer, and Humboldt modeled his *Travels* upon Pliny, but Aiken prefers "Ariel's Isle," England, to America, though neither this dying Helicon nor James is what the author of *Ushant* requires.

A poet ought to seek a genius or locality suitable to his nature and without his own foibles. It would have been better for the poet to have given his homage to a wild pear log, or to crude stones, or the cacao god and the peccary, an aboriginal feculent sow, than to Henry James. What profit were it for Rabelais to have gone to the dunghill or to mealy-mouthed Thersites? Predacious Achilles is patient and tractable in the presence of the refined, Asiatic Priam, and Helen is chaste and of modest carriage when she is beheld by a group of elderly Nestors who admire her without raising her blood. Let a New Englander go to raging Archilochus or to the choleric river Scamander; let him as Themistocles did, drink ox's blood, for what killed the Theban hero would be no more than an ejaculative draught for a writer from Beacon Hill.

The autobiography is glutted with pinchbeck, primal cries that are solely decorative, such as, "beginning without beginning, water without seam," "Whale, blow your conch, lost fisherman off the dangerous shores of Ushant." The book is a museum wrack of kelp, gulls, sandpipers, cormorant, trulls, and all composed of the dregs of Joyce, Eliot, and Hart Crane. There is a plethora of the stage dithyrambics of the romantics and of amateur art words, like "particles of the soul's landscape," "mulberry-colored red medallion of Chinese brocade," "the beer and iced coffee, in the Bloomsbury window," "magnification of rain," "a quite horrible verisimilitude," "preternaturally luminous nuclei," and "full of flux and reflux, coil and moil." All this is specious Genesis, sham, primordial sea-weather, and a Beacon Hill class in still-life imagery. There are the old salon art locutions of the Rossetti and Burne-Jones milieu. Aiken wavers between sybaritic adjectival nouns, the "rootedness of earth-living," and contemporary perversions of

Joyce. *Ushant* is in the Corinthian mood and the verbs are soft, medic adjectives. He teases the ear but does not invigorate the intellect; he is too sensual, and his words do not fall properly, or arrange themselves by felicitous accident, which is what Demetrius called "skill in love with luck, and luck skill." The book is choked with the poetaster's atticisms, "mythopeic," "palimpsest," "narcissism," "Heraclitean," and "mythos" which call to mind the "epos," "ethonic," "hubris," and "ethos" of the spurious, hellenic, academic mummer. The misuse of words induces evil in the soul, said Socrates.

There is pithless skill and a peccant understanding of the uses of myth and of hyperbole in "grand daedalian secret," or "the less Gordian-knotted." Daedalus signifies intellectual inventiveness, and Socrates was said to have been of the lineage of Daedalus, showing how intricate were his syllogisms. All the poet succeeds in doing is to reduce substantives of strong, legendary association to weakling epithets, producing as foolish an effect as if one wrote—they played in a Jovian back alley when they were children.

Fables have unusual charm and force in the nominative case, and the reader is still amazed at the labors of Hercules, or at the spectacle of Prometheus' liver devoured by the vulture, especially when these legends are applied to contemporary perplexities of the mind. Active myth dwindles when Prometheus or Bacchus become promethean or bacchic, or Icarus and Daedalus, icarian and daedalian. *Ushant* resembles the grasshoppers of Anacreon who were said to be without grief or blood. Even when the poet risks the scatophagous "cockroach riddled," or "unwashed vomit," it does not sour the gullet or sharpen the mouth with the remembrance of acerbity. The scatological in *Ushant* is aprioristic word sport, or logomachy, and is as much the toy and triffle of an idle brain as the phlegm of frogs and the spittle of newts, which are factitious and not riggish. The modern scatologist should heed the Ion of Euripides who takes his bow and aims it at the swan for dropping its ordure upon the statues.

It is written that Democritus took all from Leucippus, leaving his own folly to Epicurus. At times it is impossible to know whether it is Aiken, James, Eliot, Pound or John Dos Passos who is writing. Aiken, doubly acknowledging his debt to the debile, cliché rhymes of James, writes: "Just as the oh so precious, the oh so exquisite Madeline, the Jamesian lady of ladies, the enchantress of the Beacon Hill drawing room— who, like another Circe, had made strange shapes of Wild Michael and the Tsetse—was afterwards to be essentialized . . ." Here is another ecstatic Jamesian banality which is supposed to reek with ambiguity and covert allusion: "this radiant narcissism, with its passionate need to emphasize and identify, this all-embracingness." In referring to his childhood he remarks that the stoop, "like everything else," it has been "transitional . . . temporary; but for that it was, it remained paramount." Elsewhere Aiken tells of Aunt Jane—"she was apple pie and coffee cake and homespun clothes." He writes of "aerial flowers," "esurient shadows," and "the most meltingly diaphanous of clouded ceilings."

It is not a blemish in a poet to imitate somebody; only a humbug original derives from no one, since we are not, as Homer reminds us, begotten of stocks and stones. Aiken's defect is not that he has been influenced by others, but that his work is an ill-concealed cento. Each book, no matter what it owes to other authors, should be as distinct as was Artaxerxes whose arms reached down to his knees. A poet is the slyest of dissemblers, and, like Hobbes, who carried a pen and inkhorn in his cane, must rush to his own afflatus to rewrite with as much heat as possible the thoughts of Herodotus, Seneca, or of Statius.

All art is the working over of the ideas of others, and whether this be the rammish industry of Aspasia, or the cross-questioning elenchus of Socrates, it matters not. What is important is that Aspasia convince Pericles that though her devices be the same as Cressid's, she can do what she would fain do in a way all of her own. Socrates has the same purpose, for though Prodicus, his teacher, and Gorgias has said more or less the same as the syllogist, he has to prove to Critias and Alcibiades that he is an original. Those who refuse to be duped by Aspasia or Socrates are themselves stale witlings because Socrates and Aspasia are the most wondrous deceivers.

Aiken is not a nimble pickpocket of Helicon as were all the pothouse Autolycuses of letters in the days of Elizabeth. We do not assail these men as coney-catchers any more than we find fault with Ben Jonson who was a very gifted plagiarist, because only the most cunning scholiasts can find him out. Whether a book is a virgin or a matron only wise Democritus can tell, who, when he saw a girl pass him after daybreak, said, "Good morning, maiden," but when she returned at dusk greeted her, "Good evening, woman." This is not a pardon for low-born clodpates who either steal from bad writers, or who have too pelting an imagination to reseethe their purloinings. Once we grant, as Cicero said, that honor nourishes the arts, we will allow any man to do as he pleases, provided he entertain us, care for justice, and has not a mastiff's heart.

Aiken does not sufficiently amuse us because he pilfers from people who are too close to our own generation. By now James, Pound, Eliot, Joyce are dowds, jades and trulls of Parnassus, and we are weary of them. It may be that they will be curios again in some other time, but now they do not provide the spectacle of remoteness so significant in literature. Let a poet send me back to Macrobius, Strabo, Hecataeus, as shock to shake my satiety; ransack Nicholas Breton, or the larders of Chrysostom, for they are far from us and can provide a contemporary book with the aspect of distance. No one can come close to the pyramids of Egypt or to the Mayan oratories at Chiapas, for they so overpower the witness as to give him ontological uneasiness which causes one to believe that he may have seen these edifices in another time.

Ushant is based upon sensibility and imagery, and the ruttish joys of the ear instead of the mind. It is given over to the senses which sleepily recollect the sheets of Aphrodite and her fragrant cestus. The book is entirely too much in bed, for as the hedonist Solomon advises, do not give your strength to women, by which he means, not all of it. The American intellect is at its nadir of strength as a wild, autochthonic beast. The author of *Ushant* longs for the cits of Cape Cod, Bloomsbury and Beacon Hill, but this is enervated nostalgia and not the empiric simplicity of Heraclitus who said of his townsmen, May the Ephesians hang themselves. *Ushant* is an homage to Venus, and she is a very great goddess, for as Parmenides asserts, first of all Eros was contrived, but Eros is what the poet imagines this goddess to have been in his youth. He pines again for this deity to sting and whip him.

The more austere divinities are seldom present in this work and men require the congealed bosom of Diana which is chaste thought, and the cold, blue eyes of Pallas Minerva which are the fountains of wisdom and strife, and we cannot court these continent deities without will and striving. A book should be as chaste as it is rammish, which should enable one to understand Antisthenes when he exclaims, I would rather go mad than feel pleasure. Homer himself detests venery as much as he is drawn by it, for he has feculent Vulcan drop his seed on the thigh of Pallas Minerva, which is a fable the Priapic acolytes of D. H. Lawrence, Cocteau, and Wilde have never properly understood.

A poem or a book that does not make the reader toil for his fate deprives him of energy, which is his most tragical and valiant weapon against the cosmos, and without which man is neither epic nor universal. A book that weakens human will is inartistic, for all writing is heroic feigning, imagining that though everything perish, a book will be perdurable. Knowing that death is always brushing our backs, we write to forget death.

Everything in literature has to be enlarged to make tragedy

or comedy heroic. The fault with the modern poem or novel is that after reading it one is no longer ample enough to go to Philippi, as Brutus did, or has the swollen jocularity to be mistaken for the Persians who were said to void plains. Henry James could hardly shut a door except in a long, panicky sentence; he was too irresolute and weak to push a door to, and his nervous, worn-out psyche, like that of Fleda in *The Spoils of Poynton,* and her name suggests the most alarmed flight, just fell on the floor and screamed as it contemplated a hard, brutal knob.

The most average acts are crucial pain for the Jamesian nature, and all the wheezy parentheses are really avoidances of bestial matter. Syntax has become very circuitous and hesistant, which is another word for sensitive, and which has given us so many involved, stammering clauses, that all any reader now prays for is that a writer begin a sentence in the nominative case closely followed by a verb. This sort of plain, resolute banality makes us understand that when Ajax hurls a rock at the head of Hector he does it to kill him as fast as possible, and not because the stone tempted him or had hindered his childhood. Similarly, going to the door for Henry James was the dreariest incubus, and the reason he could not do it as promptly as any burly pedestrian Ajax could, is that he had an injured prostate gland. All the panicky, Jamesian hiatuses are the result of impotency. However, there are many critics of the Jamesian ilk who are young and virile, and who can close a door without being nervous at all, but who write as though they had sustained the same injury as their master. They remind one of the pickthank friends surrounding Dionysius, the tyrant, who inclined their heads to one side in the same manner as the despot, though they did not suffer his deafness. One argute critic, drawing upon a letter by Alice, the sister of Henry and William James, said that William James had built a house with fourteen doors, all of them swinging outward, and that this showed that he was a sane, outdoor nature. A more homely explanation is that a man who puts up a house containing fourteen doors wanted to get out of it very badly, and being a man of some rough sense, realized that he would be likely to run out of his home at any moment, and that if the doors swung toward instead of away from him, he would knock out his brains. Unless we can go through a door without it being a torment, or open a window without making a dilemma of it in nine modifying clauses, American letters is doomed. We must return to the naïve heart, without minding what is banal and average, and relating it in clear sentences. If we don't, in another generation no one will have the bravery to get through the mangling Jamesian syntax to go to the door.

The new seers of Parnassus have robbed the Muses of their strength, and though the modern cicalas are supposed to sing a street-gamin patois, their voices are too weak because they are undernourished. There is no table, hearth, or the cruets so dear to Saturn, in modern American literature. Dickens is the last writer in English to feed his characters. There was an Epimenides, a Greek Cynic of the sect of Diogenes, who kept his food in the smallest scrip so that he would have meager droppings. The characters in *Ushant,* or in any present-day book, are never at a meal, and the result is that they are too dispirited and feckless to perform the most ordinary acts.

The book has too little will in it, as the title suggests. *Ushant* signifies not deep mortification or failure, but the precautionary reluctance to risk the deeps of chagrin. A book is not Ushant, but I WILL. The author is placeless, and is as ungraspable as Proteus because he is in no single element, character or will. He is loose water, and all the glyphs, mementoes, and reminiscences are written on the unstable surfaces of the sea.

A poet should write a tree, ground, tarn, ravine or stone book to give it one sort of character and weather. However, it is easier for Peter to walk upon the sea to Christ than it is for the reader to tread this volume. The poet is homeless, and his lament is that, unlike Poe, Emerson, Whitman, Dickinson, he has not seeded his psyche in America. These piecemeal reveries—a paragraph on Brattle Street at Harvard, a fugitive encounter with a whore on Russell Square, a moment of venery with a French girl on a channel boat, a moiety of his grammar school days at South Yarmouth—are a cry for the genius of locality. But he won't let a single memory be in one place long enough to ripen or season; he has never taken the time to bury his memories in an orchard, or in some profound loam, to give them pious sepulchre.

Remembrance is a torn, placeless ghost, raw and wandering, unless we bury our griefs and pains in one specific ground, region and sod. Ghosts, too, must be seeded like fruit, rains, and despair, if they are not to return to make of our hearts their Acheron, for hell is going to and fro in the earth, and having no landmarks, or country or epitaph to define our souls.

Poetry, 1953

Herbert Read

To Infancy, O Lord, again I com, that
I my Manhood may improv...
—Thomas Traherne

Herbert Read is the most beautiful stylist in modern English. There are no better words on Herbert Read as a writer than his own on George Herbert, "The simplicity of his style is due, first to an economy of imagery, and then to a conversational ease of diction." Read's hair is already northerly; he is a misty Saxon of the Yorkshire wolds and moors, like Wordsworth. He is by nature afar; a quiet, sealed man, whose riddles are in his works rather than in his talk. He often refers to the soft purples of the heath, and this brings to mind Homer's rocky cavern where the nymphs weave purple garments on a stony loom this Porphyry asserts is the blood of the spirit. This Saxon yeoman is a stone loom upon which nature has woven scarlet raiment which is the affections of the poetic intellect.

We regard the oaten pipe of Pan as a charming anachronism in the poetry of Propertius or the *Georgics* of Virgil. Though Herbert Read has small patience with outworn words or olden meters, he is an Arcadian piper in *The Innocent Eye,* a lament for primal childhood. In *The Innocent Eye,* it is the child that is absolute conscience and art. As Traherne wrote, "Tis strange that I should wisest be, when least I could an error see." Read says that we only touch, smell, hear, and see once. All we do later is to recover these piercing Edens of our childhood experiences. It may be that Thales, who said that the first element is water, drank from a well when he was a boy, and that no rain or ocean or fog that fell upon his identity was such an angelic visitation. The same claim may be made for Heraclitus who declared that what is driest in the soul is the wisest, for he, too, may have tasted sun or fire as he had not known or felt water.

As Read says, the village in *The Innocent Eye* is in the Doomsday Book, not that it is a locality for direful ends, but because it is remote, inshut, as is fate or prescience. The family farmhouse is a square stone box with a roof of red tiles set in a dour sylvan landscape. The skies and the stones are wooly lambs, but in this frith and meadow grows the tree of life which is innocence. The children are untouched by the lewdness of a laborer, and when they go to the farm outhouse, where there are two seats, the children sit beside one another, as birds dropping their ordure on branches.

There is the pasture "pockmarked with erupted rabbit warrens . . . mole-hills . . . and watery ditches . . . inhabited by frogs, which spawned among the cess and king-cups." Here are the "sweet-briar, sorrel, and pig-nuts" which the children ate. The peonies and "patient waters," the pods and the current bushes are the apocryphal meadows of vision and foreknowledge, which is pristine childhood remembering. "Memory is a flower that only opens fully in the Kingdom of Heaven, where the eye is eternally innocent," writes Read.

The Father dies, and the childhood Georgics of fens and orchards are replaced by a stone-walled orphanage where the Read children are immured. At sixteen, or earlier, Herbert Read is employed at a bank in the manufacturing city of Leeds, where thruppenny deposits are made by weavers and mill hands. The lost green images and leaves from the tree of life are gone, and all the perils of the tree of knowledge, which are books, poetry, and reason, are his.

Herbert Read was a captain in the British Army of the First World War and he went through four years of bloodshed with a rifle and a copy of Thoreau's *Walden* in his pocket. *In Retreat* is a bucolic annal of battles done with an impassive, imagist mind in which machine guns or the death of a soldier is as much of a pastoral as a little copse of fifty trees, a "water rat plunging at dusk into the mill dam," or a "cup of misty hills." *In Retreat* is not what has happened, but is ideal occurrence, and, like all art, is a thousand leagues away in the soul.

Belle lettres is almost out of fashion. The essay is an epistolary art, full of maxims and wise sayings, which, when well done, lead us to believe that we possess all the knowledge of great men, but none of their defects. Herbert Read's book *A Coat of Many Colours* is written in that natural, artless style which is so difficult to achieve. Such simplicity, so without peacock adornments, is very seductive because it persuades the reader that the author is not vain. La Bruyère, a very plain savant, said, "A shallow mind thinks his writing divine; a man of sense imagines he writes tolerably well."

This book is composed of feuilletons on Toulouse-Lautrec, William James, Wordsworth, Picasso, Kierkegaard, Paul Klee, Eric Gill, Walter de la Mare, and others. Herbert Read says that Toulouse-Lautrec, an ugly gnome, had a zest for his chagrins. True art is self-knowledge, and one ought to be able to go to it as to the oracles for advice on everything except the wounds of Venus. It may be that Lautrec, Corbière, Verlaine, Baudelaire, thought they gave crepuscular tones to their lives, otherwise miserable and solitary, by going to the evil charnel houses of pleasure, but what they achieved was Golgotha in a brothel.

Read portrays Kierkegaard as an ennuyed Mephisto who said, "The highest thing a woman can do for a man is to come within his range at the right instant, and the greatest thing she can do after that is to be unfaithful to him." Antisthenes, the Greek Cynic philosopher, once remarked: "I would rather go mad than feel pleasure." It is a very fine epigram to be heeded by Sophocles at ninety, but of no worth to a tumulting Hamlet or Troilus. Mary Fitton of the sonnets may have taught Shakespeare that all oaths of love are written in water, but I doubt that he asked for the lesson. Herbert Read has dwelt (*The Phases of English Poetry*) on the romantic malady in Spenser,

Shakespeare, and Donne. This eroticism, almost absent in the Bible patriarchs, has been the source of anguish in the occidental world where monogamy is surreptitious polygamy.

In his lovely essay on Wordsworth, Read declares that the poet was tumored by remorse. During the French Revolution Wordsworth fell in love with Ann Vallon by whom he had an illegitimate daughter. He never married her or returned to see the child, and he was so plagued by his conscience, according to Read, that his poetic energies were harmed. Read cites the following from Wordsworth:

> To rescue my thoughts, which now and ever
> Bleed helplessly on Memory's piercing thorn.

The Erinyes, our hurt faculties gone mad, are regarded by the Greeks and Herbert Read as inferior deities. I cannot consider anguish, which is the gnawing of conscience, as a sick, demonic emotion lower than other pangs or gods of the mind. What emotions can one canonize for a poet's benefit and what is the refuse of ghosts, or do we bleed trash?

Herbert Read is sorely troubled because there is a cleavage between the artist and society; he has been a noble figure struggling for the recognition of the sculpture of a Gabo, writing about the paint-thoughts of a Paul Klee, and numerous others. One of the reasons that there is that hiatus between the artist and society, which Herbert Read laments, is that we no longer have a simple but a very ordinary people; rubber tires, automobiles, radios, enfeeble the mind, and ruin the hand; if the hand does not create, it lusts and kills. Read has wisely said that the form may slay the spirit. The best poems look as though they had been seeded, hoed and planted; they are not working-class but working-hand poems.

Herbert Read asks for a communal prose, but we have broken the communal arts to pieces. We have Babel painting and literature which only the abstract Nimrods themselves understand. Still, how can there be the art Read desires when good poetry cannot even get printed? Has the poet a right to expect society to support him? Who then will maintain society? There is a simple reply to this question that perplexes all but the innocent; it is found in Henry David Thoreau's *Walden*. An Indian, wrote Thoreau, came to the house of a New England lawyer, offering him baskets that he had woven, and when the lawyer declined to buy them, the Indian explained, "What, do you mean to starve me!"

We are in the plastic age, as Herbert Read says in *The Grass Roots of Art*. The genius we had for folk arts, the settle, the salt box house, a Pennsylvania Dutch chair, the H L, or Holy Lord hinges, all the lovely artifacts, have been forsaken for chromium, nylon, and plastic. What moral or aesthetic education can there be, declares Read, when materials are so debased. Education is, as Plato said, the training "that produces pleasure and pain at the right objects." *Fields, Factories and Workshops,* by Kropotkin, which deeply influenced Read, and should be a Bible of a civilized man, is one of the last cries in the modern soul for handicrafts. Compare the nineteenth-century weavers about which Kropotkin writes, working at handlooms in their own cottages, keeping two cows and often horses, and engaged in truck-gardening, with the groundless factory hand who rents less than a hundred square feet divided into two to three rooms. Read derives from Kropotkin, William Morris, and Ruskin, whose following remark I found in a Tolstoy letter: "It is physically impossible that true religious knowledge, or pure morality, should exist among any classes of a nation who do not work with their hands for their bread." How are we going to govern the machine? The modern auto city is a war plant; the house, as Herbert Read, quoting one writer, asserts, is "a machine to live in"; the cartels build what Read calls megalomaniac skyscrapers, which is greed ascending to heaven. It is the sin of Babel that is killing the human race; it is the one big world, the one big Nineveh.

Kropotkin suggested a return to petty trades and to small

workshops, in which the village would be an agricultural and handicraft commune. Read wants a grass roots art. This is what Hamlin Garland meant by the local color novel, for a big city literature is so subhuman and earthless that one could read fifty such novels and not see anybody sitting at a table with his family or smell a boiled potato or an artichoke.

Herbert Read's *Innocent Eye* is a Yorkshire Georgics, even his battle narrative *In Retreat* is bucolic, and that portion of his poems he calls "Ecologues" is a country hymn to "the spittle of wrens," "the fresh petals of cowslips and primroses," "where only garlic and hemlock grow." In his poem "Mutations of the Phoenix," his moan is:

> Beauty, truth and rarity,
> Grace in all simplicity,
> Here enclosed in cinders lie.

and further in his poem, he writes of the city-hurt mind of a Hamlet "musing in the gutters."

Tolstoy said that aesthetics is a false science; it is the letter that killeth the spirit. In an age when the word is the idol, what is most needed is a moral nature—like Ruskin or Herbert Read.

Texas Quarterly, 1964

*

A GIFT OF BOOKS

Herbert Read has written the finest and perhaps the only pastoral English prose in our century. His autobiography, *The Contrary Experience,** a vernal memorial of his boyhood near

---

*An expanded version of *The Innocent Eye* (1933)—Ed.

the Yorkshire heaths, can be understood and enjoyed by any imaginative child. According to Read it is the boy who has pure, Arcadian experiences; as we age, our first, Edenic pulses are no more than mildewed ghosts. Read says, "We only hear a tone once, only see a color once, see, hear, touch, taste and smell everything but once, the first time." These bucolic annals smack of the wold, beck, gorse and moor. Read lived on the farm with his father, mother, brothers and sister until his tenth year. He knew and smelled the saddle room, the shed for the dog cart and buggy, the blacksmith's shop, the flitches of bacon and "plum-dusky hams" that hung "from the beams of the wooden ceiling." No less bucolic was the ivy-clad privy with two seats where the children could sit side by side and dung like jackdaws, without shame. There were the middens and the piggeries, a "steaming morass of urine-sodden straw" and the pasture "pockmarked with erupted rabbit warrens . . . and dark fairy-rings in the grass." Before the boy is ten years old, his father dies, and his Utopian senses are urned in a wintry, dulled heart. Herbert Read writes, "Memory is a flower which only opens fully in the Kingdom of Heaven, where the eye is eternally innocent."

These reminiscences are a canticle of green, virgin sensations, which we burn, like storax, praying that some remembrance of its childhood fragrance will permeate the sere, disappointed man.

Holiday, 1965

The Classics and the Man of Letters

What do we mean by the word *classic?* Homer's *Iliad,* as Allen Tate has said, is contemporary. I know of no literature that has had such a puissant effect on me as the Homeric books. How many times have I ransacked Ovid's *Fasti* and his *Pontic Epistles?* I should be blind as Tiresias could I not thaw my dull heart in the myths of Hesiod, in the gnomic verse of Theognis, or the *Odes* of Horace.

How can a student comprehend Ben Jonson, Milton, Paracelsus, or Jacob Boehme without a knowledge of the Greek legends and the Old and New Testament? So much of Rabelais is passed over by a drumbling reader who has never heard of Antisthenes, Lucian, or Aristippus. I believe that *Gulliver's Travels* is, in some measure, modelled upon the dialogues of Lucian. Need I go farther for the origin of Walter Savage Landor's *Imaginary Portraits?*

Let us not forget that we have American Classics, and can these be comprehended unless one is familiar with ancient annals? There is Garcilaso de la Vega's *Royal Commentaries* rendered into English by Sir Paul Rycaut in 1688. Garcilaso was the bastard issue of an Inca princess and a Spanish conquistador. It is doubtful that Thucydides was any better or even as good as this aboriginal American. Professor Brinton's *Myths of the New World* is a precious source of North American fables. No less valuable is *The Book of Chilam Balam of Chumayel,* Yucatan legends and scripture. Cabeza de Vaca is a sixteenth-century American Odysseus, and he is the epic figure in the late Haniel Long's *The Power Within Us.* William Carlos Williams made a song of early American inceptions out of Prescott's *Conquest*

100

of Mexico, and that volume is called *In the American Grain.* What is now but the past converted into the twentieth century? Only recently Professor Frank MacShane published a lovely essay on Thoreau as the Buddha at Walden Pond, and there is another rare little chant, Josephine Herbst's *New Green World,* a study of John Bartram and the early naturalists in the United States. These are fables to be memorized no less than Greek or Roman ones. Samuel Francis Adams's *Three Episodes in the History of Massachusetts,* and William Bradford's *Of Plymouth Plantation* are as significant to us as Hesiod's *Works and Days.* One could also mention Adolph Bandelier's book on Lake Titicaca in which the sun and moon were said to have been born, or Fanny Bandelier's work on Father Sahagún. There is Barcia's *History of Florida,* englished by the very gifted Anthony Kerrigan. Our chronicles are no less mythic than Herodotus', and no poet, scholar, or student can afford to neglect them. But most of the labor on pre-Columbian records or those compiled by the conquistadors lie like Job's potsherd in the Sinai Desert, the archives of the universities. Students whose major subject is History have never heard of the Seven Cities of Cibola or Coronado's march through Kansas.

What is education? And the reply is a second query, What books do you prefer and in what order do you intend to read them?

Man does not have a logical intellect. A zealous student will wander from one sagacious author to another, regardless of the time in which they composed their metaphysics, poems, and criticism. Periods of literature, amputated from other centuries, become refrigerated instances of thought. One only comes to any understanding at all by comparing one book with another; too often poems written in the same era are similar in tone, cadence, and punctuation.

It is a vain delusion to imagine that one can commence with Thales and pass from one age of thinkers to another until he has come to Ruskin's *Unto This Last* or Herbert Read's *Annals of Innocence.* No man on the earth has that kind of continuous culture in his mind or soul.

Instead of going right through the alphabet of literature it is more sensible to be dialectic, going back and forth from the ancients to Chaucer and then to the present. It is better to examine the *Ethics* of Spinoza and then return to Lucretius, and maybe one will comprehend a moiety of the philosophy or the Latin poem. In endeavoring to understand the human spirit we go from Greek parables conceived in the fifth century B.C. to a Restoration play by Congreve.

The student grows weary of the same century, and though he is involved with eight to ten authors, the prose style of each one is the signature of that age.

The mind flags after reading nothing but the Greek cosmologists or the Elizabethans. What is the student's reward for several years of labor in Laban's field but a weak-eyed Leah, the dimmest recollection of his studies? Man is an angelic brute when he is ecstatic about the *Timaeus,* but if tired and bored he is a sottish lotus-eater.

Doubtless it is valuable to confine oneself to the Augustan poets for a semester, but in my empiric judgment, this sort of exclusive exploration of a particular time will not liquefy the intellect.

Could man remember a tithe of what he has read he would be a demigod. John Donne said that after he had perused 525 pages all that he knew of the volume was that it contained that number of leaves. It is said that Mnemosyne, who is Memory, is the mother of the Muses, but I believe the Greeks were considering the head of Zeus and not man's frail mind.

What is philosophy? asked Plotinus, who answered, What is most important. One attends the university in order to gain some feeling for the spirit of man. Is this a vapory remark? Perhaps it will seem clearer should I say that the most avid student can only recall a few lumpish facts, the stepmother of learning.

A good teacher is an awakener; he must also be a patient Buddha, giving his pupils the Rig Veda or the Bhagavad Gita one week, and should either fail to rouse somniferous flesh, he can offer them Hazlitt's essays on the English comic writers or Goncharov's *Oblomov*.

When can a student's faculties be kindled? A poet may seed his heart in his sophomore years, and then for a time all knowledge might be no more than the parching Dog Star. Who knows when one should be born, lie fallow, or in what season man will begin to learn. The book was ripe for me, but I was not ripe for it, says Nietzsche.

In the fag end of his life Aristotle found nothing so consoling as mythology. It is a viaticum for the old and young. However, should the Greek legends be drossy because the student is ready for the verse of Sir Walter Raleigh, does it matter?

Pound's shibboleth, Make it New, is for the sham Gideon; I say, Make it Human. "The blood around the heart is the thought of men," declared Empedocles.

What is inexplicable to a student is a book he cannot relate to his own life. Euripides' *Bacchae* is a secret glyph when one, to cite Keats, cannot use it to "prove himself upon his pulses."

How Greek or Roman is the American? We are nobody until we recognize Odysseus, Protesilaus, or Aeneas in ourselves. America is Trojan, Greek, Aztec, Mayan, and Indian. The ghosts in our civilization are being resurrected so that we can see that the Rocky Mountains, the Appalachians, and our savannahs are corporeal gods.

There can be no question but that we are in the middle of an American renascence. The interest in Jane Harrison's *Prolegomena to the Study of Greek Religion* is considerable among authors and academics. A. B. Cook's *Zeus* is an Atlean joy to the scholar. Only a short while ago the late Professor Morris Jastrow wrote his volumes on Job, The Song of Songs, and Ecclesiastes. These are Hebraic chants, but the Greek alphabet is Cadmean, and it is a song of Tyre.

103

Since a century or so is only a contemplative sigh, we cannot omit Grote's *History of Greece.* He was a mythographer, and his portrait of Socrates is a greater marvel than Xenophon's *Memorabilia.*

When Randolph Bourne, a legendary figure in American annals, was writing *The History of a Literary Radical,* one of his idols was Theodore Gomperz, author of *The Greek Thinkers.*

There is our eminent poet, Allen Tate, whose translations of the amorous Latin hymn, *The Vigil of Venus,* pierces our spirit. What fabulous use he makes of the Pillars of Hercules and the Trojan Aeneas in his ineradicable poem, "The Mediterranean." Who could expunge Professor Mackail's *Epigrams from the Greek Anthology,* which so influenced Dudley Fitts, or fail to laurel the latter for his lovely paraphrases of the same?

Nor do we go astray in referring to William Smith's *Dictionary of Greek and Roman Biography and Mythology.*

I mention these, and multifarious Greek and Roman works I have omitted with a heavy heart. Having had a little Latin I decided that French and German were more important than those archaic languages. It was a grievous error though I have a surd ear, and must read Hölderlin, Rilke, Rabelais, and La Bruyère in English.

Dudley Fitts, who knows Greek and is a Latinist, does not believe a writer should cite Hesiod, Martial, Propertius, or Pausanias unless he is familiar with them in the original. I am most reluctant to deny this though my own books are glutted with quotations from the ancients.

But a writer who is ignorant of Horace in Latin is still able to recognize whether it is a good or a noxious poem in English. Long ago I had come to the conclusion that Mackail was the best translator of the Greek Anthology, or that parcel of it he had done. Did I make a lucky guess? Perhaps. But Dudley Fitts has the same opinion.

Is Robert Lowell's Quevedo, grounded upon Spanish, just a beautiful poem in English? Swinburne asserted that Byron was

104

a far better poet in German.

The truth is that we have to take all learning on trust. How do I know how much confidence I should have in Buffon, Humboldt, Lyell, Bates, White's *Selbourne,* or Darwin on plants and animals. Is not Sir Thomas Browne's *Pseudodoxia Epidemica* abstruse, and cannot it be misread just as quickly as Whiston's Josephus?

Let no one imagine that I do not think Dudley Fitts is far more right than I am. What would not I give for his Greek and Latin?

As for Eliot and Pound I was never able to slake my thirst in their Hippocrene puddle. One can agree that Gilbert Murray's Euripides is exsanguinous, but what of Eliot's sere conceits in his Introduction to Seneca's tragedies?

Can one be in earnest about Pound's neologisms which come before and after some nonsensical allusion to a Greek deity?

What does the literary scholar make of Pound's uncouth dismissal of Milton? There is more English in the *Areopagitica* than in all of Pound's wind. Ezra Pound regards himself as a literary iconoclast; he abhors facile rhyming but recommends Arthur Golding's version of Ovid's *Metamorphoses,* which I find not much better than doggerel.

La Fontaine alleged that he who loved his own age more than ancient times was insane. Having his veneration for the past, I am not prepared to knock down an olden writer. In doing that one is likely to be a stupid Ajax who slaughters the sheep instead of his foe, Agamemnon. May I be shriven if I err, but I believe that the most tedious of all the antique books that I know is Philostratus' *Life of Apollonius of Tyana.*

Let me conclude this small paper with a few rambling remarks on education.

Most of the courses in English literature are recitations in grammar. Montaigne said that he did not know one case from another, and whenever I had classes in composition, it was necessary for me to learn the rules each time.

Fowler has never been an advantage to me; read his long passage on the use of the subjunctive mood. After giving you forty to fifty reasons why it is a heavy vexation to begin a sentence with "if," he advises the author to avoid it altogether. Manuals of grammar are no better; the ideas that are put into correct sentences are puerile and repulsive. One is told that the conjunction "because" should not follow the copulative "is," only to discover that this was a common practice with Sir Thomas Browne.

To a great extent it is futile to separate the laws governing syntax from literature itself. If I am to learn anything about English—and this is my passion and despair—I can only do so by going to the Masters of that glorious language. Seeing how a word is used in a line by Dekker or Swift is a replenishing experience. However, I often read Skeat's *Etymological Dictionary* with jubilation, and am sometimes calmed by the *Shorter Oxford Dictionary* because of the citations from Sir Philip Sidney, Samuel Daniel, Addison, and Steele.

There is a cairn of pedagogical fustian in Dryden's marvelous *Dramatic Poesie* and far more in Coleridge's masterly *Biographia Literaria,* and at moments the great William Hazlitt is a child. But what a simpleton I should be without their precepts!

Still, had I to repeat my youth, I should look for the olive of Minerva in our pantheons of learning.

The American college is no cloister. In the close future the university press will take the place of the venal paperback houses. Recently the Yale University Press published the colonial poet Edward Taylor, the peer of Traherne and Smart.

Too much honor cannot be given to the work that is being done by the University of Texas for writers. In spite of natural human error, and the influence of the Mammon literary agora, it is conceivable that our Thoreaus, Melvilles, and Poes will not be obscure wraiths in our own day. For there will always be

106

some rare person in the American Academe who will print the poems of our scribes. The parables are more important than the raiment and the meat; for the poet can somehow endure indigence but not the neglect of his books.

Arion, 1964

Majorca

For the past fifteen years I have been a reluctant traveler. Like most other people I think somewhere else is Utopia. Moreover, I have never ceased looking for a cheap Elysium. Then, islands have always tempted me. D. H. Lawrence commences one of his short stories with: "There was a man who loved islands." There was a brief sojourn at Bustin's Island in Maine; Hven, a scraggy, barren jot of Swedish earth on the sea, attracted me because it was an isle. Someone once told me to settle at Bornholm, above six hours by water from Copenhagen. I heard that the natives used paint mixed with cow's dung on their houses. Backward places fetch my imagination, and so I took a ship for Denmark. However, Bornholm made me nervous because it was windy most of the day. After that I came to Majorca. A man, who had just been released from a New York State hospital for mental patients, said this Mediterranean mountain would be an ideal spot for me. But no matter, I need an island for good or bad or insane reasons. A famous philosopher, Pascal, has said that all of man's troubles come from his inability to remain quiet in one room. Those who don't wish to take advice from the wise will do as I have done—travel.

In 1954 I arrived in Palma de Mallorca and thought I had discovered Prospero's Isle in Shakespeare's *The Tempest.* I was unreasonably sure that I could be contented here, or, at least, that I would not be stung constantly by the desire to go elsewhere.

This sensual, café town was not at that time glutted with evil herds of automobiles. The fifteenth-century, golden sandstone edifices eased some fierce city wound in me. Here I was not punished all day long by grating cement and cruel iron. Every dirty, Arabic alley was a voluptuous experience; nearly each house, humble or rich, had a patio filled with feminine lemon and orange trees, massy pots of geraniums, begonias, tears of the virgin, aspidistra, and the empurpled bougainvillaea. Reared in the Midwest I had been indifferent to that slut of the garden, the geranium; but there are about two hundred different classes of this flower in Majorca, and they bloom twelve months a year. How tender are her vestal petticoats to me now!

Too, I was ecstatic when I learned that I could go to a restaurant at the Plaza Major and get a beefsteak, with several vegetables and a bottle of wine, and all for about fourteen pesetas. For two pesetas and a half I could buy a liter of palatable, ordinary table wine; Seco del Monte, a wine both sweet and yet dry, and thoroughly delightful, cost five pesetas. I had rented a pair of rooms, furnished in a traditional Spanish style, with a fine, sun-fed balcony overlooking the sea. The rent was twenty-five dollars a month, and that was expensive. In Soller, Deyá, Valdemosa, Inca, and in other Majorcan hamlets it was no hard matter to find a house, wholly furnished, for eight or nine dollars a month.

Palma is a very ancient city, perhaps as old as wind-swept Ilium, Homer's epic town. It is mentioned by both Pliny, the great natural historian, and Strabo, the geographer. Majorca and the diminutive island, Minorca, originally were called the Gymnesian Islands. They were colonized by the Phoenicians as early as 1000 B.C. Later, the Carthaginian and Roman armies overran Majorca. Moorish influence began about the seventh or eighth century. Majorca is an island of olive yards and Moorish walls. Most of the walls are in perfect condition, and many form terraces which journey right up the steep flanks of the Majorcan mountains. There are countless granite steps going up to the peaks where the olive has stood since the Phoenician and Greek mariners went as far as the Gates of Hercules. Bañalbufar, one of the jagged, sea-swept towns, is built on these stony staircases; in each rustic village you will see wide, granite mule steps, and the wells and huts are composed of this rock and earth.

109

Palma is still a licentious, golden sandstone town with antique museum streets and many fifteenth-century buildings with sylph-like columns. Havelock Ellis said that the church in Palma is the finest in the world. Though charming, it is by no means the best in Spain, far from it. The royal palace adjacent to the cathedral, and now a military office, is an enchanting *casa,* and I never grow weary of beholding the Renaissance gallery and the columns of the small Maritime Museum.

The main entertainment here is the cheap and pleasant café life. Without sidewalk cafés and plazas a city is a mortuary. There is very little one can do with his life: you can either sit or stand, and you need savory and viable places to do both. The Spanish *rambla* is a special walk lined with plane trees and with many benches. Fortunately, walking still costs nothing, and café sitting can be purchased at a bargain price. One can stay all afternoon at a table for a five peseta coñac, without being persecuted by a Gestapo agent, the modern waiter.

Naturally, there are many more beaches, or *playae,* than I can count or remember; but swimming holes like Cala Mayor, just outside of Palma, have been spoiled, at least for those who hate to see the sands littered with garbage-like heaps of people. Cala San Vincente, a short while ago, was surrounded by fishermen's cottages, but now a hotel has been put up there. A hotel is the nemesis of all Edenic raptures. La Calobra, a pensive, salt lagoon, girt with small stones, was marvelous for a day's picnic; now the gross, tin buses from Denmark, Sweden and Germany disgorge their contents there. A brand-new hotel was sprouted up out of the granite, but if you have a barbarous tourist's gullet, La Calobra will still enchant you. The same has happened to Paguera, Illetas, and Palma Nova, which are not many kilometers from Palma. Formentor, the most idyllic beach in Majorca, is also the most remote. Worse, it is a place of lucre. One can bathe at Palma, but the water is not bracing or tonical; the vessels throw their oil and refuse into the sea, and there is no sand.

110

Spite of the claims of the sundry travel agencies, there is no bathing year round in Majorca; the winters are often very rainy and arthritic, and when the sirocco blows over the inhabitants they go out of their heads. A full moon here is the time for the crazy to go out into the streets and shriek. However, one February I sat on the patio and at my typewriter without a jacket, and was marvelously serene and comfortable until four o'clock in the afternoon. In winter a coal or wood fire in the hearth is a holy altar, although outside the sun may be your quail and manna.

Almost any part of Majorca is worth contemplating; there is no village, orchard, or the meanest street that will not appease or even humble your eyes. Valdemosa, where George Sand lived with Chopin, is a rapturous little hamlet. The damp, monastic cellar where Chopin wrote some of his music far less so; here Chopin coughed and quarreled with George Sand. Both were regarded as atheists because Sand, that female free-thinker and novelist, felt obligated to tell the Catholic peasants that they were not married. Now this illicit cell is a shrine; a caretaker prevents persons, who buy their tickets of admission, from touching the keys of Chopin's piano. The piano looks somewhat new to me; besides I have forgotten the ascetic, pulmonary cell he occupied, but I will always remember the terraces of wise olives, the Moorish walls that are songs of stone, and the amorous almond trees. The almond pinks and flowers in February, and these blossoms of desire will charm those who have fatigued souls.

The journey by automobile from Soller to Formentor is a rhapsodic sensation: along this route near Lluch there is a cemetery of natural rocks which looks like Ezekiel's Valley of Dry Bones in the Old Testament. The short excursion from Palma to Soller will also replenish jaded eyes; along the entire route are orchards of olive and almonds.

Soller is a handmade town; most of the houses are of granite, earth, and particles of loose cement. The streams, or *torrentes,*

111

dry bedrock the greater part of the year, were walled in by the Moors; the bottoms were formed by stones rolling down the mountains, or laid there by the Arabs. These hollowed-out rivers would be a glory to behold did they not stink. One of the principal industries here is skinning rabbits and goats, and the smell from this is abominable. One can go by tram from the town of Soller to the Puerto, and the Mediterranean bay, passing fields of lemon, tangerine and orange trees, furrows of lettuce, tomatoes and *judias verdes*—Jewish beans, an odd appellation for a comestible in an anti-Semitic land. The mule and the burro have not yet disappeared, although the horse-fountain has since been removed from the main plaza, and is now situated close by the *mercado,* the market.

In spite of the sierras, a sterile terrain that must have been volcanic in origin, the ground and the vales are a delirium to the sleepy senses. Austere, rocky plateaus produce fortitude in a people, and it may be that the great Spanish literature of the past was dominated by the Pyrenees rather than the sheep, the goats, the citrous groves and flowers that delighted the licentious inhabitants.

Majorca, from one promontory of the isle to the other, is a vineyard; the foliage is a continuous vein running through the blooded clay. The olive trees along the road from Soller to Valdemosa have been in their dotages for centuries; their huge, wrinkled trunks are so old and brittle, they seem masses of twisted dust. When we consider the cult of youth that obtains everywhere in the world, and then regard the senile olive whose fruit is the symbol of Minerva, the goddess of wisdom, we know that where there is no veneration for the aged there is no real civilization either. Old people are not unwanted castaways here as they are in so much of the western world. Who, with any human feeling, can contemplate the untouchable, old man who has that repulsive, latrine solitude about his clothes? People not needed or loved smell bad. In all Majorcan towns, decrepit, spent men have their clubs where they can sit and drink moderately; they have the only nostrum that can somewhat cure the sorrows that come when the bones are sere, dried leaves—companions.

Though the island is an orchard the land is thirsty, and water is the gravest concern of the natives. One goes to the well rather than to the uglified spigot for water. About five years ago there was rainfall for only eleven days of the year, and this was a great hardship. In summer the hotels absorb most of the water and the people occupying apartments or houses either must buy it or wait until the early hours of the morning when they can turn on their faucets without despair. Three years ago a luxurious hotel advertised its newfangled bathrooms; they were miracles of progress, and there was nothing wrong with them except that there was no water to fill the tubs.

In Soller the Majorcans built an up-to-date housing settlement; it contained seven good-sized buildings. There were cement walks outside going from one dwelling-place to the other, a grubby, stunted lawn in the shape of a lozenge, and modish fluorescent lamps. The townsmen came on Sundays to view this astounding American architectural theorem. Completed two years ago it is still unoccupied; when all the work was finished, the contractor discovered there was no water.

There are two pests which have not yet destroyed Majorca: the machine and Sunday. In Soller all the shops are open on Sunday until one o'clock; what a difference it makes to saunter through a town that is not a shut graveyard. However, the Puritan Sunday has come to Palma; it is not the church but the *sindicados,* the specious trade unions, that have closed the city. When everybody has the same holiday nobody can do anything; since browsing in the shops, and spending money is the last recreation left to the people, Sunday has become a day of void.

Of course, the automobile is here; but the native is still a ridiculous Quixotist with a machine. A European artist once said that the house is a machine; what a refrigerated definition of a home.

113

Though progress and the auto are now here, it will take at least another generation for the real estate Attilas to kill the earth. As for myself, I would renounce all modern, occidental improvements—the watercloset for which man has given up poetry—for the Roman arch at Aleudia. It appears impossible to maintain both a savory lavatory and an ancient civilization. Man has relinquished the glories of the past for a flush toilet.

To the Spaniard the auto, like the bull, is a dangerous toy with which he likes to play his ritualistic game of death. Still a peasant, though often wiser than a professor, he cannot comprehend the machine. At El Terreno, a bistro dump for foreigners, an electrician came to my cottage to connect the hot water heater. He cut the cord without bothering to measure the length of it to see whether it would reach the socket in the wall. The gloomiest Andalusian or Mallorquin is optimistic; he will tell you the worst is the best because he knows he will die anyway. The electrician, finishing his work, said quite proudly: "Todo es listo," and went away. Afterwards, when I tried to take a shower, the cord was a foot and a half too short.

Besides progress and the auto, the curse in Majorca is the high standard of living. To the local people it is an acute, economic sorrow. In 1954 a house of six to eight rooms, all furnished, and with a romanesque patio, could be rented for eight to ten dollars a month. One could hire a servant, a *criada*, for 250 pesetas monthly. But in Palma rents have soared; you now pay four and five thousand pesetas a month for rent and a chambermaid costs a thousand or more pesetas. In a semi-feudal land the middle class can still afford to keep a servant, whereas in the United States the wife has become the cook and the scrubwoman.

Some food is still quite reasonable, at least for the tourist. Last year a head of lettuce sold for a peseta and a half; tomatoes in season were as little as one peseta for a kilo, which is slightly more than two pounds. Butter is expensive and not for a worker's table. In the markets you can see forty to fifty sparrows hanging by a string and offered for table meat; thrushes are sold for the same purpose; in ancient times this bird was a great Roman delicacy. Rabbits and doves are raised by the lower classes for eating. When Rome had colonized Majorca, the island was overrun by hares and the natives begged their conquerors to help them eradicate these pests. The Majorcans then imported cats from North Africa to destroy them. What is a bane in one century is a gourmet's delight in another, at least, for those unable to purchase liver or other animal flesh.

Before the civil war the milk was marvelous; now it is the bad water and whey that passes for milk in New York.

Spain has always been a wondrous winery; wine is more plentiful on this isle than water. During the civil war there was such a dearth of water that soldiers stationed in the Majorcan mountains shaved with wine. Until a very short while ago the cheapest wine was refreshing and every workingman drank his bottle of wine while he ate his loaf of bread. All beverages are ecstatically reasonable: good champagne, and very dry, sells for about sixty cents a bottle; coñac costs fifty cents a liter; liqueurs, crème de menthe, anise, crème de cacao, are about the same price. A bodega, a wine cellar, is enchanting; one of the most famous drinking cellars in Majorca is at Inca, the shoe-town. You can moisten your gullet and then buy the most chic shoes for walking—provided you can still stand on your legs. Shoes too are cheap; however, in a couple of weeks the soles and heels will drop off, but if you take them to the shoemakers in America and have them repaired you will still have a bargain.

Wine that used to be two and a half pesetas a liter is now six, and it is made with a powder and turns sour rapidly. The same economic idiocy prevails in all countries—the more you pay for a thing the worse it is.

Spanish bread is rough but good; what a pleasure it is to observe a peasant woman walking at dusk and carrying under her arm a vast, round loaf weighing about seven pounds. *Sopa mallorquina,* which is mostly vegetable water, the crude dregs of oil, and morsels of bread, is the principal meal of the lower classes. But wheat is now dear, and the small bakery will soon disappear. Then the machine-made loaf will be sold in the shops—that terrible bread baked in Styx, and wrapped in the winding-sheet called cellophane.

The inhabitants of the Balearics speak Mallorquin, a gross mixture of Spanish, French, Italian, Arabic and a little Portuguese. Nothing like Castilian Spanish, it is a nasal dialect which sounds like the melancholy trumpet of the burro one hears about five o'clock every morning. Their customs are in many essentials derived from the ancient colonizers. Until about twenty years ago there were no regular prices for fish, vegetables or meats in the markets. The old Phoenician habit of bargaining prevailed.

In speaking of their racial ingredients one should not omit the Jew. Common opinion holds that most of the Jews quit the land during the Spanish Inquisition. When Columbus set out on his second voyage to the New World, he saw long queues of Jews making ready for their exile or Diaspora. But many remained; they became Catholics, or practiced Judaism secretly in their cellars. The local people today can tell you who among themselves is Jewish, though no one has admitted being Jewish since the persecution began in 1492. The Spaniard is a tragic and a droll paradox: the late Bishop of Sevilla was a fanatical Catholic, of Jewish origin, and very outspoken in his sympathies with Israel.

Death is a national fetish, and also a parcel of Latin realism. In Soller, a classic Moorish town of 14,000 people, the same man that carries the cadavers to the graveyard also takes care of the garbage when not employed for holy purposes. Such naturalism may offend the trembling heart of the Westerner, but to the Spanish mind what is not spirit is carrion.

The children are just as realistic as their elders; one day in Soller I saw a small boy with a square box painted blue, and containing four wooden drawers; in one he kept pesetas for

116

clothing, another was reserved for *pan,* or bread, the third for his offering, and the last for funeral expenses.

Tombstones are extremely expensive; but the poor in Soller, unable to pay for a slab of granite (called *piedra muerta*—dead rock), are entitled to free ground for the interment of their dead. There is a beautiful little city of the dead, with painted and tiled funerary houses, outside of Andraixt.

If a neighbor dies, even though he were a pile of malice when he lived, a Majorcan must leave his work that day and go to the house of the bereaved one and express his sorrow. Otherwise, he is likely to be ostracized. Death notices are extremely popular, and are distributed every day.

Ordinary corpses are buried in the evening; nuns are carried to the cemetery in broad daylight, because, perhaps, their sins need not be hidden. Both men and women attend the ceremony at the church, but they are separated from each other. The women sit on the right side of the altar and men on the left. This absolute division of the sexes is doubtless the result of some primitive tabu, but what, I do not know. One seldom sees a man and his wife on the street together during the weekdays.

The tourists who come here will be overwhelmed by the villages; each town is a work of art; however, the foreigner himself is not. The outsiders are a bizarre baggage; most of them try to look as disorderly as possible; their raiment is wild, representing some kind of protest against dull respectability. Their shirttails hang out as well as their stringy beards. Most of the persons who come to Majorca want to be parasites or artists. Almost all of them are lonely. As a result they are great chatter-boxes. The main aliment of the foreign colony is scandal; there is always a good story to be heard. The artist is no less eccentric than the bourgeois traveler, and the English are just as crazy as the Americans, and no less voluble. The other day I was in a shop, and a woman from Yorkshire, whom I had nodded to on several occasions, suddenly said to me: "I've had such a dis-appointment today." I looked at her sympathetically and she

117

went on: "My husband just ran off with another woman." Thinking of the price of olive oil, I replied quite vacantly: "Young or old?"

There is a seventy-five-year-old chick from Devon who is a notorious gossip and who bitterly complains to everybody because her ninety-two-year-old husband is impotent. Another English bantling of about sixty-eight is always looking for the veterinary because she says her poodle, who has pink polished nails, is sickly. A short while ago a woman coming from England asked the clerk of a very fancy hotel in Palma for twin beds, one for herself, and the other for her dachshund. She had occasion to ask for a veterinarian, who sent his nurse. As the nurse arrived without a uniform, the woman asserted she was not qualified to take care of her dog. Twin beds, incidentally, are not popular in Majorca; these people still prefer *la cama matrimonial,* the marriage bed.

Some of the Americans who come here are real crackers also. One man, who claimed he was a poet as well as a millionaire, an improbable combination, was a devout alcoholic. Once he informed me that he had a wife, and when I happened to ask him what her name was, he said, "Wait a minute, I've got it written down on a card in my suitcase upstairs in the hotel room." He was a solitary figure and so I introduced him to a charming pair of Americans who ran a ballet school on Calle Jaime Segundo. He was so taken with them that he said when he returned to the United States he would send them a check for $3000. He never mailed them any money, but he was not coarse either; for when he wrote to them he enclosed his best regards.

Three months ago a pseudo-painter arrived with his wife; soon as they came to Soller they wanted to buy a little house with an orange grove. Towns like Fornaluxt, Deyá, Alcudia and Biniaraix, a suburb of Soller, are such ecstasies to newcomers from the grum, iron cities, that almost at first blush they are attacked by this fever. These two were living off the revenue of

118

a houseboat they had sold on the installment plan to a widow in Marin County, California. Like the majority of the others, they were outlandish. In the Majorcan heat the wife wore Wellington boots and heavy homemade Mother Hubbards, usually of a gangrened hue. She even appeared unsightly to others who imagined they dressed soberly though also garbed in some outrageous filth.

A few years ago a Brooklyn zipper salesman, fifty-three years old, arrived in El Terreno, just outside of Palma. With him were a wife and two children. The first night they stayed at a hotel, and hours after they had checked out he discovered that he had left his money-belt beneath the pillow in his hotel room. It contained $1300, all that they possessed. Frantic, they hurried back to their room, and the criada very quietly returned the money-belt and all the money to the frenzied zipper salesman. So elated by such probity he asked her to become the family house-servant, which she did. She did the housecleaning, shopping, cooking, and when he made a bad painting she told him so. But this did not grieve him so much as when she informed him she would no longer work for him. Hating to lose such a fine housekeeper and art critic, he promised her an increase in wages. When she refused he asked her what she was going to do. She replied: "I am going to be a prostitute and save enough money so that I can get a husband."

The zipper salesman was a most zealous nature; he locked himself in his room all morning, only appearing for a rush lunch, and then returned to his labors until six or seven in the evening. His wife was extremely lonely, and pined for her rapturous days in Flatbush; how she missed American butter, meat, eggs, and fresh dairy milk. She began to hate her husband, and worse than that she had nobody to whom she could pour out her full, ripe scorn. She found me. Every day she arrived at seven in the morning at my house on the Calle de la Salud, the street of Health! When I defended him she became more exasperated. How could I get rid of this fellow countryman

119

without being too common? I told my wife Rlene: she is so miserable with this man that I have not the stomach or the heart to mangle her righteous feelings. One morning, after listening to an hour of her rage, I said, quite upset myself, that if her husband was such a rascal I never wanted to see him again. She looked at me with positive horror, picked up her handbag, and never returned.

Most of those who come here on holiday are English, French, German, Scandinavian and a few Americans. Only a very immoral person will be immune to the beauties of this island. However, as Socrates once said, "I can't talk to trees and rocks." So bring your friends, your wife, or your friend's wife. The disease that is ravaging the Western nations is solitude, and not even the Balearics will ease that.

There is privacy for those who crave it; I have all the quiet I require amidst the almonds, figs and oleanders. Since people are discontented everywhere, the choice is quite simple: where would you prefer to be bored? In the big, cement cities or in Majorca? It is a dilemma, at least for me. I knew a young couple—he was a painter and his wife artistic—they were on the deck of a Yugoslavian freighter about to leave New York for Tangier from which they were going to take a boat to Marseilles, and then proceed to Palma. Both were involved in a serious dispute. He said: "What do you think we ought to do? Maybe we should find an apartment in Hoboken; rent is cheap there. Why not go out to Big Sur, Henry Miller's sex colony? What about Athens or Istanbul? I hear the Turkish coast is wild and a real bargain." Still waving good-by to friends as the ship pulled away from the pier, she could not take her eyes off two children who were busy trying to split the dock to pieces; one had a hammer and the other a saw, two ideal tools of the progressive school child. Still their argument gave them enormous pleasure. As the freighter began to move into the East River, he said: "I think we ought to renew the lease on our Avenue D slum." She replied: "Who in God's name are those pair of bomb-throwers on the wharf?" He looked at them narrowly, and then screamed: "Where are we going? Those two nuclear animals belong to us!"

Holiday, 1965

Hart Crane

The Letters of Hart Crane, 1916-1932,
edited by Brom Weber

The life of Hart Crane was a Bacchic orgy; he knew no other way to live or compose his poems. As Quevedo wrote: "He rode post to perdition." Though I realize that humdrum everyday existence cannot be a gloss upon the poem, it might be of niggish interest to the reader to have some intelligence of Crane as a person. I knew him, and there were some similarities in our lives which, though no more than gossip, tease the blood and the veins.

Hart Crane was born July 21, 1899, and I on July 22, 1900. When he was a soda fountain clerk in his father's fancy ice cream parlor and tea room in Cleveland, Ohio, I was then an inmate of an orphanage in the same city. For a short space of time Hart Crane was a navvy in a munitions plant in Cleveland, and so was I. In 1928 he went to Paris where we met. Crane had already published *White Buildings,* of which I had never heard, and he asked me, though God knows why, to read the ms. of *The Bridge.* Though I had studied pre-Socratic philosophy and Middle English in the graduate school at Columbia, I knew little about the Boulevard Montparnasse seers of the U.S.A. vulgate. I was exceedingly anxious to be a part of the covey of roaring, spastic exiles who contributed to *transition* and *This Quarter,* little expatriate magazines. Hart Crane and I already had encountered Robert McAlmon, Kay Boyle, Eugene Jolas, one of the editors of *transition,* and Harry Crosby, a disciple of Lautréamont, author of *Maldoror,* and the high priest of surrealist Satanism.

I was prepared to offer Crane all the genuflections necessary to quell his doubts. We became friendly and he introduced me to McCown, the artist, with whom he lived in a Left Bank atelier. Both had read my first novel, *Bottom Dogs* (for which D. H. Lawrence, one of Crane's deities, had written the Introduction), and Constant Huntington, director of G. P. Putnam's in London, had given me a contract for the book. Huntington asked me to look up somebody in Paris who would design the wrapper for the volume and Hart Crane had suggested that McCown should do it.

When McCown gave me the drawing for the dust jacket, I conveyed it to Mr. Huntington who, after receiving it, sent me an acerb reply, saying that he knew that I had written a dirty, picaresque Americanese, but he had never imagined I had believed it was lewd. Eugene McCown had drawn a map of the United States emphasizing a phallical Florida which I had noticed with a nebulous and naïve uneasiness. Of course, I had heard about pathics, but had not the scantiest suspicion that Hart Crane was homosexual. Crane was a stocky, virile male with a Jovian square face, mizzling, foggy eyes, gun-metal gray hair, and a smouldering, amorous mouth.

Though Crane and I knew many Americans in Paris both of us were overwhelmingly alone, castaways of American letters. On the outside of this riotous, visionary coterie, we were solitary mendicants looking for the rotten grapes of Pisgah, and living like cut-rate Montezumas in some dump near the Select or Coupole, Parnassian meeting-places for deracinated chatter-boxes of literature and gamy, venereal whores.

Crane and I were part of a senseless Babel of economics. Impecunious most of his life, he was then receiving a handsome subsidy from the banker and patron of the arts, Otto H. Kahn. *The Bridge* was to be published by the millionaire sybarite of letters, Harry Crosby. No less poor than Crane, I was then involved with the niece of a very puissant industrialist who later became the fervid crony of Khrushchev. I mention these pocketbook ironies as an aside.

Harry Crosby also invited Crane to write in a castle whose eighteenth-century proprietor had been the duc de La Rochefoucauld, hoping he would finish *The Bridge* there. Meanwhile, Crosby, a tenderhearted sufferer who also longed for Dionysiac trances, and detesting a world suitable for pithless salesmen and fusty, monied dowds, committed suicide. It was Crosby's widow, Caresse, who published *The Bridge* in a beautiful, recherché edition of the Black Sun Press in Paris.

Although Crane had fallen into adust ecstasies over Paris, absinthe, Gertrude Stein, and the French language, he went back to America. Penniless by then myself, Hart Crane suggested that I go to Otto H. Kahn and say I was his friend, which I did, and with felicitous results. In New York I saw Hart Crane just when Boni and Liveright had brought out the American edition of *The Bridge.* He lived in a one room apartment, somewhat beneath the sidewalk, with a gallon of whiskey on the floor next to his cot, and a pile of Sophie Tucker records for his Victrola. Though not thirty years old, his hair was the color of a seagull. In the daytime he was deeply pooled in moldy sleep, and at night he ran about Red Hook, the libidinous docks of Tarshish in Brooklyn, soliciting the favors of sailors.

Many times Crane had been beaten by seamen; on one occasion, living on Columbia Heights hard by his iron seraph, the Brooklyn Bridge, he complained to me that a young man whom he thought had the milk-white shoulders of Pelops (I am paraphrasing Christopher Marlowe, Hart Crane's demigod) had stolen his clothes and forsaken him. He was sorely wounded by this ill hap, but, as I have said, when he was not humiliated, or had not drunk hyssop in some waterfront pothouse, he was unable to achieve that Apollonian composure which he needed to enable him to sit at a table—a poet's guillotine—and write. "Unless you are broken up, you are not alive," said Wyndham Lewis in one of his remarkable letters, but as Hart Crane has worded it, he wrote verses, roared, and

124

quarreled with all "the zest for doom."

What drove Crane crazy was the humid torpor between poems. An odalisque can be idle and recumbent, and her languor is the joy of Eve and the serpent in Eden, but when a poet is supine, just a rotting unthinking corpse, he is beside himself.

Still, he was glutted with remorse and shame; he wrote: "Our tongues recant like beaten weather vanes." Later I saw him at a party given in honor of Mae West, who had completed her autobiography, the usual elite *merde* of the cinema star. Crane arrived late; though extremely drunk his clothes were seemly and his manner cavalier. In one of his missives he said: "I've been cooking my own meals, and doing my best without the help of a flatiron to keep myself looking spruce." Crane, copying the dandyism of Heine, explains elsewhere: "Despite my objections to cane-carrying, I find it very pleasant. Puce-colored gloves complete the proper touch."

He doted on a soirée, and on this occasion he had found the side of a carton which he was offering to authors upon which to sign their names to petition Mae West to sing "Frankie and Johnnie." Why Mae West, a mildewed and synthetic dame of the theater, was considered such an aphrodisiacal morsel I will never know. Edmund Wilson, who was there, thought she was as desirable as a Sabine virgin. I don't think any poet has ever had luck with these dumpy Hollywood dolls whose agents inform us they adore Proust and Dostoevsky. He had sent *White Buildings* to Chaplin, supposed to be the sorrowful and educated Quixote clown. Chaplin's secretary sent him a sere, laconic note acknowledging that the book had been received. I believe Hart Crane's idolatry of jazz, Charles Chaplin, and his mechanolatry, was, in part, the slag of Acheron in his poetry.

There is a doleful chasm between Crane's epistolary comprehension of a mechanized commonwealth and the veneration of brand new gewgaws which are so apparent in Crane's poems.

In one of his letters Crane asserts: "All this talk about being gay . . . and painfully delighted" with "the telegraph, the wireless, the street-cars and electric lamp posts annoys me." A model T. Ford is more precious to the unshriven up-to-date mind than St. Paul's occiput which was said to have been found in a sheep-cote. We are now near the Last Judgment, making ready for the gaseous declamations of a celestial missile.

The *Letters* have been marvelously arranged by Brom Weber; and though Crane shows lucid knowledge of a society grounded upon money, an opiate phantasy that has no relation to work or the moral values of products, it is necessary to take a fugitive glance at the poetry. Hart Crane desired above all to make an American myth, and notwithstanding his contempt for pessimism, he was a "revolutionary" in the sense that Wyndham Lewis defines it, "a man of the tabula rasa."

The American poet is a nihilist, and because he has no past or any sure, graspable tradition, he starts with nothing and then imagines that is his godhead. Crane's principal faults come from his misuse of language; English is our stepmother language, and we speak, giving the scantiest thought to the reasonable order of words. The music of logic in literature is the sublime use of the metaphor. Crane took swollen and almost deranged risks to make a startling phrase. Crane says: "I now find myself baulked by doubt at the validity of practically every metaphor I coin."

There is no science of literary criticism, and whatever remarks are offered come from countless errors. A man can misread a poem at twenty, fifty or at my age. The critical faculty is no less splayed than Vulcan's foot. May each one accept as much of this as suits his purpose, and if the reader mislikes what I say let him throw it out of his mind, and stuff himself with lentils, cabbage and a tithe of Aristotle.

At his best Hart Crane was a Magician of the Logos, but when he fell down he wrote turbid, amorphous doggerel. His work

126

is glutted with neologies, solecisms, and jazz dada locutions which have nothing to do with the sexual feud between his father, a Cleveland candy manufacturer, and his mother, a Christian Scientist. There is no doubt that he was the brunt of bestial, Faustian altercations between his parents. Hart Crane tells his mother: "... my youth has been the rather bloody battleground for yours and father's sex life." "Must every man entomb a withered child?" asks the poet Stanley Burnshaw.

No matter what one's childhood is, a seeming Elysian remembrance or a parental vendetta, the understanding of the afflatus of a poet lies elsewhere. Crane was a neo-American Elizabethan who ran mad for new words. Nor can one assert that his electric shock tropes were the result of a sundered, homosexual nature, for this makes no sense. He could have been drawn to Aphrodite, inflamed by her peplum, and have had no sensibility.

It is too easy at this time to be a canting adorer of Crane's poems; or a pedant who falls upon his work as if he had not eaten a full meal for a week. Crane combined music, color and sound and made of them the "prayer of pariah." His concern with sensations perfectly wrought and gemmed in his mind like the sapphire, emerald, or ruby in Paradise, paradoxically resulted in many of his most turbid lines. Oddly enough he quoted limpid lines from the Book of Job, *Tamburlaine the Great, The Alchemist,* or a poem from Emily Dickinson, while he himself hurled thundering and forked diction at his auditors. He would have burnt Troy for a memorable stanza and swallowed Hell's sulphur to be laureled a poet. One should allege straightway that his genius was a parcel of the gargantuan follies in *White Buildings* and *The Bridge.* At times there is no grammar in his verse, or he employs, to make an oxymoron, an heroical bathos. I have prowled sundry volumes to understand his poems, which are pages of bedlamite shrieks of a soul sunk like Atlantis, and then there are those green sea cries towering out of the foam. He could be a syntactical zany as is apparent in some of the passages I have culled from *The Bridge:*

Into the bulging bullion, harnessed jelly of the stars
lead-perforated fuselage, escutcheoned wings lift agonized quittance
Ghoul-mound of man's perversity at balk
And Klondike edelweiss of occult snows!
And white legs waken salads in the brain.
The conscience navelled in the plunging wind.
Umbilical to call —

As a Café Dome expatriate he dropped into rapturous U.S.A. jargon:

Stick your patent name on a signboard brother—all over—going west—young man Tintex-Japalac—

But then who can be the surd adder after these fleshed locutions: "Gongs in white surplices, beshrouded wails . . ." Or not pity the spirit, thirty years old, only thirty-five months from his Caribbean winding-sheet: ". . . snow submerges an iron year." Hear this lachrymal expletive: "wounds that we wrap in theorems." And this could have been the magic of a Fletcher or a Tourneur: "Like pearls that whisper through the Doge's hands." Or remain immune, if you can, to this canorous rhetoric:

> . . . take this sheaf of dust upon your tongue.
> Ask nothing but this sheath of pallid air.

Be compassionate and drop a tear for this orphan unhoused in Abraham's bosom, with no place to lay his head save on "the pillowed bay." And though the poet of these States, he was landless: "And fold your exile on your back again . . ."

Those who spat upon his identity were not even "dull lips

128

commemorating spiritual gates." How many who knew him had that honeycombed wisdom, his self-knowledge: "Thou sowest doom thou hast nor time nor chance to reckon . . ." An acolyte of Keats he wrote, "I think the sea has thrown itself upon me and been answered." In "At Melville's Tomb":

> And wrecks passed without sound of bells,
> The calyx of death's bounty giving back
> A scattered chapter, livid hieroglyph,
> The portent wound in corridors of shells.

I once saw the portrait of Melville in the house of his grand-daughter, and I wondered how Hart Crane could have known this: "Frosted eyes there were that lifted altars . . ."

A poet is a prisoner of his wounds. One could also attribute some of his cranial belchings to alcohol, but he wrote to Waldo Frank: "Lately my continence has brought me nothing in the creative way." Doubtless the long bouts of penury maimed him. In one of his novels, Quevedo says the Spanish sharper sprinkled crumbs on his beard so that it would look as though he has just had a splendid dinner.

His lodgings in New York or Brooklyn Heights was a scabrous room, which, if one can think of a fugue as a color, was lit by a beige abscessed electric bulb, the rent for which he often had to borrow from one of his friends. "I have helped to empty several other pockets also," said Crane.

Crane had received a hundred dollars as an advance for *White Buildings*, and Allen Tate, who wrote the Introduction, doubtless only got desert manna for his work. When a writer can count on as much for his labors as a charwoman we will have an American El Dorado. Let anyone tell you that the situation is better now than it was is babbling: there is a great deal of humbug about the twenties, the thirties, and the forties; what difference can one or three decades make? Does anybody really

129

believe that the poet in other centuries was not less hindered than now or forty years ago? Imagine the plight of the poet at the time of the Caesars when Domitian relieved the Roman economy by abating the price of a eunuch. If this sounds bizarre to the doubting Thomases of Philistia, let them ponder the days of hunger of Baudelaire.

Though the writer is reckoned some kind of parasitic Ariel, nothing will prevent him from producing what is absolutely essential to a commonwealth which otherwise exists for millionaires, wastrels, and stupid and immoral articles which nobody needs.

Hart Crane never finished high school, and this seems to trouble his biographer, Philip Horton, who imagines that had he gone to the university he would have been a more cultured poet. A biographer generally is the epicure of a poet's faults. It would be more accurate to describe Crane's lack of formal education as a "blessed dearth," to quote Christina Rossetti. By the time a student can be called a doctor of philosophy he has very likely never heard of Porphyry, Philostratus, Antisthenes, or the Rig Veda. Crane wrote: "I have been reading the philosophies of the East until I actually dream in terms of the Vedanta scriptures." And "The people I am closest to in English are Keats ... and the dear great Elizabethans like Marlowe, Webster, Donne and Drayton."

Nearly all of his canicular days he belonged to the brotherhood of beggars. Both Harriet Monroe and Marianne Moore mangled his verse, and he asked "how much longer will our markets be in the grips of two such hysterical virgins"; the former was the editor of *Poetry* magazine and the latter the arbiter at the *Dial.* He was also assailed because he was not a *whole* man, which, like the Absolute, according to Duns Scotus is *nihil.* Crane was everyman's cully: Waldo Frank, his steadfast friend, was hemlock to his work. The *Complete Poems* appeared posthumously, and the Introduction by Frank is a masterpiece in astral platitudes. Says Frank in his opening line:

130

"Agrarian America had a common culture, which was both the fruit and the carrier of what I have called 'the great tradition.' "

He had published poems in the *Little Review,* Joseph Kling's the *Pagan,* the *Fugitive, Broom,* and had gotten nothing for his jubilant pains. He hoped to buy a pair of shoes for the money he would receive from an article on Sherwood Anderson that had appeared in the *Double Dealer,* a New Orleans literary paper. He had beseeched Thomas Seltzer to publish *White Buildings,* assuring him he had a grandiose audience of five hundred readers, but Seltzer declined to do it. After much pressure from Eugene O'Neill and Waldo Frank, Boni and Liveright brought out the small volume for which he was given one hundred dollars.

Meantime, he was generally looking for "jobs in limbo," his purgatories were the office in which he wrote advertising copy for hot water heaters or in the "bellies and estuaries of warehouses" of his father's candy factories.

Hart Crane had no social creeds, and to Allen Tate he wrote: "Poetry as poetry . . . isn't worth a second reading any more. Therefore away with Kubla Khan, out with Marlowe, and to hell with Keats." Crane was never baited by the social paroxysms that are the Cain's curse of each generation, be it feminism or Marxist dialectics. Covering a strike in the cotton mills, when I was an extreme advocate for the working class, I slept in the house of a Portuguese laborer; above his bed was a tryptich, on one panel was the Virgin Mary, on the other was Shirley Temple, and in the middle Karl Marx. Crane had no inclination, as he averred, to "sum up the universe in one impressive pellet."

Again the letters reveal a comprehension of the perplexities of the American visionary, and despite the influence of the good, gray poet, he says to Tate: "It's true that my rhapsodic address to [Whitman] in *The Bridge* exceeds any exact evaluation of the man." Then, scolding his friend, Crane adds: ". . . you

131

like so many others, never seem to have read his *Democratic Vistas* . . . decrying materialism, industrialism." Few poets have perused Whitman's *Specimen Days,* but neither of these books will be yeasty pabulum for a good maker of verses. He was far closer to what he hoped to do in expressing his admiration for MacLeish's *Conquistador,* once a renowned poem, as finely wrought as an Aztec lapidary's work on turquoise but now skulled in anthologies.

In Mexico, as a Guggenheim Fellow, he discovered that he could fall into as much of a passion for Venus as he did for "calla lilies, freesia, roses, calendulas, white iris, violets, cannas . . . geraniums . . . feverfew, candy tuft." He wrote: "I must admit that I find conjugal life, however unofficial, a great consolation to a loneliness that had about eaten me up."

But the alcoholic frenzies continued, and his flesh ached for Gehenna and the Gates of Jerusalem. "Suffering is a real purification," Crane said. "What is beauty, saith my suffering?" wrote Marlowe, his savant and master. His demise was deliriously close; unable to abide the ignominy of level, average days, he either was ecstatic about the fiesta of Tepozteco, the ancient god of *pulque,* or shuddered with fright as he envisaged himself once more as a penniless urchin in New York. Violence sharpened his intellect; as Plotinus has said: "the . . . Corybantes continue their raptures until *they see what they desire.*" But Crane craved infinite Bacchanalian seizures, or the bliss of the shroud and the tomb, and so aboard the *Orizaba,* on his way back to New York, he leaped from the rail of the deck into the sharkish Carib sea.

Exile, wanderer, homeless in all latitudes, strife was his god, and his oracle the sea.

Is the agony or the fury of nonsense any different today? Three decades ago or so, the customs officials insisted that D. H. Lawrence's urned ashes were a work of art and should be taxed; Waldo Frank had to call upon a clergyman to prove to

132

our warders of sexual hygiene that the title of his novel, *The Bridegroom Cometh,* taken from the New Testament, was not obscene.

So we, who cannot conceive the books without sinning, are outcasts and pornographers, our brains void of cassia, ambergris, and camphor until they are dead, and then deemed priceless in the venal agora, a bookstore, a university, ay, a textbook!

Leopardi "saw the world as a vast league of criminals ruthlessly warring against a few virtuous madmen."

New York Review, 1966

Beautiful Failures

I am not obsessed with the apocryphal trash of any lustrum or decade, nor do I intend to canonize what is fustian because it is a particle of the past. For the poet there is in fact no time passing.

About 1924, a shoal of authors, seldom mentioned nowadays, appeared in a quarterly magazine that came out every two years or so, whenever the pair of editors, Ernest Walsh and Ethel Moorhead, had gathered together their ecstatic errors or truths. Among those printed in *This Quarter,* the little oracle, were two sibyls of American letters, Kay Boyle and Josephine Herbst, besides Ernest Walsh, Emanuel Carnevali, Robert McAlmon, Ezra Pound, James Joyce, John Hermann and Ernest Hemingway.

Most of these contributors were mendicants, but he who resolves to be an honest author takes the vow of poverty. Then, thinkers frequently come from the gutters of the earth. The poet of the *Thebaid* was called Statius, a common slave's name in Rome; Proclus, the disciple of Plotinus, was a porter; Epictetus, the philosopher, was freed by his master; and Plautus, the waggish Latin playwright, hired himself out to a baker. Penury is a stepmother, but how often are her peeled and chagrined sons the most valorous ones in any society? Antisthenes, the Cynic and contemporary of Socrates, looked upon the barest walls as warm tunics, and any roof as a thick blanket.

Those who left the United States for Europe have been described as deracinated exiles. The Greeks regarded ostracism as the cruelest punishment, and there was no reason any one of us should go abroad to be more homeless than we were. Besides, there is never any place for the waifs of the Muses to go, for, as Josephine Herbst says of the writer, "our fate is desertion." Charles Baudelaire was completely lost in his native Paris, and more miserable in alien Belgium. How well he knew the "grandeur of the pariahs."

Unable to secure asylum for his verse and energetic judgments, Ernest Walsh happened to meet Ethel Moorhead in Paris, and she suggested that they found *This Quarter*. She had studied painting under Whistler, was a dogmatic feminist, had marched to Whitehall with other suffragettes, and whenever this becrazed procession of Irish and London furies came upon a man, they cried out: "Shame!"

Since Walsh had all the fever of a tubercular who knew his days were few, he journeyed with Ethel Moorhead from Milano to Nice and to Monte Carlo. It was at Roquebrune, where I had gone to greet Walsh, not knowing that he had died in October 1926, that I met Miss Moorhead. After the death of the youthful Walsh, she liked to gamble at the casino at Monte Carlo, some fifteen minutes by train from Roquebrune, to fume away the empty hours or to cover her grief.

Her pinions maimed, and now alone, Ethel Moorhead continued the magazine in a villa hanging over the Mediterranean Sea, whose three or four rooms were cluttered with the manuscripts of her small commune of illuminati. She had a lean, stiff figure, a long, theoretical nose, an acrimonious mouth, and wore thick lenses over which she darted her suspicious glances. She railed at Ezra Pound (the first issue of *This Quarter* was dedicated to him), and despised the pragmatical Calibans of the bookish world—Arnold Bennett, Chesterton, Van Wyck Brooks, Waldo Frank, Gorham Munson and Ernest Hemingway, one of whose first short stories she had published. Walsh, no less waspish than she, called these well-known hackneys whose creed was self-service, "dilettantes of passion."

Absolutely disinterested, but a highly intelligent she-bigot, Ethel Moorhead emptied her purse, not obese by any means, to her juvenescent geniuses, particularly for Walsh and Emanuel Carnevali, and opened her pages to me.

135

I was supposed to be coeditor of *This Quarter,* number 4, but I could not accept her anti-Semitism. She declared that if the great Hebrew prophets could not redeem the stiff-necked Jews, they were indeed a hopeless lot. O indignant droll, did you not realize that no seer has ever healed a nation, which, according to Giordano Bruno, John Ruskin, and Walsh himself, is always a mob?

On those occasions when we were making ready to go to Monte Carlo, there was the inevitable search for her keys; beside herself because she could not find them, she scarcely failed to give me a flensed and untrusting look accompanied by, "You're a Jew, have you been rummaging through my papers? Where are my keys?" Bewildered, I did not know how to reply, but I still remember that other Celt, James Joyce, who gave a party in honor of Paul Valéry, who was to be seated in the chair at the head of the table. The late Humbert Wolfe, arriving and seeing that the chair was vacant, sat down in it, but was unable to decipher the glowering face of Joyce until he heard him say: "You're a Jew, aren't you?" To which the English poet Wolfe answered, "You're a writer, aren't you?" However, Ethel Moorhead misplaced her keys too often for our friendship to endure.

Before we separated I showed her a lot of disconnected words I believed was a short story; she read it, and said: "Why don't you write a novel?" It had not occurred to me to do that, but who ever knows what he is doing or going to do? She printed a heavy parcel of the novel in *This Quarter,* and later it was published in London bearing the title *Bottom Dogs,* with an Introduction by D. H. Lawrence. I detest my three novels; one is humiliated by nature, then by the world, and afterwards by one's books. I bless Ethel Moorhead wherever she is; stoic that she was, she concluded her labor, and disappeared.

Something of Ernest Walsh's aspect should be mentioned. He had been a pilot in World War I, had fallen in a plane at a

Texas airfield, and been discharged from the military hospital as an incurable invalid. He looked so ill that strangers often avoided him. Once a fat, healthy gentleman, upset by Walsh's appearance, asked the patron of a French hotel to tell the consumptive to leave so that he could enjoy his meal. "I hope he is guarding his health well enough to enter the army of the next war," Walsh said afterward, but usually he accepted his illness without mumping it: "Like other beds, the bed of a sick man has its conventions."

He detested the "dilettantes of passion," and the cutpurses who then and now attempt to destroy the honest writers with whose ideas they lard their own haggard and hungry pages. They are "picking their teeth after a cheap lunch on other people's notions," Walsh said. And again, they "remind me of gentlemen who advertise in the *London Times,* 'Intentions respectable.' "

In spite of the wild friendship the marvelous youths of *This Quarter* had for one another, each was a solitary. But who can dissolve the wall between himself and other spectral persons? "The hills are nearer to me than to themselves," Walsh remarked. I quote these lines from his pseudo-middle American-English (and I do not mean this unkindly):

> Even the towers of the cathedral speke
> Like old men and wimin coming hom.
> And the legginges of the black trees loosen,
> The earth's elephant skin wrinkels.

Ernest Walsh endeavored to compose Chaucerian verse in the American vernacular. It was a valiant effort, but I believe he seldom achieved what he proposed to do. As for my judgments, let them lie or die. Thinking flesh is generally senseless, particularly the weakest part of it, the head. Except for Kay Boyle and Josephine Herbst, I am concerned with the beautiful failures. When anyone refers to me as a successful author, I wince.

137

Walsh might have been a great figure, had he lived longer. It is quite possible; however I find it difficult to say that one does not complete his character before he expires. This may be wrong and it is a risky remark. I do not patronize the shades in Orcus, or the living, who have no less sorrows.

When Walsh died, Ethel Moorhead asked Ezra Pound to commemorate the poet. The two editors had dedicated the first number of *This Quarter* to Pound because Walsh had venerated him. But Pound declined to eulogize the deceased. I assailed Pound several years ago, and have no stomach to berate this fissured Polonius with more than a touch of Hamlet's ghost about him. He is eighty-two years old and glutted with remorse. Each one of us has to live with his tumulus of errors. Let those who admired Ezra Pound's *Personae,* and his *Lustra,* as I do, judge him. I shall not.

But Walsh was not to die without a bard's epitaph. In a carnal monody not surpassed by the early Pound, Hart Crane or Allen Tate, Kay Boyle's marmoreal moan (republished in her *Collected Poems*) is most pertinent—and those who prattle about our American exiles, notice the title: "To America":

How shall I say there is no desert except beyond him
And that your soil is rich dark banners flying under the plow;
That the clay of his bones is a hard famine . . . .
. . . let there be pillars of song to set over him . . . .
But in years lean as the locust you shall listen in the crops for him . . .
There will be flutes of stone and javelins at his fingers . . . .

Her other orison for Ernest Walsh is called "For an American":

Not plumes of the sea did you offer, but gaunt feathers, bare rigging of ships . . . .
      . . . the dark sap singing
    Aaron, Aaron, I would be a great tree over you
    Aaron, I would be air running like a sea in your nostrils . . . .

I have not seen or heard from Kay Boyle since 1928. I met her and Robert McAlmon at the celebrated bohemian café in Montparnasse, La Coupole. After a short conversation she jotted a scrap of words on a pastboard introducing me to William Carlos Williams, the poet-doctor of Rutherford, N. J. Kay Boyle was a moneyless poet, drudging as a saleslady in Raymond Duncan's shop. He wore a Greekish clout, and sandals, and was a poseur of Hellenic civilization which he affected in order to hide a Stygian parsimony.

One afternoon Kay Boyle, Hart Crane and I went to the chic apartment of Harry and Caresse Crosby. Crosby was a Sur-realist, follower of Lautréamont, and he was the nephew of the partner of the grandiose J. P. Morgan banking house. I have heard uglified allusions to Harry Crosby, but he published Kay Boyle's tales—and I believe helped her—as well as Hart Crane's *The Bridge* in the recherché Black Sun Press. Like the majority of writers, he was a sidereal nervous wreck, and com-mitted suicide a number of years later. He had been kind to the tubercular, splenetic D. H. Lawrence, who squabbled with his host and publisher, calling him a burnt-out cinder, forgetting that he himself was rather dilapidated. One day I assisted the frail Lawrence across the street to the hotel where he was stay-ing, and I thought there was nobody inside his clothes.

There was Emanuel Carnevali, who came to the States from Florence when he was fifteen years of age, with no knowledge of our language, yet at nineteen had learned to chant in a Levantine English. Carnevali was a part of the Chicago group that included Theodore Dreiser and Sherwood Anderson. He wrote verse and prose, and aided dear Harriet Monroe, editor of *Poetry*. A mendicant, Carnevali may have put his hands too often in Anderson's famished pockets. After a brace of years distinguished by poems and starvation, he thought he would have better luck in the brutal megalopolis of our new Attica,

139

New York, where he became secretary to the learned Joel Elias Spingarn. Spingarn, an American Jew who founded the NAACP, was the author of *A History of Literary Criticism in the Renaissance,* a dry prose elegy in scholasticism.

Carnevali's employment came to a brusque halt. There was a scant difference between him and Spingarn over the books on the scholar's shelves. Carnevali was of the mind that quite a truss of them would be more useful to him than to Mr. Spingarn, a remarkable person who introduced the works of Benedetto Croce and Vico to American thinkers. There was behind Spingarn's frigid but not uncivil exterior a tender regard for other people. When *Bottom Dogs* appeared, I asked him if he would make a statement for it, and he declined, but offered me money, which I refused; and we were both right.

Long after Spingarn's demise in 1939, I heard of a bookshop in a loft on 23rd Street which was glutted with volumes that came from merchant marine ships. Browsing through thousands of dust-girted books, I saw a miraculous title, *A Chronicle, Conteyning the Lives of Tenne Emperours of Rome,* by Gueuara, Bishop of Mondoñedo in 1537. A passionate gambler whenever I am in a bookshop, I quaked as I handled this rare first edition, and studied the printed matter on the fly-leaf, "Ex Libris, Joel Elias Spingarn, 1900." I purchased it from the dealer, whose name was Carnevali, the uncle of the writer.

After Carnevali-the-writer was dismissed by Spingarn, he acquired an occult misfortune, encephalitis lethargica, sleeping sickness. Without that devil, lucre, he wandered about Washington Square, picked garbage out of a can and, weeping, tossed it back again. Shortly thereafter he returned to Italy, praying, as he declared in one of his verses, that his former kinsmen would not kick him out with the toe of that land.

Carnevali went to Bazzano, a small, medieval hill town, two-and-a-half hours from Bologna by *le train de vapour.* I remember because I visited the young author of *A Hurried Man,* published by Robert McAlmon in the Contact Editions. Why these stories, squibs and poems, although not at all lubricious, were banned by the customs officials, I will never know. But then D. H. Lawrence's ashes were regarded as a work of art by these agents, and perhaps they were.

Carnevali was not forsaken, for though we were Lazaruses of American literature, Ethel Moorhead, Ernest Walsh and I visited him at Bazzano, and brought him fantastical pastry from Bologna, cartons of cigarettes, and money none of us could spare. There was no feline jealousy among these jolly freebooters of letters. As for myself, my hopes have never been graved because somebody wrote an extraordinary book. The Elizabethan Dekker holds: "For he that can so cosen himself, as to pocket up praise . . . makes his braines fat with his own folly." Moreover, he who hoards his praise for others starves himself to death.

Carnevali's forehead was an upland slope the skin of which was delicate as the brittle papyrus in the mummy-pit; he had the mouth of an amorist; not yet in his thirtieth year, he was doubled over as he walked. He was in a sanatorium at Bazzano, too ill to see me when I arrived, for the light of the day was a rapier in his eyes. I strolled about the olden Catholic hamlet until he appeared many hours afterward. We went to a workingman's café, and we chattered, drank red wine, and I was overwhelmed by the ebullient friendliness of this cruelly stricken man for a brand-new acquaintance. Maybe one has to be sick to be a virile singer.

I cite as ample evidence of his strength some lines from this picaro in comic socks and the tragic body. The jibing, undefeated Carnevali called the fetid spital house, where he was confined, the Villa Rubazziana, which he took from the Italian word, *rubare,* to rob. His table was "half an apothecary shop," containing a bottle of scopolamine, "my oil for walking and

141

writing, my lubricating oil for my wretched dreams." His best medicine is his ironies: a sensual sufferer "among a caravan of encephalitics," he says his room had "such lordly intimacies with my soul," though its floor is "diseased . . . and badly splotched with grey cement."

The hospital was a refuge for crazy cripples and their ridiculous quandaries and amours. One patient is perplexed and tells Carnevali: "I wish I could see my face!" The poet, never a complicated bore, has a plain answer: "Stand before a mirror and you certainly will!" Still discontented, the madman retorts: "But I wish to see it without a mirror. And my intestines too." After his agony of Chicago and New York, he curses the city that "eats the country, slowly, but relentlessly." "Its wombs are the dirty streets." Mercilessly crushed, he has found a piece of sylvan quiet in Bazzano, with its distant mountains which are "a black assembly." His song is a swagger though he alleges his "ink bottle is as empty as poverty."

For him, most women were Venuses, even the deformed sluts: "I loved your eyes because they were violets hid in the grass of your ugliness . . . your snub nose defying seriousness." The "worm of sophistication" never devoured his majestical simplicities: "Why should I live today? Because I have two new pairs of socks." "This desperate poet who cannot write of his despair; that's myself." "This man who is not strong enough to hate anybody; that's myself."

The blood in his arteries was the wine in the chalice. He never forgot those who attempted to bless his broken life with what gifts they could bestow upon him. Hearing that Ernest Walsh had died, he wept: ". . . he's dead, he's dead . . . I should have died before him. He brought me a wagonload of cigarettes. He brought me eau de cologne and wetted my forehead with it." His appreciation of Robert McAlmon, "my princely giver," was a little psalmody of gratitude.

We revere his Spartan courage but know the joys he emitted

werc steeped in gall. A poet carries his Golgotha with him wherever he goes, though he feigns it is an enchantment. He falls down every day and resurrects himself with a smile or a gentle quip. Carnevali translated his pain into a chant to delight his readers, but his own felicities were brewed in hell. Even such a cairn of ironic raptures may be too much for those who flee from the misfortunes of others while imagining they are free of them. The people who think they are happy should rummage through their dreams. Emanuel Carnevali, like Ethel Moorhead, vanished, but I shall never forget you, O honeycombed singer, until all the wailing ghosts within my own veins have died.

Robert McAlmon was another castaway, and though not poor he was to be a beggar at the fag end of his days in an American treeless mesa. He had married the heiress of an extremely rich manufacturer of perfumes in England, and had spent more than a moiety of his income on his Contact Editions, which he created for the publication of neglected people he regarded as talented. (It has always taken the hackney reviewer a long time to arrive at a judicious indecision.) What remained he spent on alcohol, which I think was his nemesis, but then self-destruction is one of the most delirious pastimes of mankind. Aside from whisky, he wallowed in the crowd that consumes the vitals of a man. Woe to him who gives most of his force to living. He scrabbled a graveled, riffraff prose, somewhat resembling the yellow purslane which grows along the wayside among rubbish.

He was up to date, and it would seem that he had aimed at the vulgus, but he was positively no mercenary littérateur. An extraordinary figure, I cannot laud his novels, among which are these few, *A Hasty Bunch, Post-adolescence,* and *The Distinguished Air,* now sold as red-light-district pulp in that most obscene street, Broadway.

McAlmon was a tabula rasa novelist, but no book can be zero. One is either the vassal of the wise books one has studied or at least affected by the debauched fiction one never saw. Those who fear that someone might influence them should realize that only the insane are impervious to the world. Though McAlmon's work was brought out in the 1920s, it is really new, and should gratify the academic porkers who root in the mire of dates, the merchant neologies and what Milton referred to as the "pamper'd metafor." The only reason they have not yet exhumed him is that they haven't heard of him, but they will!

Robert McAlmon was a failure as a writer, but otherwise an epical figure. He was useful to many authors, essential to some. Some of his judgments are right, very acerb and septic, and so many of the contemporary criticasters still do not comprehend what he knew half-a-century ago. A close companion of James Joyce, the mundane Jesuit of Irish thought, McAlmon alleged Joyce recited "Dante as though he were saying Mass." He quotes Lincoln Gillespie, a Montparnasse zany from a wealthy Philadelphia family, who introduced himself as follows: "I am Lincoln Gillespie, and find you the only formpacking symbol realisticator tuckfunctioning modern commodity." This may be the colloquy of a man smitten with delirium tremens, but it is a far more sagacious comment upon Joyce than any of those myriads of keys to *Ulysses.* He found T. S. Eliot's slinking, clerkly humility intolerable, and I must say I don't trust the meek, who not only have inherited the earth but American literature as well.

McAlmon parodied Gertrude Stein, "the sumerian monument," her "ancient, mastodonic slow idea, with slow suspicion moves agedly . . . resting to pause in the ancient slime." Her brother, Leo Stein, had this to say: "She hasn't much intuition but thickly she has sensations, and of course her mania, herself."

McAlmon was scornful of Ford Madox Ford: "Mr. Ford assured me that he was a genius." But then a writer is not necessarily wrong when he praises himself; often he can't find anybody else to do that for him. He rejected Wyndham Lewis, gave him money but would not publish him. Lewis thought he resembled Shakespeare, McAlmon said, and on other occasions "he was looking like Shelley or Swift." One gets quite tired of oneself, and would like to be somebody else. Our friends grow weary of us since we are always the same, and even nature gets rid of all of us and maybe for no other cause than that we are tedious and monotonous.

A man unblessed by emotion, McAlmon could divulge that "the doctor pumped cocaine into Joyce's eyes, to relieve the agony." Could he have foreseen his own end, he might have viewed Wyndham Lewis with more compassion. The writer and Vorticist painter was even more afflicted than was Joyce. One day he left his atelier in London and went into the streets to buy a paper, and, on a sudden, said to the news vendor, "What time is it, please, about noon I should imagine?" To which the puzzled man in the booth replied, "No sir, it is eight o'clock of the evening." Lewis was blind. Had McAlmon lived long enough to examine Lewis's letters, the important annals of a tremendous person who was the prey of "sub-arctic" solitude and the snows and sleet of impecuniosity, I believe he might have reconsidered his judgment.

He had no enthusiasm for the holiness of the artist, and despised all humbug, the noble, the humble, or the serious mood. He refused to be anybody's cully, but we are all the hoaxes which others impose upon us, and he who has no trust at all in life is not likely to partake of the most precious parts of it.

An international chatterbox, McAlmon liked literature well enough, but wouldn't bother to go to a museum, and did not care a whit about a cathedral, that massive pile of excogitative spermal stones, or anyone who was too earnest and soulful. He wanted comrades who could swallow gin and Pernod until dawn, and so little wonder that Djuna Barnes, a beauty in her heyday, author of *Nightwood* and one of McAlmon's favorites, exclaimed: "I came to Europe to get culture. Is this culture I'm getting?"

By the time he had settled in Desert Hot Springs, a sandlot spa in California, he was utterly forsaken. I went to see him every month or so, and endeavored to assist him. He was tubercular, with a skinny, distempered frame, still youthful except for a slender fillet of gray across the forepart of his head. He rarely spoke except in billingsgate, and he was exceedingly bitter. Each one is entitled to his scruple of wormwood, and I did not mind that. He asked me to peruse his manuscripts, which I did with the intention of finding a publisher or printing his memoirs. On guard against any show of sentiment or affectation, he either guillotined everybody or was mawkish. When a man cannot achieve the sublime, he is sure to drop into bathos.

There was another difficulty: when I suggested I take his manuscripts back to Santa Monica, where I then dwelt, he was suspicious. Alas, had I been a plagiary, what could I have filched from his bare larder of words?

His orgies of alcohol continued, but he never stopped writing, though there was not a soul who would do anything for him. One might wonder why I had offered to aid him. I was far more moved by affection for a man who had done so much for authors, and who now threw himself away, than I was by my so-called critical faculty.

Not long afterwards he died in that servants' entrance to Palm Springs. Always a desperado in his literary realm, Robert McAlmon was no philister, and he was relentlessly himself. He never stooped for money or reputation.

Ethel Moorhead transferred the publication of *This Quarter* to Edward W. Titus, who had been the husband of Helena Rubinstein, the cosmetics millionairess. I used to go into Titus's bookshop on the rue de l'Ambre, around the corner from the Left-Bank Dôme. When I saw D. H. Lawrence again, he asked me whether he should allow Titus to publish a trade

146

edition of *Lady Chatterley's Lover.* I told him Titus was a gross person whom he should avoid. But when a man asks another for counsel, he is simply arguing aloud with himself. I am the only one I ever met who took advice.

After the dissolution of *This Quarter* came the fiction of the mystical pleb. The Marxist assumption was that those who were not proletarians were hardly people. Impoverished authors who had had long bouts of misfortune, which were only bourgeois and did not count, were ordered to carry their empty suitcases to the mines, the steel mills and the canneries, and there fill them with working-class experiences. A fellow-traveler complained he could not describe death because he had not died, and I suggested a very easy solution to his perplexity.

Now that the proletarian corpse has been dug up, the platitude is sovereign, and what is not implacably ordinary is dismissed as effete sensibility, aberrations of the imagination. Along with this lunatic shibboleth is the temporal misconception of literature which has led to the most vulgar and specious values. The golden calf of the new academic anthologists is time, the 1920s and 1930s; fustian is canonized solely because it was scrawled a generation ago.

Often the grubby and inchoate beginnings of a writer are presented as the major opus of a ripe individual. When the early stories are memorable, as were Josephine Herbst's in *This Quarter,* they are ignored, and her later miracles in prose go unnoticed. I allude to her monograph of Nathanael West, who commenced as an iconoclast but ultimately submitted to Hollywood dollars; I also refer to her carnal word-paint about the Spanish earth and the Loyalists who reddened it with their blood.

Why are these sociological geese cackling about a generation which is no more than a sigh of a pyramid or broken pylon in ancient Egypt? Even a millennium is just an angelic flight of a thought. This fetish of time is the rational commerce in the agora of the ignorant literati. It is the cash logic of this world, and is there any other kind? The result of this venal stupidity is the tinsel apotheosis of the pigmy.

I believe in the imperial reality of the absurd. Once Dreiser said to me that he wept after he had read the bizarre adventures of the sad knight, Don Quixote. Do you want to understand the ideal trance in literature? Be ridiculous, and ask your grocer for a bag of woe, three pounds of poverty and four of humiliation, and then you will be prepared to compose a truthful book.

New York Times Book Review, 1967

Return to Kansas City

Can one ever go back?—to a withered amour, to a childhood friend or to one's native city? No matter how trashy our memories are, we cannot relinquish them. In some way Kansas City, Missouri, is as important to me as an El Greco painting. I don't know why, for I cannot understand what I am save that I am the result of all the streets, shanties, livery stables and gim-crack stores of this buxom, hilly town I knew in the early part of this century. Its grass, dandelions, sunflowers and stones are a song in my blood. I walk upon each olden footprint as if it were Christ's Capernaum and Bethlehem.

My mother and I came to Kansas City about 1905. We lived in a lodging house, a wrinkled, rocky building at 714 McGee, near Admiral. McGee was a street for the pariah and the un-loved poor. Still, there was grass, and the crickets chanting in the elms softened our indigence. Pots of geraniums, the frowsy dowds among the flowers, stood on the window sills. There was then some respect for penury, without which the heart is a mildewed carcass.

Admiral Boulevard, where we later lived in a humble, two-story dwelling that had an honest porch and rough, wooden steps, was idyllic compared with the cold big-city tenements of the East. One could lie in a hammock at dusk or lounge on the stairs. The first Ford sales office was established here when the auto was a novelty. Not far from this was a Baptist Church that looked like the pile of rocks Jacob the Patriarch set up to worship Jehovah. There was the Jewish Educational Institute that preceded the YMHA. It was a street populated by gentiles, Jews and Negro children who came to frolic in the grass and to pluck the dandelions.

When we came to Kansas City, Admiral was a dirt road; a

149

couple of years later rectangular wooden blocks were laid on the earth to support carriages and buggies drawn by stallions or pinto ponies. Hard by were the livery stables for mules, brood mares and wagons. This is in the north end of town, and cobblestones were far more ordinary then than macadam highways. In the wealthier districts brick thoroughfares were common. The streets were littered with horse manure, ambrosia for the Homeric olfactories of plain Missouri people. The wagon, too, was a heroic vehicle, and now that I recall the hucksters bawling, "Cantaloupes, melons, strawberries, cherries and apples!" I imagine I am hearing Homer's *Iliad.*

Admiral Boulevard has dwindled; most of it is a freeway; Independence Avenue, the old Jewish ghetto at the same end of the city, has almost disappeared. Many of the grum, trashy stores are boarded up or look dead. One can see an occasional Negro in work clothes sauntering along Independence, and he has the same languid gait of the old-timers. The Kansas City Jews have grown prosperous and have moved out into the Thirties and Troost Avenue or have bought expensive homes in the country club district. In 1908 I thought Woodland Avenue, which is now downtown, was an Eden for the swells. There was always a large colony of Jews here, a fair number of whom became Christian Scientists; also, some lonely celibates and sere spinsters, unable to meet others or get married, found the health and science of Mary Baker Eddy a cure for their difficulties.

The Negroes have left northeast Kansas City, and the Paseo, formerly tenanted by well-to-do citizens, ironmongers, proprietors of stables and dry goods stores, is a Negro neighborhood today. Otherwise the Paseo is about the same; it is green land for at least fifty blocks. Near the beginning of this artificial meadowland is a Greek pavilion with fluted columns, and a rondured rampart of wrinkled rocks; the other day I saw a few Negroes fishing in the pond on the Paseo. One professor at the University of Missouri told me that he had occupied a flat here, but when it was taken over by a Negro landlord, he was told to move because he was white. Just how much enmity there is between white and Negro in Kansas City I do not know, but there is certainly a division between the two. Yet Negroes attend the University of Missouri at Kansas City, live in the dormitory and eat at the cafeteria, and I have never heard any white student speak ill of his Negro classmates.

Swope Park is also unchanged. It is acres of Edenic verdure, with countless trees and a lissom lagoon. The entrance to Swope is marked by two stone pillars, and a rocky house where holiday people shelter when it rains. It is unspoiled by moldy vendors or stupid candy stalls. Those who have been to Dublin are rapturous as they pass through Saint Stephen's Green, but though I like Dublin enormously, I doubt that Ireland is more grassy than Kansas City.

All over Kansas City are ponds and lakes, and one is startled to discover that many of these are the art of human hands. Somewhat beyond the city limits is Lake Jacomo, whose name sounds Indian, but actually means Jackson County of Missouri and is man's rather than nature's work, though I would not have known the difference had I not been told. There are sixty-eight parks in the city, and one can go almost anywhere and be eased by the blossoms of the magnolia in the spring, or fall into a soft, moody melancholia when autumn has unclothed the oak, maple, cherry and forsythia. Kansas City is a blowy Trojan town, and the breeze coming from the forests, the Missouri and Kaw Rivers, will furnish one with juvenile or vernal expectations that so soon die.

The climate is about the best I have known. There is no smog, and the skies, usually azury or clear, are at times covered with ragged clouds that remind one of the household laundry, the shirts, drawers and petticoats that hang on the clothesline in the backyard. There is almost none of that burial fog or mist that hovers over the West Coast of California.

151

Now, when I return to McGee, the side of the block where we had a light-housekeeping room is a forsaken vacant lot. All of it is the ghost of gravel and nothing remains there but a skinny, thorny cairn of stones that hid one of the rooms my mother and I occupied. As a child I thought this skeletal dwelling place was the tower of Ilium. Transients are still there; the windows are broken, decayed beige teeth and crumpled curtains shawl the crannies in the rocks.

The north end of Kansas City is cemented, quite progressive and grassless. Still, Kansas City, or at least a moiety of it, is rural, built on more hills than ancient Rome. Those who dwell in the refrigerated, abstract megalopolis, New York, and walk on Avenues A, B and C, macadam lanes in Styx, will be healed by the names of these bucolic streets: Walnut, Oak, Locust, Cherry, Woodland, Forest and Rockhill.

The alders and cottonwood have not died, and in spite of cement and the uglified tin cars, this is Midwest. Kansas City is full of jubilant knolls, and country wooden bridges lie over the small brooks.

At Walnut and 8th was the old viaduct, held up by dropsical iron legs. On one corner was the Jenkin Cigar Store, where a Buick or Stutz was raffled on Saturday night. On the other corner my mother and I stood and waited for the midnight owl streetcar after she had closed her barbershop at the end of a long, hard day. Beneath the rusty viaduct was a steep cobbled slope on which stood shoe-repair shops, a bawdy house, rooms for transients that were often places of ill fame, Basket's Lunchroom, and the Electric Oyster Restaurant, patronized by rugose-throated cattlemen and wild, milk-fed trollops who were crazy about clam chowder, fried smelts or a bowl of oyster stew.

On Walnut between 8th and 9th was a nickelodeon known as the Subway Theater, a rueful name and a tawdry pantheon for moving-picture deities. East 8th was busy; switchmen from the roundhouse, motormen with a day off or a rosy-rumped

152

chick just out of Sedalia were always on the sidewalk.

The viaduct that trailed down beyond Wyandotte has been demolished, the red-brick depot and the streetcars that chanted as they rolled over the tracks are gone. One cannot lament their disappearance unless they were a part of his memories. Today it is septic and up to date, and the carrion alley back of my mother's Star Lady Barber Shop is now the expensive Walnut Towers. The alley was a slough of filth, and how many bad dreams have I had that are a shadowy remnant of all the rot, mire and hallucinatory rodents I saw there. The platform of the Grand Opera gave on to the alley, and there was a slope of clay behind Levi's pawnbroker Jewelry Store that looked like the gold of Ophir to me.

In going back to my native city I missed the landmarks of my boyhood, but we cleave to what we remember no matter how desolate and rubbishy it was. I liked the heavy, joshing stock-men and thought every lass clad in calico was Venus. I preferred the depot simply because I think the name gamy Americana. I cherish the yard, the caboose, the steam locomotive—a proud mechanical horse—and the freight trains—all of which remain —and the Troost Avenue trolley, which is no more, inflames my mind more than Chartres.

There was the Grand Opera House at 7th and Walnut; it is now a garage. I heard Chauncey Alcott there, saw *The Question Girl* and *Beverly of Graustark*—elite garbage, no doubt. Opposite the Grand Opera was the ticket office of the Burling ton Railroad. The building is still there, though it is no longer the Burlington headquarters. Main Street is quite different, but who is not willing to relinquish any Main Street in the United States? It was a scrofulous, lecher's Hades filled with pawn-brokers and storekeepers who offered merchandise at bargains because of a fire or flood that had never occurred. One can still see slouchy railroad Johnnies, sapless crones in curried kitchen cottons here. There was a shooting gallery, and a penny arcade with machines one cranked by hand to observe pictures of

153

women removing their clothes.

It was a riffraff assortment of lewd shops, but now brand-new skyscrapers have taken their place. These soulless, epicene buildings are better than what was there.

As far down as 5th and Walnut were the commission houses and wholesalers in eggs, butter, grain, bananas, peanuts and general produce. Here also was the Gillis Theater, where one saw pulp Wild West shows, and it was right near the farmer's market, where country people came every Saturday to sell chickens, dogs, kittens, rabbits, vegetables and fruits.

On lower Walnut are the Hardes Seed Company and the Oklahoma Barber Shop, embalmed remains of a gaslight town. I thought I was looking at one of Charles Burchfield's dated oils. There are Americans who will look with glazed, museum eyes at Clarence's Shoe Shine Parlor and Star Employment Agency, over at 12th. Some will regret that the Orpheum, where I heard Eva Tanguay sing "I Don't Care," has become an area for cars. Anna Held appeared at the Willis Wood, a specious Gothic cathedral, now extinct, as is the Baltimore, once a rendezvous for moneyed bachelors, show girls and out-of-town drummers. But the northeast portion of the city is still glutted with the same kind of patrons, customers and transients.

Those who stay at the Muehlebach may recall that Clyde Griffiths was a bellhop at a hotel at almost this spot in Theodore Dreiser's *An American Tragedy*. Those who have feeling for this great, torn man won't forget that he viewed Kansas City with much of the nostalgia with which my own heart is stuffed. There was the Jefferson Hotel, where Tom Pendergast, the Borgia of Mafia politics, elected senators and gave Harry S. Truman his start. There is still a great deal of talk about Truman, and about his former partner, now dead, the haberdasher Eddie Jacobson. I think their store was on 12th in the early days of this era; this had been a wanton, wide-open street.

154

Now there are several Eddie Jacobson men's apparel stores, one uptown in the chic, elegant shopping district. Harry S. Truman's clapboard house at Independence, Missouri, just outside the city, is a classic specimen of idiomatic American architecture. There is nothing showy or pretentious about it, except that in these days of insane inflation it requires a great deal of money to maintain such a home. There are countless wooden houses very much like it throughout the city; they are smaller, but good, homely structures that the unaffected will admire.

To return to the north end—there is the Aladdin Hotel, where businessmen from Kansas used to toy with fast women. On 4th and Wyandotte was a chic house of ill fame operated by Ann Chambers, who gave parties from about 1890 to 1920 for gorbellied cattlemen. This particle of the city is still a hushed and underground red-light district. There is the Puritan Hotel at 9th and Wyandotte; it is a sound, truthful edifice, and despite its pewed name, it was a place of assignation for rakehells who smoked Turkish Hassan and Sweet Caporal cigarettes. Another dated piece of architecture is the Coates House, built by Colonel Coates. It has a ceiling of leaded glass and iron that is reminiscent of the railroad shed in London's Victoria Station. The entrance to the Coates House has an archaic veranda supported by iron posts; above the first floor is a naïve wooden porch from which the paint is peeling away like papyrus. The Stanford White building that was the Board of Trade has three upper stories that are genuine red brick with arched windows; the other half is sandstone or Missouri granite; the side is rondured and feminine. (Some may recall the tragic liaison of Stanford White and Evelyn Nesbit, which was ended when her husband, Harry K. Thaw, assassinated him. Perhaps only a man who is capable of 1,001 nights with a woman can construct a good, erotical building.) Inside the Stanford White edifice are iron staircases, and there is a carved wooden balcony overlooking the pit where stockbrokers used to bid against one another. What a spectacle this would have been for Frank Norris, the novelist who wrote *The Pit,* and who found a publisher for Dreiser's *Sister Carrie.* All three of these men were amorous rebels, and entirely American in their genius.

How different was Stanford White's art from the flat, sexless new boxes, Nimrod's modern towers of lucre. A medieval or baroque house or church is voluptuous. Paris, originally known as Leucotia, according to Rabelais, signified the white thighs of the Gallic women. The Manufacturer's Exchange at 210 West 8th is in some respects an Americanized Rabelais; the corners of this interesting building are like the loins of a licentious woman. The entrance resembles a portal of a European church. The Bunker is a classic example of a Midwestern cathedral of commerce. In this section of the city there are many such business pantheons, and one cannot refrain from contemplating them. Plain and puritanic in some aspects, they have something surreptitiously carnal about them. Buddha himself, who was supposed to be ascetic, said: "But if those sensual pleasures fail the person who desires and wishes for them, he will suffer the arrow of pain." Still in the north end of Kansas City, the visitor is likely to find virile entertainment at the Folly Burlesk on Central and 12th. The proprietor of the Shake House claims it is the only cocktail lounge that offers burlesque.

On 12th and Main is the dowdy Paramount moving-picture theater, where I saw Gloria Swanson and the late Thomas Meighan in *Male and Female,* the film based on Barrie's *The Admirable Crichton.* In 1918 it was considered a holy Mecca of amusement. At that time I had not read one great book and I thought this film was a masterpiece. Nearby on Petticoat Lane was the Champs Elysées department store, Harzfeld's Parisian. It is still there, and so is Emery, Bird, Thayer, with its robust arcade. Not far from these elegant shops is Pennsylvania Street, where there are numerous 1895 homes in which the blood still flows through the brick. They contain bay windows and sincere porches. How essential is a porch to the health and laughter of a people. All of them belong to an agrarian America, and the city fathers have moved quite a few of them to a place that will be a museum.

Some of these homes have the long, narrow Romanesque windows one used to observe in schools and orphanages and in the toilets of the Edwardian period. Most of them are two stories high, with unpretentious glass panes large enough to let in the sun during the January snows and not too wide for the August heat to cudgel the head. A picture window is a phlebitis in a room; one usually finds them in a domicile wrought of false materials that make the entire abode seem as though it had no interior or entrails.

At 710 A East 8th, where my mother and I were tenants, is a dump. Opposite it is Sam's Auto Park. It was a row of scurvy flats that sat on a slope. As you entered at 8th, there was one flight of steps to be climbed, but the latticed back porch was four stories high. There was a weedy yard down below that was littered with sunflowers and speckled light.

Going uptown and south is the residential district, much of which wears the garb of rough-hewn rock or honest wood. Take a walk on Holmes between 52nd and 64th, and the jubilant grass and the maples in front of the cottages will be a balm of Gilead for the eyes. The forsythia, magnolia and redbuds will April the sleepy blood. At Linwood and Main is a stout ledge of fieldstone. Mexicans and Negroes dwell in Penn Valley Park. They occupy Midwest Gothic houses. There is a large Italian colony on Harrison, and the U.S.A.-vernacular homes on that street are worth seeing. Summit Street, though an asphaltic pasture for autos, is rural; the gabled roofs are not humbug asbestos, and the brick still lives. For a block south along Karnes Boulevard, there is a low stony wall from which elms sprout. There are some caitiff ranch houses rendered in boudoir pink, but there is always a front yard in the midst of

157

which is a basin to catch rainwater for thirsty, rusted robins. Roanoke Road is bricked and lined with ledges of rocks. Kansas City is composed of Bethany and Argentine limestone, Missouri granite and sandstone.

Valentine Road is Silenus's garden for the rich. On Oakridge Drive one is likely to view Italian colonnades or false English Tudors with mansard roofs. The Paseo, mentioned earlier, goes out to Cliff Drive. In the old days a buggy ride to this steep bluff, covered with elms, oaks and the sycamore, was an excursion. It still is. In late March the rouged cardinals wing from rude gray branches to natural stone ramparts. It is a pensive declivity, and when the sky is crabbed and a quarry of clouds, the veins look ruminative and seem to know that spring is near. Below is the East Bottoms, a ruck of factories. Despite my fear of the machine, my pulses are giddy as I regard the Gold Medal Flour General Mills or a dock where freight is unloaded. Among the countless industries fathered by Kansas Citians is the Empire Grain Elevator, where shoals of pigeons gather to peck the wheat; its pipes of steel are windowless; on top is a two-story galvanized shed.

The West Bottoms is also a factory canticle of warehouses, tracks and boxcars. A few of the names painted on the walls of plants located here are the music of commerce: Kansas City Bolt, Nut and Screw Company, Columbia Burlap and Bag. There are also the stock runs where cattle are moved from one pen to another. Kansas City has the third largest stockyard in America, and is an immense railroad center. The freight trains are epitaphs of an America for which I ache: Southern Pacific, Great Northern, Union Pacific, Rock Island, Santa Fe, Nickel Plate, the Katy (or M.K.T.), the Missouri, Kansas and Texas, the Milwaukee Road, Louisville, Nashville and Rio Grande. After going through this litany of sacred names, I came upon the former Heim Brewery, which is now a Safeway. The words we use are what we are, and I can taste saloon, silo, caboose, but cocktail lounge and streamlined Diesel engine are chaff on my palate.

Travel out to the southeast of the city on Rockhill Road and you find the University of Missouri. The William Volker campus is woods and meadow. Along Volker Boulevard, each side of which is a knoll of grass and trees, are four fountains whose feminine sprays are like broad-hipped candles that drop their wax at the feet of the Virgin Mary.

Most of the halls of learning at the University of Missouri are built of rocks hewn out of the hills. The students can roam through eighty-five acres of woods or sit beneath an oak, saucer magnolia, Douglas fir, mimosa, cedar, gingko or redbud. The campus is a bucolic poem that seems to be guarded by the forest god Pan. The school is now a branch of the University of Missouri at Columbia and has about 6,400 men and women students.

Close to this rolling hillock of learning is Country Club Plaza, which is perhaps the most cohesive shopping center in the United States. The stores are of a Kansas City Spanish style that is as good as California Spanish Mission. (In Spain they are now copying American-Iberian architecture.) There are bronzed water fountains, statues, and benches for the peripatetic who is tired. The Plaza lacks sidewalk cafés for conversationalists, and a second-hand bookstore. It is a Utopia in many ways for most citizens, but as Milton would say, "bokeless and museless."

Kansas City is still a populist city: one that would have teased the blood of Sherwood Anderson, the psalmodic novelist of Midwestern America, who wrote a book called *Hello Towns!* People will greet you, address you as "Sir," and this is as true of the well-to-do who live near Cliff Drive in the country club district as of the humble and tattered whose huts are northeast or near the East or West Bottoms. Courtesy is the strength of a nation, and rudeness, according to the ancient historian of Rome, Livy, is the symptom of the decline of an empire.

Holiday, 1967

159

A Letter to *Prose*

My dear Coburn: In our recent festival colloquy we had occasion to mention the drying up of our oracles, good books. We agreed that wise books, like the brash deciduous willow— your phrase—should be renewed each year. A book published once is scarce in print, little- or ill-read, or only reaches a shoal of auditors. Such neglected folios or octavos lie in the calms, and are parched by the Dog Star, and must be exhumed; you might, my dear Coburn, reprint some albic passages from them in *Prose*.

We live, as John Milton would have had it, had he writ in these pithless machine days governed by dour Saturn, in a "museless and bokeless" era.

This is no newfangled occurrence; it may be more woeful

160

than in former times; I cannot be sure, but allow me to list a few titles that may truss up our mirth: I cite Holbrook Jackson's *Bibliophobia: or Fear of Books*: ". . . Bishop of Ossory, in his Preface to Leland's *New Year's Gift to Henry VIII,* says, 'A great nombre of them whyche purchased those superstycouse mansyons reserved of those librarye bookes, some to serve theyre jakes, some to scour their candelstyckes, and some to rubbe theyr bootes.' "

Most of the precious volumes lie upon biers in our monolithic funeral parlors called libraries, and are seldom removed from their ritual ossuaries. Callimachus, the third-century Greek poet, was the custodian of the celebrated papyri at Alexandria referred to as the Healing Library. A sage quarto is a balsam for a blowsy hour. This puts me in mind of the ancient purification ceremonies of the Greeks who chewed buckthorn to expel evil spirits, according to Dioscorides, and the reading of Sallust's *Catiline,* englished by Thomas Heywood, or George Chapman's *Bussy D'Ambois* is such a rite. We exorcise our chaff, our fell wastes and doric glooms as we gather the analects of the Rig Veda or Dekker's *Plague Pamphlets.*

We have to cure our days as best we can, and a book we enjoy is more likely to be the remedy for our soul and body than the physician. When Coleridge was in the dumps, his friend, Charles Lamb, suggested that he go to Izaak Walton's *The Compleat Angler* for a sedative.

After a pair of grum hours in a drugstore, where the eye is dried up by a bilious display of balloons, galoshes, clocks, chewing gum, scales, and a nerve-wracking assortment of nose-sprays, hair-lotions, patent medicines, bath salts and postcards, half an hour of an evening with *The Life of William Blake,* by Alexander Gilchrist, published in England in 1863, will cleanse you. Gilchrist's widow was so enamored of Whitman's *Leaves of Grass* that she came to America to see the bard, who then occupied a humble clapboard cottage in Camden, New Jersey.

The poet no less than the secular enthusiast of booklore is an apprentice-reader. Who can remember one page or even a line he has gone over with much exuberance? It may be that the memory of human beings depends in great measure upon what they have forgotten. However that may be, John Donne remarked that after he had perused 525 pages all he recollected was that he had turned 525 leaves. One is always a prentice-friend, and an inexperienced reader. We pick up a friend where we left off and are amazed because we do not know him, and return to writings we supposed we had diligently examined and are surprised that as we look at the pages we wonder how it was we could have missed them. Dryden opined that he perused the comments of the scholiast Macrobius on sundry poets in order to discover a sovereign sentence he had slubbered over or omitted. Should one find any of the books I mention in a second-hand bookstore, never let a friend take them for one may lose both the book and the friend. He who borrows the work of an author you prize often fails to part with it in order to prove he cares more for erudition than you do. Should the borrower be a kleptomaniac who steals books and paintings, he is not dishonest, but is simply keeping what he needs to reassure himself.

The viaticum of the soul oftentimes unfed and crestfallen is Seneca, Cicero, or Virgil's *Bucolics.* When I am incurably dull, and can find no Northwest Passage to Cathay, I am best medicined by the *Fasti* or the *Pontic Epistles* of Ovid. Considering the *Fasti,* I have the vapors for this is February, the month of the shades, which presses hard upon my pulses. Ovid says that February comes from the word *purifiers.* Yet with rapture as well as February emotions does the bibliolater champ the *Fasti;* he licks Ovid's pages on the kalends as the priestess of Apollo ate the laurel leaf. No author, regardless of his darkling excogitations, furnishes us with the swamp of desolation, morose concupy. We are no different from any vessel lying idle in a sluggish wash, whose hull is eaten into by sea-worms.

162

Do not imagine I am wholly preoccupied with buskined conceits. I wear my comic socks often enough, and am just as glutted with nonsensical prate as garrulous Democritus. However, I abhor that hysterical convulsion the motley think is laughter; what a form of debility is this feral spasm. Charles Baudelaire in *The Mirror of Art* declares that: ". . . the comic is one of the clearest tokens of the Satanic in men . . . this laughter is the perpetual explosion of his rage and his suffering."

As a pelting aside it is my impression that Henri Bergson, who composed a tractate on laughter, pilfered his conceptions from Baudelaire.

But to return, it has been remarked by Rozanov, author of the arcane *Solitaria,* and acolyte of Dostoevsky, that Christ never smiled; Plato seldom did, and I doubt he laughed. Baudelaire announces: "Holy books never laugh." Let us not misconceive Baudelaire, believe him to be a Saul sitting beneath the pomegranate tree at Gibeah and continually brooding over his sorrows, or conclude I cannot joy in the fond, smiling navel of Venus Mandragoritis. I am no bumbailiff of any man's lubricious appetite, for I am as amorous as Holofernes who lost his head over the pantofles of Judith.

Elsewhere in *The Mirror of Art,* Baudelaire says: "I have found myself wishing that the poet, the connoisseur and the philosopher could grant themselves the enjoyment of a Museum of Love, where there would be a place for everything, from St. Teresa's undirected affections down to the serious debaucheries of the ages of ennui."

The literature of the *caballero* (the Spanish gentleman, and this word sounds almost as ridiculous to pedestrian ears as "lady") and all the delicate refinements we associate with amorous pangs and the miraculous gusts of infatuation, have been replaced by boring bedroom scenes. Women and the romantic sensibility are out of fashion. The obscene scribbler has omitted one glorious four-letter word, love, now in the index purgatory. As for me, I find the pornographer altogether wearisome; he is venal, a starved man, and anti-feminine. There is a saw in olden Moslem: "Even suppose the effeminate has put on a coat of mail; as soon as he feels the blow, he will become a captive."

Those puzzled by our world—and who isn't?—will find the *Letters of Eric Gill* a great excitement for the mind. Eric Gill was the artisan par excellence. And so far have the manual arts decayed that Gill had to cut the stone for the famous French sculptor, Maillol. He abhorred any sort of bilge or affectation, especially literary and art criticism. Why is it that long tracts on aesthetics, the so-called science of beauty, are written in such a morose and unkind prose?

Few words on art are worth five minutes of a reader's life. But some while after I had so luckily come upon *The Mirror of Art* in Copenhagen, I went by sea to the Danish isle of Bornholm where I met the American-Negro painter Harvey Cropper, who gave me two slender volumes containing essays on Chinese artists. One is entitled *An Essay on Landscape Painting* by Kuro Hsi. The other one is called *The Spirit of the Brush,* full of apothegms, writ by sundry Chinese painters who did their work from 317 to 960 A.D.

The beef-witted artist of today should adopt the following remark as his diurnal orison: "Every circle he drew, he went over again to make it perfect. From beginning to end he worked as if he were guarding against a strong enemy."

A devout adversary of the villainy of the little, I am pleased by this: "Chang Yen-yuan laments the fact that the mountain peaks of the period were drawn like combs or hair-pins." I cannot repress the impulse to decorate my letter to you, Coburn, with this sensual aphorism: "Watercourses are the arteries of a mountain; grass and trees its hair; mist and haze its complexion. . . . Water is the blood of heaven and earth."

I like to ramble from one author to another; sometimes I am so beside myself as I dote on a book that I burn in the flames of Troy. Since my nineteenth year I always assumed a divine writer to be a god. Ovid relates the "Arcadians are said to have tenanted the earth before the birth of Jupiter," and I say the Muses were created before that divinity. At this instant, I am dismayed that the modern Attic wag, Norman Douglas, is out of season. Douglas's *Birds & Beasts of the Greek Anthology,* published in London in 1928, has not been exhumed since then, and I have not encountered one person who has mentioned this galliard little fable of natural history grounded upon Aristotle, Theophrastus, Columella and others. It is full of sweet, plain learning. A single citation may whet the appetite of a few: "There is an interesting epigram on the figure of a wryneck jynx, engraved upon an amethyst and set in gold as a love-charm. According to Kruper, the wryneck is a rare bird in Greece and Asia Minor. I have seen it on the islands during migration, but not on the continent. 'Not rare in olive groves,' says Lindemayer." Ben Jonson says some are "born to suck poison out of books"; for the majority these unwanted waifs of the Muses are not even known or touched, and the book or man, who is starved for Touch, is simply starved. Touch is the Genius of all flesh. I pray the reader will range the whole town, and land, if necessary, as sorrowful Demeter did in her search for Ceres, in order to lay hands on Douglas's *Birds & Beasts.*

Before naming another brace of volumes, I must relate I am in the suds whenever I see an ugly, raddled cloth binding; what carnal satisfaction is there in handling a cheap fusty folio? It's no hearth, and is about as repulsive as the llama dung, fuel for the Indian on the barren island of Titicaca.

Since the earth is God's sphere why should not a boke be a venerable circle. The Babylonian baked clay in the form of cylinders on which were inscribed burial names, customs and the vegetables and liquors the deceased devoured and drank. The Hebraic Talmud is a scroll. A learned vellum copy should be cavernous or give the impression of the Orphic caves. Porphyry, in his little known chapbook, *On The Cave of the Nymphs,* tells us: "Ceres educated Proserine with her Nymphs in a cave. . . . Saturn fabricated a cavern in the ocean itself and concealed in it his children."

If I may be ribald for a moment, certain books should have the shape of a codpiece, a gourd or seashell in which the native Indians near Darien kept their private parts.

So much for a libertine moment, but then a divagation is a path to an accidental perception. Porphyry's *On The Cave of the Nymphs* is an Orphic scholium upon the *Odyssey*. Apocryphal or not, the *Odyssey* may be composed of divers chants and lore bequeathed to the people of Greece and recited by roving Homeridae. No matter; this volume is as much of a secret to contemporary people as the Sibylline papers; as for me, I would rather lose a covey of foamy Nereids or a dram of rhapsodic expectations than part with my Porphyry.

Lately I saw the obituary notice of Charles A. Pearce, who published a sweet book based on Cabeza de Vaca's relation of his journey from Florida to the Pacific, 1528-36, and written by the deceased Haniel Long. It is fabled that Pindar was born with a honeycomb in his mouth, and I venture to say this chapbook contains some of the flowery aliment furnished us by the bees.

Haniel Long, singing out his last swan-like hours in Santa Fé, New Mexico, and afflicted with glaucoma, sat in his adobe house, whilst he took this peregrination with Cabeza de Vaca. Would you perambulate this mizzling globe, sir, be seated like sagacious Buddha. De Vaca, after countless Odyssean mishaps, walked naked from the Floridian Atlantic seaboard to the Rio de las Palmas, the Rio Grande, subsisting on roots, herbs, bark, foliage, and the carrion shellfish he could find on a bleak wintery shingle.

The name of Haniel Long's discourse will vex some: *The Power Within Us;* but it is no verger's treatise gotten off by one sweeping up our turpitudes with a theological besom; rather it issues from loving organs, and what a gift that is in a Laodicean era.

166

How many will give me a flensed, wry look when I speak of Swinburne, whose false vinous verse was never my beverage or potation. However, he wrote an acerb and energetic criticism of Ben Jonson. Though I am gravelled by Hazlitt's secular and peevish remarks on Master Ben, Swinburne's philippic nourished my paltry head. I refer to Swinburne's *A Study of Ben Jonson.*

The aforementioned study of Jonson's work calls to mind another inhumed volume, bearing a drab title, *Miscellanies of Literature,* and at first blush just the mention of it is likely to put off an enthusiast of letters. In the thirties I stepped into the Raven bookstore, and came upon its three volumes bound in mediocre cloth. What caught my fancy was the name of the author, and be sure, O unknown and discerning readers, Isaac D'Israeli, father of the English Prime Minister, was no sciolist or dunce.

With what pain and dolour he chronicled the penury, the factions, and the sulphurous jealousies of Elizabethan scribes. Some of them were forced to take up bastard underworld trades since they could not scramble up enough pennies for feeble meats, small beer, or "bald unjointed chat" at a London hedge-tavern.

Thomas Nashe, who gave us immortal idiomatic English, was a loller and mendicant, and had just cause to call his protagonist *Pierce Pennilesse,* and Robert Greene, who authored a book on the confidence-man, was himself a cony-catcher. How odd it is that the ill haps of geniuses, dead ones, I should add, give drama to our lives, and are likewise a relief from wormwood satiety.

Once more I must meander; after ransacking Xenophon's *Memorabilia,* a record of the corporeal rather than the Platonic Socrates of the agora, the learner (and one must learn until his demise, or live dead) might well dig into Grote's *The History of Greece.* Grote's long chapter on the great gadfly is astounding; nor should one overlook his remarkable pages on mythology;

thinking on this, the author or reader should not squander an instant before consulting William Smith's *Dictionary of Greek and Roman Biography and Mythology*. There is enough Thassian wine in these three tomes to assuage the hydropic bibliomaniac and to make him oblivious of ever-present woeful Avernus.

Should you have a taste for gnomic prose, La Bruyère's *Characters,* modeled upon Theophrastus' opus of the same name, is a feast for the book-gourmet. One of La Bruyère's sayings I have never forgotten: "What decays most quickly in any society is sense," defined by Langland and Chaucer as "kynde wit."

There is the Spanish picaresque author, Quevedo, and his mordacious *Visions;* his irony is no less keen than was his Toledo blade. He was splay-footed, and at court the finest swordsman in Spain offered this cripple an insult, and a few jibes, challenging him to duel him. Quevedo accepted, and killed him. Would that I had his skill in dealing with rapacious salt rogues and skulking plagiaries.

Then there is the Egyptologist Gerald Massey, and his famous *Natural Genesis* into which Robert Graves slipped his cutpurse fingers without referring once to this imperial scholar.

A. B. Cook's fantastical masterpiece, *Zeus,* appeared in 1925. At present there is a truncated edition of his august labors by Biblo & Tannen, Fourth Avenue booksellers, but they are not to be considered trumpery anthologists, for thus far they have been unable to gain rights to the entire *Zeus.*

An edible history of the Greek Cynics, Diogenes, Crates, Zeno, Aristippus and their followers, honorably garnered up from witty Diogenes Laërtius, was published years ago in London and written by Donald R. Dudley, and is called *A History of Cynicism.*

Nowadays, when publishers want tomes, what a gem of wisdom is Maxim Gorki's *The Remembrances of Leo Tolstoy.*

I gave a copy of it to Theodore Dreiser, a great pensive animal, whose death is still a monody in my blood, and one to Alfred Stieglitz, the photographer, who introduced Cézanne, Derain, Degas, Monet and others to the Americans. Both spoke of it with rapture, and if you can afford to spend an hour and a half of your days consider the price very cheap.

My dear Coburn, I have merely suggested a very small phalanx of authors, but let me say, and I know how deeply you are of my mind in this, that one who does not fall into a Dionysiac passion over a profound book is a burden to the earth, and a barnacle one is not likely to get rid of, and withal such a drone, bore and sapless clodpate should be mewed up like any predacious and senseless haggard. To paraphrase Herman Melville, Cato fell upon a sword, I fall upon a book.

Prose, 1970

Old Masters

The most prodigious mishap of the young American writer is that he has no Master, or an elder of letters to guide him; and so he relies wholly upon himself, a very unreliable teacher. I was lucky; I knew Theodore Dreiser and Sherwood Anderson.

Alas, my encounter with Dreiser was too meager, and it was my fault! I had heard vile gossip about him— that he received visitors seated in his kingly chair on a dais, for example. Then there was the story that Sherwood Anderson, arriving in New York from Chicago, came to pay his homage to Dreiser, where-upon the latter said: "That's kind," and shut the door. (The next day he gave Anderson a party.)

I had met the affected and busy popinjays who were either starting a puissant opus, in the midst of one or just finishing it and who would ask you to call on them a year later. Would not Dreiser be creating another *Titan?* How could I interrupt him? Besides, what had a raw prentice like myself to offer him except a few moldy reflections? Should I telephone him, he would surely hang up the receiver, and I would be mortally wounded. Finally, I took the penultimate hazard.

Theodore Dreiser asked me if I would not come right over to his pair of rooms at the Rhinelander Apartments on 11th Street. The building, unfortunately, is no longer extant. The American is a recherché collector; after he has destroyed every remnant of the past, he looks for any relic in order to create a museum of nineteenth-century clapboard cottages, an old-time boulevard, even a model T Ford. Get rid of the Old; Be New! That is our schema in poetry, our Mammon Towers, our raiment and our lives. How droll it is that we now have a *Moby-Dick* postage stamp! Poor torn shades of Herman Melville, who also had no Guide and who was so apart from his own writing kin that he dedicated one of his books to the Berkshire Hills!

My meetings with Dreiser continued, but I always was of the mind that I was ravaging his precious hours. Long after his death I read that, at the time we became acquainted, his closest friend had died and he hoped that Edward Dahlberg might take the lost friend's place. What a glut of mulligrubs I had when I perused that single line in a biographical study of Dreiser. Time and again since then I have been bitten by the ever-hungry tooth of remorse. Good God, Theodore Dreiser needed me, and I, who have always been the beggar in any relationship, did not realize how desperately I required him!

Occasionally I would meet him on Eighth Street. If it was a flinty winter night, he would be walking without an overcoat. His appearance was never *outre;* he had little respect for the *artiste;* once he reminded me that I needed a haircut.

This cogitative man taught me more about books than I had garnered up in our academe. Nor did he mind my hetero-doxies. By chance I learned that he relished my iconoclasms; obviously he was looking for an American idol-breaker and felt he had discovered one in me. Once at his Mount Kisco home I had the effrontery to argue with him about Rabelais, whom he loved and I had misread. I knew little of the giant Gargantua, having merely slubbered over forty pages of Rabelais's erudi-tion, which I proclaimed was scatophagous! The hectic dispute went on for hours, and Dreiser put up with my opinionated foolery. What a musky heart he had!

I seemed to be meeting him on cold nights but was never to realize he was my human hearth or that he endeavored to be my Buddha. One evening at an Eighth Street restaurant he spoke to me of Shakespeare's plays as man-eating fables, and so I learned how to decipher the historical tragedies. He also gave me insight into the Sermon on the Mount, and through him I learned of local-color authors, of Henry B. Fuller's *With the Procession* and *The Cliff-Dwellers,* Edward Eggleston's *The Circuit Rider* and Hamlin Garland's *Main-Travelled Roads.*

171

He dug up that rare man, still an unread myth, Randolph Bourne, who wrote *The History of a Literary Radical* and *Untimely Papers*. These are our truths, still buried. Besides, he mentioned to me another trove of his, Gustavus Myers's *History of the Great American Fortunes*.

During our friendship—I wish I could name it that—perhaps we had ten disputes—that is, we saw one another ten times, and only once was I in the right. Dreiser compared a morose Tin Pan Alley catch, "Annie Rooney," with Beethoven. That afforded me a regal occasion for irascibility, and Dreiser too waxed rancorous. Coming to my senses, for I was commonly out of them, just as the fire between us blazed, I reminded him of the Sermon on the Mount; he laughed and suggested that we go and see a couple of girls.

I cannot repeat too often, choose a seer! Never mind being the great original. If you've got a dram of talent and are influenced by Erasmus, Gustave Flaubert or Charles Baudelaire, you'll still be yourself; without them you are likely to amount to nothing as an author.

How many exsanguinous grammarians are prepared to announce that Dreiser was a clumsy proser. How easy it is to diminish him, but where is the man who can write *Sister Carrie* and *Jennie Gerhardt?* Little doubt, without Dreiser's novels I could never have composed *Because I Was Flesh*.

I remember one Christmas about 1937 I spent at the home of Mrs. Sherwood Anderson's parents at Marion, Va. Anderson, without a tincture of malice, said to me, "This is the way Teddy writes: 'It was a terrible, pitch, dark night; in fact it was a horrible night.' " There is a good deal of truth in this parody, but there is a physical presence in all of Dreiser's works seldom to be found in our newfangled fiction. If a book is not physical, the words are empty as gourds and dry as the sherds in the Mount Sinai Desert we hear of in the Book of Job.

Every book is a mistake, just as life is, or mine is. What I cannot stomach is the cult of originality which obtains today—

the cult of nonentity. Writers who are solely concerned with originality scribble addle words and are at the same time obscene and epicene. Pornography is a folly because it is positively asexual; a man who is starved for a female or a wife cannot satisfy his hunger watching nudes in films or privy bedroom erotica.

I remember also any number of scullion reviewers who denounced Sherwood Anderson for being confused. Anybody who supposes he has a clear brain has a vacant one. If the author was not obscure to himself, a glut and flux of nebulous sensations, what urgent necessity would he have to make a clear, lucid book? Art in a way is a grandiose hoax. The merciful reader is of the opinion that an author is a savant, is not likely to select a squalid consort for a wife, or be senseless most of his days, improvident and his own hangman. One only has to refer to the wretched existence of the French poet, Gérard de Nerval, who returned to Paris after a long absence with a very expensive piece of marble, although his patron saint was Poverty.

Then there is the myth, at least to me, that Shakespeare made a fortune out of his plays. I freely own that there are many Shakespeare scholiasts who know far more about Shakespeare and can quote lines I either missed or are absolutely unknown to me. Since we do not know who William Shakespeare was, how is it possible to be what Le Sage calls his "bookkeeper of the other world"?

Despite the many serious commentators who conclude that the saint of all literature was shrewd, who can conceive of varlets, popinjays, rakehells paying money to hear dilapidated Lear rail at his pelican daughters, Regan and Goneril, whilst abandoning the one who loved and esteemed him, the faithful and seraphic Cordelia? Could the same playwright and imperial poet accumulate a vasty sum of coins from an audience who had to hear Timon of Athens swear at the whole human race? A writer is a simpleton, a cully rather than a sharper; and, as I in a way belong to that joyless period referred to with jubilation as the thirties, I can say that just about all of us were mendicants.

Maybe a poet is a great thinker in a book, but sure to be a fool in his life. Actually, the writer has little or no life; his autobiography is close to zero, so he has to invent incidents; in short, his everyday humdrum hours are not worth a pin and certainly not a quatrain or a whole volume. It is his legendary or apocryphal life that is important to him and to his readers.

One of the reasons I object to naturalist fiction is that the reader can find the same dreary, banal conversations in the book he heard in the streets, the shops or in our wormy, desiccated subway. Who goes to a book to discover what he already knows? All colloquies, or nearly all, should be ideal; it is what people are supposed to say (that is, words in their imaginative hearts), and not what is *actually* said, that quickens the pulses of the reader. It is the letter, and not the spirit, that killeth the entire man.

The realism of the guttersnipe is not art, and we squander our natures when we weep over a bathetic film, a fatuous novel. Only the best is worth our tear-bottle, and one feels tawdry and disgusted with his own soul and skin after he has wailed over a dunghill novel, or a stage dolt who is only mimicking the Duchess of Malfi, without any comprehension of her interior identity. We can only be relieved of our own sorrows which are our many gibbets by the greatest dramas; otherwise, instead of leaving the book with a puissant understanding we depart from it dwarfed and dirty.

A vile book that exacts some sort of feeling from us is a conycatcher; and no one cares to be fooled by a friend, a drama or a woman. Myself, I am of the mind that after witnessing a fourthrate ill-wit tragedy I have been fleeced, trimmed and flea'd. Let me say once more, everybody is a mistake and I am an imperial one. People often reproach me for impugning what I know is a marketplace fiction without having read it. Is this being opinionated, dogmatic, or is it experience? I can smell a Mammon volume; and, as Thoreau advises us, if you read all the rubbish that is published you won't have time to peruse the memorable authors.

There is also another contradiction in writing that should not be omitted: often a valetudinarian can mold the most salubrious passages. Schiller, the German poet and a consumptive, kept rotten apples in the drawer of a chest, finding in this decay health and a tonic; Hölderlin, another German poet, spent his last days in a madhouse. But what mountain air and pure snows of the Alps are in his poems! One who has never had any afflictions will not have any compassion for others either. A man with a very sound constitution is almost sure to provide us a work in very poor health. It was Heinrich Heine, commenting on a writer of his own times, who said that one could catch a terrible disease by just reading it.

In 1928 I met Edith Sitwell in London at a tea in her flat, and at her request I gave her Emanuel Carnevali's *The Hurried Man*, since republished by Horizon Press and edited by Kay Boyle. The day afterward she beseeched me to come and get the tales at once; I had told her that Carnevali, who had authored these gamy, picaresque stories, had encephalitis, sleeping sickness, and the frightened dame was sure she would catch it by merely handling the book. I meet with students at the universities who write me letters asking to come and see me. They expect to be quaking in the presence of a pompous man, full of himself, and are surprised to find one with the same quandaries they have and who always views himself as a beginner.

The heart is always inexperienced, says the eloquent seer Thoreau. One is sure to be fatuous at any age; and senility is not just a malady of the old; many youths have the same complaint. However, there is an adage, go not to the aged for wisdom, go to those who know. I must here conclude this little essay with a mirthful incident, furnished me by Sherwood Anderson. He related that he had been living with an enchanting sylph, pilli-cock or trull, whatever she was, and that one day she called him "Master," whereupon he packed his suitcase and left.

New York Times Book Review, 1971

Ignorance and Malice
at the *New*

*... why he has no more judgment
than a malt-horse ... he should eat
nothing but hay: he was born for the
manger, pannier, or pack-saddle.*
—Ben Jonson

I had a thin connection with Jakes Gorbelly, editor of Our Peace Loving Nations Publications. This Jovian editor printed mungrill pamphlets on Lenin, Stalin, Plekhanov and Radek. Jakes, as his familiars commonly called him, was something of a squib that Nature had palmed off on her captives. He wore wide slops to cover his low Balkan paunch, had a puddly complexion, the merchant bulbous nose of Laban in the Old Testament, and resembled a street peddler of Turkish halva. Jakes was the Stalinist arbiter of American Literature. He had a sneaky, abdominal intuition that all American fiction was worm-eaten capitalism, and that the muckrakers who had invented the proletarian novel were arcane imperialistic warmongers.

However, Jakes wanted to start a Party magazine devoted to belles lettres, and I was asked to attend three of the ghostly consistories. The Central Committee selected Saul Hobinol and me as the cofounders of a literary Stalinist periodical.

Jakes also elected two cronies of his to be editors. They were Lob Miching and Cog Murrain, a rustic from Iowa. Considering their unexpected presence a muckhill indignity, I resigned, and the two by briguing soon eliminated Saul Hobinol.

Their knowledge was prodigious, mainly deriving from the

176

Communist Manifesto and sundry aconited paper bullets on rallies, coal diggers' meetings and the wages of workers in the canneries. Despite their immense abecedarian erudition they could not discover a name that seemed cultured enough for their magazine. Lob suggested Self-Love, but Cog Murrain said that was too introspective, and then he thought Self-Interest might be closer to the Truth, which so exasperated Cog Murrain he struck Lob several times on the head and face, and they fell foul of one another for a fortnight. Then they came together and agreed on the *New,* which both were sure would attract the lily prosers of Helicon. At first it was a Stalinist periodical, then it was Trotskyite and ultimately High Church Comma.

Some small mention of Cog Murrain is in place. Although he made the most zealous efforts to be known, he had so much character that he antagonized that strumpeted dame Fame, and to his credit. Through Hearsay, a tallow-colored, ill-born fellow, he learned he had two sons, Morpheus Ignorance and Ignatius Malice. Cog Murrain, a man glutted with the subtlest emotions, declined to give either his noble surname, Murrain. The pair were said to be horse-leeches. However, only a woodcock has any confidence in Rumor, a cautelous fellow. Besides, Ignatius Malice has quite another habit; whenever he grinned at his Father, Cog Murrain, and the latter was not sufficiently vigilant, he bit him. Cog Murrain bore so many teethmarks on his cheeks and hands that he sought the following remedy to dull Malice's molars. He took the white seeds of Bitter Vetch, sprinkled water, stirring them together, and mixed with wine; he made Malice drink it to inhibit him from biting everybody he encountered.

Another churl, Ugly Report, claimed that Thomas Dekker had delineated these two loveable boys as having "bladder cheeks puft out like a Switzer's breeches." It is doubtful there could be a jot of truth in this since Dekker was a seventeenth-century poet. And moreover, it must needs be added that I know nothing about the editors of the *New,* and that, anyway,

177

the town is full of "bald unjointed chat."

Other remarkable characteristics of Good Father Murrain should not be omitted; he had the nicest faculty of gathering together a legion of foes, and for no other cause than that he graved the books of authors, a surly factious tribe who took this in ill part. Cog Murrain considered writers a band of ill-bred conies who could not even hide their feelings from themselves, and, worse, from others. The latter claimed the sons resembled the parent, which was unkind and likewise pelting communist doctrine, for Cog Murrain did not look like anybody else in the earth. Which must be attributed to vituperative wretches, for a man should have some kinship with the human race.

To soothe Cog Murrain, the writers, whose palsied English was widely noticed in the *New,* told him the misbegotten imps had actually been authored by his adversaries.

It would be unjust to speak of Morpheus Ignorance as a bad person. A slug, he was near to self-understanding, for had Ignorance known how stupid he was he would have been intelligent. Be it said he was an exuberant biblioclast; if he happened to pass a library or enter a bookshop he carried flax in his pocket for burning it. But he denied this, and since nobody knows his own experiences, he was never charged with arson.

However, Ignatius Malice seemed as vicious as Catiline, although his appearance was plain as his nature. Whenever he had a spiteful thought his face broke out; his short squab forehead was embroidered with vermillion and saffron boils. Otherwise he was in perfidious sound health. This worried Malice, for he feared that should he have an unexpected attack of goodness he would die of it, since people who have never ailed are sure to expire abruptly.

Jonathan Swift's caveat that critics are "the drones of the learned" had no effect on our august editors. They had such agile nostrils for the rammish scent of learning. Horace affirms, "My nose detects more accurately a rank armpit than does a keen hound where lurks the boar."

They could scamp any book and run through the index to see if the liar Herodotus, milksops like Virgil or Milton were mentioned. Were that so, they gave the volume to Morpheus Ignorance, who built a fine timbered coffin for it. Though Ignorance made the casket, it was Malice who inhumed these crazy honest skulls.

It should be plain to anybody who has studied Lavater's *Physiognomy* that Cog Murrain was a queasy person. When he received a scholarly waif of a volume that was so out of its wits as to come to the *New,* his first tender impulse was to take it to the almshouse. Were he undecided, he would carry the ragged threadbare truth under his arm and bring it to his son, Malice, and averting his face would say: "Malice, my child, you bury this book. I can't do it." Malice was more constant than his brother, Ignorance, for he was always overflowing with saffron bile, and when he met with a person who showed any symptoms of hope he kicked it out of him to make sure the poor fellow wouldn't catch that contagion again.

Once Malice was asked to inter Erasmus' *Colloquies,* a compilation of limping adages, and quite out of date. Before giving this dotard volume its rightful burial, Ignatius slubbered over a few of its pages and came upon a bewildering citation, actually written by an ancient beef-witted poet. It was about a Mammon suppliant who after offering public sacrifice and loudly calling on Janus and Apollo—gods of light and of day—mutters under his breath this prayer: "Fair Laverna, grant me the grace to seem just and pious. Cast night over my sins, and a cloud over my frauds."

Ignatius Malice was so enraptured with this orison that he told Father Murrain to print it as an epigraph in the *New,* and Good Father Murrain gave his foot to the boy's pin buttocks, and quite deservedly.

What deeply saddened Cog Murrain was that he could never be as renowned as Ignorance and Malice, even though he had been eulogized for having composed four phallic essays in thirty-five years. But who can expect to rival Ignorance, who gads about the globe, or Malice, known to everybody? None can assert that Cog Murrain was weak, or that he was not successful, which he showed in his contempt for Virtue, who had never done particularly well in this world. Iago remarks that "honesty's a fool, and loses what it works for."

Cog Murrain has denied he sired either of these oafs, which leads us to suppose that the *New* begat them. There is not a dram of truth in this whole rumor, but I dote on a gamy tale which cures my dumps more quickly than Mercurius Vitae.

Prose, 1971

The Gold of Ophir

Now is the eventide of the historiographer; the news-historian gives his false public kneel to FACT, the Baal Peor of our pedants. What concerns me are the three Americas, and not a discourse of a truncated continent we name with putid ignorance the United States.

Alas, we know as little about our beginnings as the tapir that hides in the swampy growths when the morning appears. Our best ethnologists and explorers are no better known than the relics of Cholula. Their works, often merely titles, are cenotaphs. How common it is to epitaph a noble scholiast or poet by remarking, "I have heard of him."

Who may claim he has a dram of intelligence who is unfamiliar with the soil that nourishes his body and higher faculties? Worse, our earth by now is the avenging Erinyes of the North American people. Can it not be said that our veins are the great floods of the New World, the Amazon, the Rio Negro and the river Magdalene, and that our most virile thoughts are the ingredients of porphyry, feldspar, limestone, and gneiss? Pliny alleges that emerald clears one's sight. It is worth noticing that many cities in nether America lie at the foot of volcanoes and that the houses of the inhabitants are built of lava and rocks of igneous origin. The volcanic Cordilleras furnished the light for the Indian, just as Etna was the torch of Ceres, the goddess of grain.

For the most part, my concern is with the cormorant man who sought the cruel auriferous ore, gold, but most often found instead marcasite and death. The misfortune of Columbus we know; he says in one of his epistles that he made the voyages to the New World for lucre.

There have been numerous apologists for the conquistadors.

Perhaps without exception they were bloodthirsty and avaricious. Las Casas indignantly stated that forty million Indians had been extirpated by the Spaniards. This is doubtless hyperbole, but that is of no moment, for it is hard to find fault with Las Casas's virtue.

Pedro de Alvarado, the lieutenant of Cortés, annihilated four to five million natives in the peninsula of Guatemala and Yucatán within a few years. On the day 4 Quat, according to the Quiché Maya calendar, Alvarado had a king and three caciques burned alive because they were unable to supply him with as much gold as he coveted. In a letter to Emperor Charles the Fifth, Cortés explains that he had only refrained from razing to the ground an entire village because the flames might attract the natives nearby who would come to the aid of the wretches. When a band of these red Indians, fearing that their tribe would perish at the hands of the Spanish adventurers, came to spy on their camp, Cortés cut off the hands of fifty of the Indians. De Soto lopped off the heads of Indian couriers because he was too fatigued to remove their iron collars. Gonzalo Pizarro threw numerous Incas to the dogs, which devoured them, because they were unable to tell him anything about a land of the cinnamon trees. Endeavoring to find out where the remains of Yahuarhuacac and a vast store of gold had been secretly buried so that the Spaniards would not trouble his remains to gratify their greed, Gonzalo Pizarro tortured many Incas until he discovered that the grave was at Xaquixaguana.

Fray Motolinia, a mild and good man, blamed the Spaniards for the ten plagues in Mexico. The worst, the monk said, was the gold mines where the Aztecan laborer had to toil until he perished. He was compelled to furnish all the materials for the mines and even his own food. Often he ran for thirty leagues with the little maize he had and died on the way. For half a league from Oaxaca, the principal mining town, the ground was so bleached with human bones that one could not go in that direction without stepping upon skeletons. The Indian was the mule; he was forced to walk one hundred and thirty leagues, his naked back loaded with artillery or an anchor weighing seventy-five pounds. Had the poor Aztec no food, he went to the oratory to look for a slain victim that had been offered to an idol, and after the priests and their followers had feasted upon the flesh of the captive, he ate what was left.

Another plague was the taxes; the Indian had to sell his children and land to meet this robbing. Often having nothing except his drawers or a loincloth, he took his own life.

Human flesh has been for sale in all ages. Columbus captured Indians and kept them as slaves. Las Casas, overwhelmed by the frightful plight of the Indians, recommended that Negroes be imported to Mexico to take the place of red bondsmen. Las Casas agreed that each Spaniard be allowed to import from Africa a dozen Negroes as slaves. Africans were heavily engaged in this bitter marketing of black flesh which they exported to America.

Another plague was the Spanish overseer and his black servant. Too lazy to collect whatever he could from the Aztec workmen, he sent his Negro vassal to extort maize and land, and the black man was more ferocious with the Indians than his master.

Errors, rituals, and greed drive men to their Odyssean destinies. An apocalyptic cutthroat, the Spaniard dissembled, cheated, robbed and murdered whilst he paid the most humble homage to the Holy Ghost. That he was a true believer cannot be misdoubted, but his guile was no less genuine.

Commonly the Levantine freebooter and voyager was only by mischance a discoverer. The Portuguese were so indifferent to the *sertão,* the forests far from the Atlantic skirting Brazil, that they lived along the coasts like sea-crabs. When Columbus came to Hispaniola (Haiti), he was crestfallen; he saw a few huts made of reeds and covered with palm leaves and woven grasses and scattered villagers. Where were the ginger, pepper and the spices of the Moluccas? He found a little gold, mastic, and cinnamon, but this was no pelf for his sovereigns Ferdinand and Isabella. Of course, the simple, rural manners of the people astonished him. He was delighted with the albic, glabrous skin of the maidens at Isabella and Navidad who wore nothing except gourds and seashells to cover their privy members. How enchanting it was to learn that these timorous natives did not covet property, had no martial passions, and prized broken glass more than gold.

The Spaniard mapped the headlands, estuaries, morasses, and vales the best he could, giving the appellations of saints to riverine hamlets and ranges of basaltic hills to conceal his chagrin and cupidity.

Columbus, a man of far more refinement than rough Balboa, was no less greedy. Neither knew what he was doing. Columbus never realized he had come to the New World. Although Balboa fell upon his knees when he saw the South Sea from the peak of Darien, it had not occurred to him that there was another ocean. Balboa viewed this infinite dropsy, an unknown ocean, with religious awe; for man is the only animal on earth with beliefs in the supernatural. No one can be more intelligent than Homer who is always telling us about prodigies, the anthropaghagous Polyphemi, the Elysian Fields, and moly, which the bard says is a plant that cures protean men of their distempered humors, and unbearable seasons of phlegm. Dioscorides informs us that moly is only a species of garlic.

How rapturous is one when he hears that in Huancavelica of Peru water flowing hot out of a fountain turns into rocks, or that at Laguna in the Canaries the roofs and walls of the houses are covered with houseleeks. Yet this is a source of rituals; Pythagoras states that one should fasten leeks to his door to avert evil. The Greeks of old did the same to avoid disappointment, disease or death. Jane Harrison relates that before the victim, the *pharmakos,* is slain, he is beaten with leeks.

Were not all races people-eaters we would think men as

naïve and simple as the penguin. Though we are repulsed by the Spaniard's cruelty we also admire his extraordinary fortitude. Orellana and his soldiers were looking for the lands of the cinnamons. They had been floating in a bark upon a massive river, not knowing in what direction they were going. After they had consumed a thousand dogs, they had nothing to eat but palm shoots, fruit stones, fungi, or their belts and shoes cooked with herbs. One day they imagined they were close to the Atlantic because they *felt* the pulse of the great river. They had no compass or loadstone and none of them was a sailor. Orellana and his men had not intended to undergo miserable deprivations, the wildest rains, and thick tempests, even for cinnamons, and certainly not just to discover a body of water, now called the Amazon, and then known as the Orellana or the Marañón.

Man is always starving; there is almost no sorrow he cannot abide; for the whole earth is a groaning brute, and the cause of his endless aches is that the ground and the seas suffer too. What he cannot endure is his inanition, his Guinea calms; his most severe ill is his torpor and this is as periodic as the scab which occurs after the rising of the Pleiad.

Mischance is a deity; Pluto, our eternal darkness, lay in the arms of Tyche, who is Chance. In the *Iliads* it is told that Paeon the physician healed Pluto after he had been wounded by Hercules. What a rare myth, for it suggests that death is not death, and that the deceased can be hurt. Nearly every discovery of the Spaniard was a mistake. All discoveries and sovereign ideas are accidental.

America is a great, negative continent. Almost every conquistador reaped the penury and death which he sought, since men are automatic, and know not what they do, but must perforce do it. When the Spaniard referred to this land as *terra incognita,* he was describing his own darkling nature, that Orphic cave. The men who went with Champlain encountered

185

snowy mishaps, sleet, blizzards, and the hardest terrain. They explored the St. Lawrence and its perfidious rapids, and Champlain pondered the fierce weather in his own soul, saying that the New World was a *terra damnata.*

The rites of the sundry nations are more similar than not. The Inca offered maize, coca, shells (*mullu* in their language), and old shoes to hills, gullies, and to the junction of rivers or paths. Hecate was the Greek goddess of the crossroads, and Lares guarded the roads that meet. In Guatemala the natives, informing Pedro de Alvarado, their ferocious enemy, that they were at war with him, sacrificed a woman and a dog and placed them betwixt two mountain passes that merged.

All people have legends about the beginnings of the world and how each nation sprung from dust, plants, or the seas. The inhabitants of Hispaniola thought that mountains, streams, and the prodigious waters flowed out of a gourd. Nearly everyone throughout the globe is familiar with the great deluge. After the Peruvian flood the survivors were said to have come out of a cleft at Paritambo. Ravines were venerated by the Inca, and a chasm, known as a *magera,* in the *Prologemena,* was a sanctified place to the Greeks. Porphyry, in his commentary on the thirteenth book of the *Odyssey* writes: "Ceres educated Proserpine with her Nymphs in a cave" and ". . . the ancients made a cavern to be a symbol of the world [and] Saturn fabricated a cavern in the ocean itself and concealed his children." Empedocles held a similar belief in crevices. The women, during the festival of Demeter, dropped a pig into a cave.

The Indians were no less pious than those who peopled Latium under the dominion of Saturn. The Romans paid devout observance to ovens, hinges, doors; Hera for the Greeks was a log, and Terminus, the god who divided Roman land between neighbors, was a stone or a bole. The idols of the Aztecs were wrought of basalt, terra-cotta, or flint, and the eyes of their demons were composed of grains of maize or beans, and the teeth of glass or hyalite.

Quetzalcoatl, Mexican god of wind, who first appeared on the coasts of Panuco, taught the people to pierce their sinning tongues and ears with the thorny maguey leaves until the blood flowed. Their idols were covered with reeds dabbled in human gore. He instructed them in the rites of sacrifice and penance. Styx is the darksome underworld of our wicked imaginings; the Inca believed that bad people who died were tormented by demons called *supay.* The Greeks assuaged the ghosts, bringing them victims and grains; the deceased fattened on their sorrows. Whoever is glutted with the pains of his foul acts feeds on the dole of the dead, and they in turn provide him with the festal meal of remorse.

The Aztec priest wore the skin of the slave he had offered to his idol in the *teocalli,* the temple, and the Greek hierophant put on the same garb, certain that this integument had "medicinal properties." The Greeks had many braziers and so had the Mexicans who used incense, *copal.* Jane Harrison thinks that brimstone was a sort of incense which was supposed to cleanse the sinner. We are acquainted with the Christian injunction, purge me with hyssop, and we may well wonder if the Mexican did not share the same faith in the purgative virtues of *copal.*

Many nations deify the shades; Demeter protected the tombs, and the Indian paid such reverence to the deceased that he imagined any conic hillock "covered with bushes, molina . . . and cactus" was a sacral tumulus. A petty king at Hispaniola placed the ashes of his deceased son in a bitter gourd which he hung from a balsam tree. Father Sahagún, referring to Aztec sensibilities, says, "When one dies they are wont to say he is now a *teotl* [god]." When a girl was inhumed in Mexico the mourners placed a besom alongside her, signifying her devotion to her parental household and her purity, and laid roses and maize cakes on the stone that covered her. Indians of Brazil thought it inhuman to allow the worms to feed upon their beloved ones, and so they ate them and believed they were their living sepulchers. The same people interred in

187

a coca orchard or in their homes. The American dumps his kindred in a morose factory cemetery, and allows them to starve; of course, it's a superstition to imagine we can feed the dead, but there is much feeling in it.

Spleen is common to all human kind. An Indian of Brazil who was vexed ate dirt. When a captive was taken, these Indians held a festival of insults; they heaped invectives upon him while playing flutes made of the bones of human legs. A similar feast of vituperation obtained in Greece; the victim was beaten and treated with every form of insolence before he was slain to honor Zeus.

Vestals were esteemed by Romans and the autochthonous Americans. Romulus lamented the rape of the Sabine virgins. Ovid states that in the Golden Age of Latium maidens were taught by Pallas to card the wool and to unload the distaffs. The Latin poet says that the eldest vestal burned the calves in the fire that their ashes might purify the people on the day of Pales. Mexican girls of unspotted virtue fed the idols with meat and loaves shaped like human hands and feet; they sprinkled incense upon the altars, swept the "fane" with feathers, and busied themselves spinning, weaving, and making blankets. Anyone who violated an Aztec nun was punished with death.

Who is civilized and who barbaric? The Indian priests lay on the ground in the *teocalli* with no covering except a loincloth. They abstained from food for many days, did not touch salt or garlic, and had no sexual commerce with women. Martin de Valencia, a Christian zealot, could not humiliate himself enough, and who can? He was restless and loathed his cell because it did not resemble a maggoty grave. Unable to endure his seclusion, and inconsolable after prayer and fasting, he began to regard the trees surrounding him as demons. Beside himself, he threw ashes into his broth, and still he could not overcome that inward dryness that is a feral affliction to a contemplative man.

Motolinia, the highly intelligent padre, living two millennia after Aristotle wrote his book, more of a fable than the natural history of animals, believed that griffins, having the heads and wings of eagles, and the bodies and hindquarters of lions, dwelt on the ridge of the volcanic Popocatepetl. Man has and always will be the irrational brute with hands. The Franciscan monks at Santo Domingo, doing all they could to extirpate the larvae of ants, and failing in their efforts, selected St. Saturnin as their defender, and shortly thereafter these pismires disappeared. Women who were pregnant and whose lives were in jeopardy were said to survive after they had touched the cord of St. Francis. In Ovid's *Fasti* the invocation is: ". . . ye ants, O spare the sown grain."

It is trite to assume that the Indian was savage, no better, as the French who came to Canada said, than a wild weed. The Indian was quick to learn languages, and to discern Occidental cant. Often the natives of New Spain were exhorted to renounce their concubines, and on one occasion when so admonished they replied that the Spaniards had many wives. Upon being advised the Spaniard kept these women as servants, the Indians retorted that they retained them so that they might weave their mantles and take care of the fields. Observing the religious Spaniards kneeling to the Rood, they asked why they had no better sense than to worship a tree.

The Incas had a Genesis, more promising as a legend than the Gilgamesh epic, but not as psalmodic as the Old Testament or the Gospels. It is revealed that at Tishuanaco, Pachacamac the Creator raised up divers nations wrought of clay. Pausanias claims that he saw the original primate of the Greeks made of penguid marl by Prometheus. It is fabled that the first red inhabitants were turned into stones because they were disobedient. Lot's wife was translated into a column of salt for hankering after Sodom. Only foolish persons are homesick for their past, and long before they are old they are in their swaddling clothes.

The Indians of Callao held that the sun and the moon were born in the waters of Lake Titicaca, and the Arcadians assured the Greeks they were older than the moon. Zeus is a god of thunder and lightning; he is also Helios the sun, and these two planets and the elements were worshipped by the Indians. Isis, the Ancient One, is the moon and Osiris, her consort, the sun, in Egyptian theogony. Quetzalcoatl, we know, is the wind, and Agamemnon, though rancorous, is highly intelligent, but that does not prevent him from sacrificing his daughter to appease Artemis and the Winds. And Socrates, deemed the wisest of men by the Pythian oracle, says: "Do you mean that I do not believe in the godhead of the sun or moon, which is the common creed of all men?"

Greeks and Incas paid the strictest attention to youths: boys from eleven to fourteen years of age went to the sacred hill of Huanacauri; Inca girls who were in the procession carried vases of *chicha,* boiled maize, to the foot of this mount where sacrifices were made. In the month Capac Raymi, Christoval de Molina tells us, they held their principal feasts; at this time the youths were given breeches, the toga of virilia, shoes made of reeds and of the color of saffron, and slings. After the fasting and the orisons were over, the parents and their near relations flogged them to make sure they bore them the proper filial regard and did not forget their ancestral valor.

Then they marched to the square of Cuzco, the holy city of the Incas, where the embalmed lords and the *huacas,* the idols, were exhibited, and the youths were once more whipped. Aristophanes, dismayed by the truculence of the epheboi, who crossed their legs wantonly, and sat in an impudent and licker-ish manner, and who had small respect for their elders, speaks of former times when no boy would ever anoint himself below his navel.

Without some degree of shame, insolence is rife and modesty is considered provincial. The populace given to rabble habits and practices is as phlegmatic as the sloth who moves on its belly, never standing on its feet. In an age of male and female sluts, the attitude of the people is ignominious. It is fabled that Venus assigns a civil attire for men and women, but today there is an addle show of virility which indicates that sexual love has sharply abated. When virgins and boys are garbed to show their shame, and the hunkers are accented, the pudenda of the nation is flaccid.

The Chichimecas were naked giants and as uncultivated as the man-eating Polyphemi. Polite nations of the world were attired with appropriate modesty. Backward Indians ranged the plains, or *ilanos,* without any clothing except leaves or gourds to cover their private parts. The rude Canadian Indians, as it is disclosed in the Jesuit Relations, wore only the bark of a tree to hide their privy members. The Chichimecas, who inhabited Mexico before the arrival of the Aztecs, were naked giants who plucked up trees as if they were lettuce. They were uncouth, ill-languaged, had no houses, and like Cyclops knew nothing of the grain of Ceres, for they did not till the soil, and ate roots, vipers, and jaguars.

According to Torquemada, Xiuhtlato told the people how to make bread of maize; and South American Indians used cassava and the root of the yucca for bread. Before the Greeks learned how to bake loaves they ate seeds and laid pots of uncooked porridge on the altars of Zeus. The Egyptians used swamp roots for bread.

Nations close to plants, herbs, and rocks do not despise poverty, the modern stigma, or the five Christly wounds in the body of the poor. Ovid says that in rustic Latium the altars were loaded with savin and crackling laurels. Nor did Demeter disdain grains of salt, spelt, or a few violets. The Inca having no coca, maize, or shells to pay his homage to a river or mountain, offered a stone, green weeds, or a blade of grass to win good tidings from a flux of water or a summit. The other day I discovered that wild thyme flourishes in barren hills, and was pierced by this bit of natural history. Who could believe

Shakespearean poesy thrived in sterile land?

The natives of Central America were content with the bare ground for a pallet, a piece of wood for a pillow, and regarded a tree in the forest as their summer house. Penury is a caitiff god that brings much woe to men, which is the price of understanding. However, Plutus, an arrogant and greedy deity, eats up the populace and its legends. Without fables the people wax mad and are as poisonous as henbane that grows near dunghills and highways, the rabble altars of the North American.

The Indians and Greeks observed human sacrifices. Motolinia says that when the corn was palm-high, a boy and a girl about the age of three or four were killed. After the stalks of maize were knee-high, four children were slaughtered to appease the water god, Tlaloc, and to make sure there would be no want of rain. It is not what happens that causes men to cower so much as that which may occur. His fears are the origin of his theogony. Animal uneasiness is man's clearest understanding, and no one should dismiss his qualms or misgivings. There was also a merchant festival; during this ceremony a woman was clothed as the goddess of salt, and after the throng had danced all night she was sacrificed the following morning.

Mexican children were docile, and were adored by their parents who slashed their throats to assuage a demon because they could not bear to rip out their hearts. Not always capable of murdering hundreds of slaves that they felt necessary to quiet the idols, they made an unction of spiders, scorpions, palmers, salamanders, and vipers which they burned and mixed with a seed. Of this they concocted a beverage that was so intoxicating that they were senseless enough to murder about four hundred captives in the temple of Camaztli. Manetho asserts that in the dog days the Egyptians burned a man alive, expecting that this would bring rain. The Greeks observed a harvest festival, the Thargelia; during a plague or famine they selected a captive, struck him with leeks and dried figs, and then burned him in order to save the stricken city.

Those who are repulsed by such horrid rites must ask themselves whether there is any difference between human sacrifice and modern war. The youths of the country are also captives, enslaved soldiers sent to remote lands to be slaughtered to sanctify the new merchant god named Petrol.

There is not a nation in this piacular earth that does not require dittany, a sharp hot herb, the juice of which taken with wine is said by Dioscorides to be a remedy against serpents. Every man has adders in his soul. The saint, the savage, and the divine lawgiver go into the wilderness or to the mountains to expel their Satan who has a thousand gluttonous mouths in his body.

How men make civilization smell sweet as fennel is an enigma. Men are too protean to be just; no one can weigh his acts in Job's Balance without cringing. Nor is there an enlightened legislator who, if given absolute power over his subjects, will not become the hierophantic assassin in order to establish a penitentiary Utopia.

Mention should be made of the gold of Ophir. The ships of Tarshish are a proverb unto this day. We first came upon the former name in Genesis where it is told that Solomon sent out a fleet to fetch the gold of Ophir. That Ophir was any particular nation José de Acosta doubts. St. Jerome asserts that Tarshish had many significances; it may mean Crisolite, Jacinth or a region of the East Indies. Ophir was thought to have the finest gold. The Spaniards, as de Acosta relates, sailing for Peru supposed they were bound for Ophir. Peter Martyr, the first historian of America, believed that Columbus had located the Antipodes. He writes in an *epistola* that Columbus, touching the shores of the New World, was sure he had reached a parcel of the earth near the Ganges. It was also assumed by Columbus that he had arrived at Marco Polo's Cipango (Japan) or Cathay.

New Ground was a kind of imaginary savannah loaded with angelic miasma. The Atlantic, called the Sea of Darkness, was considered a vasty, bottomless gulf. It had been rumored that on an early date the Carthaginians had made voyages to the Canaries which Pliny alluded to as the Fortunate or the Purple Islands. Homer was acquainted with these blessed isles he imagined were Elysium.

Nobody knows who was the first to have broken the Pillars of Hercules and ventured into the pelagic deep. There were various legends, but no historical annals. When a fable becomes a humdrum fact, man is the worse for it.

The Canaries consist of seven islands, the most fertile of which is Tenerife; the western slope of Tenerife is verdurous and zephyry, whilst the eastern loins of this smoking peak are more sterile than lava. But we are discussing the phonolites, the acoriae, the mica slate, and quartz of the intellect, or, if you will, the soul. One part of the human spirit includes palm trees, mangroves, oaks, laurels, arbutus, and the other watery mists, the salt marshes of Avernus and the mire of grievous Cocytus.

It can be affirmed that the winged caravels that broke the Pillars and furrowed Oceanus, going past Gades (Cadiz) knew whither they were going, but that the Admiral of the Ocean Seas did not. With no compass or loadstone that always points north, his pilot sat in the prow of the carrack depending upon the stars, patches of seaweeds, or the flight of a frigate bird to determine his course.

Fifteen hundred years after Pliny had described the loadstone, the seafarer had no intelligence of its useful properties. Two years following Columbus's discovery, ships going to Hispaniola carried mariners and astrologers to assist the captain.

Not Columbus, but the Jews, banished from Spain by the Inquisition, were the eminent hydrographers of the time. The unfortunate Jews who remained in Spain were robbed of their money and jewels in order to build pinnaces and furnish the men for the second voyage of Columbus. The purblind voyagers relied upon ancient cartographers, Strabo, Ptolemy, and

Eratosthenes. Aristotle believed that the Burning Zone was uninhabitable, and St. Augustine thought there were no human beings beyond the Tropic of Cancer.

Late as the seventeenth century, José de Acosta, the Jesuit who lived in the equatorial zone, disclosed that when the sun entered into the Aries, the weather was extremely cold, and that Potosí, renowned for its gold and silver mines, was environed with caustic winds and void of grass or herbs.

The ancients, with what prescience we should not diminish or fleer at, had the utmost reluctance to go past the Pillars, and venture into Oceanus. Pindar the poet, having similar prophetic qualms, warned the Greeks: 'That it is not lawful, neither for wise men nor for fools, to know what is beyond the Strait of Gibraltar."

Had Terra Incognita risen from the seas long after Asia, Africa, or Europe? Humboldt misdoubted that. Why then was the New Continent meagerly peopled, and why had they no domestic animals? There were the forest hen, but no poultry as we know it, the sloth, the ant-eating tapir, the llama, the Peruvian sheep, the peccary that has an evil-smelling gland, described by the first explorers as a navel; and the *manatí,* the beef of the Indians, which feeds on mangrove leaves, but lives in estuaries and saline rivers.

Columbus shipped horses to America and De Soto brought sows. Turquoise was here, but no jade, though jade hatchets have been found in the plains and in the Andes. There were remnants of gigantic cetaceous animals, the bones of a species of elephant; in Uruguay the bones of the megatherium were discovered.

Indian rituals were astounding in many respects, but agriculture was primitive, and there was almost no poetry, and no alphabet. Diodorus Siculus alleges that the Atlantides were ignorant of the use of corn because they were separated from the human race long before it was cultivated.

Our knowledge of the triune Americas is still as nebulous as the origin of the Guanches; the remnants of that people consist of a few mummies and one hundred and fifty words. The Guanches at Tenerife were no more than eighty leagues from Africa, and yet they had no flax or corn, and they plowed the ground with a goat's horn. Their humble aliment was an un-domesticated grain, *goffo*, a word in their extinct language, which after it had been washed and toasted was bruised in a hand mill like the ones employed in Spain for grinding the grease of bullocks. Does not this custom smack of a remark made by Sancho Panza?

Humboldt states that one-fourth of the extraordinary altitude of the Cordilleras is a region of snow. Would that our humid Occidental civilization afforded us a hard wintry metaphysic or a kind sensual poesy. Man without freezing steppes in his nature will have no equinoctial sun in his conceptions either. Since man is less than zero, he imagines his quest is a plus. Did he not suppose so, he would have a caitiff portion and the destiny of a hemp seed. The thinker is a restless ontological mariner, seeking the Moluccas, Terra Incognita, and other planets, to find himself. For neither man nor the volcano of Gotopaxi has august heights except at a distance.

It is said that after Ynca Yupanqui expired, a thousand of his servants were murdered and inhumed with him so that they could attend to his wants in the underworld of the *manes*. How can one account for the Inca so civil in other ways? No North American has equaled the Inca architect. Without knowledge of mortar or cement, the titanic rocks of his temples were joined together with such miraculous skill that the walls of the edifices were as seamless as the coat of Christ. Compared with the pyramids of Cholula and the chapels of the Inca, what are we to think of the Mammon Towers in our concrete Acheron.

The Mexican and the Inca were remarkable lapidaries and goldsmiths; each Aztec and Inca cut the stones and the timber for his house; he was a weaver, shoemaker, carpenter, mason, and tailor. The artisan in the United States has almost vanished. The machine will never replace the genius of the hand.

The paralysis of the Promethean will is the result of mechanical vehicles. The machine has turned the American into the most epicene and lonely automaton in the world. Solitude was not the malaise of the Indians who dwelt together in communal tribes. Even the Zamura vultures in Mexico roost in a flock of forty to fifty on coca trees. The titanic steel furnace is the chimera that breathes forth noisome flames, but not the volcanic fire that attracted Empedocles and Pliny.

The North American mammalian thinker, having no place in the cruel iron cities, will be forced to migrate to the two Americas below him, for the naphtha that flows out of the primitive rocks in the peninsula of Araya may yet feed the lamp of Pallas Minerva.

Prose, 1971

II

Shorter Reviews
and Prefaces

Roman Literature

CATULLUS ON 14TH STREET

The Complete Poems of Catullus,
translated by Horace Gregory

Mr. Horace Gregory's distinguished translation of Catullus has
the vitality and freshness of a new book of contemporary verse.
The poet, full of invectives, metropolitan irritations and heated
diatribes, is curiously modern. The poems themselves are a
remarkable and violent self-portrait, so vivid that any biography
would seem gratuitous.

Catullus was a poet of the city. Coming out of the sticks, like
a number of our best American writers, he wrote about the
politics, the hacks, the homos, the pussyfooting leaders of a
Tammany Hall Rome that in many ways suggests New York
today. How current are the following lines, how apropos these
paeans to a veritably Hooverian prosperity:

Furius, you've no slaves, no box to hold your money,
for you have no money,
no spiders (and no walls where spiders live) no hearth, nor fire—

All's well and it's no wonder:
you still digest what food may come your way: no falling
house to fear (no home) to be destroyed by fire, wind, or rain or
thieves, no poison will end your lives. Ill fortune
cannot perfect your ruin.

Why here's prosperity!
You cannot sweat, saliva
shall not drip from your lips, you have no phlegm and therefore
no running nose.

Catullus is very near to us and to our times, much nearer and much less of an anachronism in these alrightnik states than Harvard, Princeton or Congress. There is a definite connection between Catullus and the current reader. There is a common meeting ground, a sociological tie-up which our Eastern exchequer colleges have failed to preserve, with a living, mobile and economic America. Why, even our penny arcades with crowded dirty-postcard movie machines, our vaudeville gags and snickering jokes about pansies and fruits, are nearer to us. They are a richer library: there are more imaginative prose and verse lines in our ribald music halls than in our antique-shoppe corridors of learning, politics or literature.

The energy of Catullus, which comes to us as a surprise, is the quality that Horace Gregory has caught and rendered so well in the colloquial idiom. In communicating to the reader the directness and the temper of the Roman poet, Mr. Gregory has judged that living speech would be more effective and accurate than a factitious sixteenth- or seventeenth-century English vocabulary. And of course he is right. Moreover, he has used the idiom with sparing economy and a rigorous selective taste. Where Catullus himself is artificial, where his lines are obviously rhetorical and imitative of the Greeks, Mr. Gregory employs a more literary vocabulary. Elsewhere he has tried to be as simple as possible, while retaining the cadence and movement of the original. He has endeavored to penetrate the layers and layers of Anglo-Saxon traditional literary patterns that have dried like a thick cake over the original Catullus. As a very simple example (I do not know Latin and have had to consult with one who does; however, I have read enough dull translations to know what is alive and what is dead) the following lines testify to the freedom of style he achieves:

> Now warm-smelling Spring has come
> and here's our sweet weather,
> and the gallant West wind

clears dark April skies,
Say goodbye, Catullus, to the plains of Asia Minor,
leave these spawning farmlands
and heat-sick Nicea.

Here Mr. Gregory has substituted "West wind" for the customary "Zephyrus," and "dark April skies" for "Equinox." I suppose another translator following his predecessors would have preferred "farewell" to "goodbye." I have never been able to understand why the one is considered more poetic than the other. Nothing seems so absurd as this kind of effete eclecticism in language, this remnant of verbal aristocracy. Before Lessing's time, it was bad taste to have the stage center around working people: they were only fit to be clowns, butlers, harlequins; they had no drama in them. Now it is their language that we still apologize for using.

It would have been silly, as some previous translators have done, to have rendered the epigrammatical lines, the poems on pederasty and other Roman-New Yorkese perversions in the stale euphemisms of the drawing-room. Moreover, it would have been out of keeping with the splenetic profane Catullus. The direct speech in the poem to Gellius, and in that to Suffenus the scribbler, the dainty esthete who wrote his stanzas on "magnificent vellum bound in parchment with neat ribbons," makes it all the more incisive and alive. An almost unexpurgated Catullus will doubtless scandalize a number of readers and university professors. Nevertheless, I believe that Horace Gregory's warm and living translation will survive their revulsions.

New Republic, 1931

*

The Portable Roman Reader, edited and
with an introduction by Basil Davenport

Why should anyone read the small, pelting commonplaces of Basil Davenport on Roman civilization when he can turn to Livy or to Suetonius or to the Latin poets themselves? And why should a reader bother with a fragment of Terence and a moiety of Martial or piecemeal Lucretius when he can spend the same amount of time exploring the whole vision of a single ancient author? The mind is the higher stomach of man, and it cannot sustain helter-skelter change without confusion. The intellect at its best is a pastoral milch cow that rejoices when it has continuous meadow and pasture; uncoerced by fashion, it is not likely to forsake the cribs of Virgil's *Bucolics* to graze upon a bit of Lucretius and then rush off to Catullus and to Caesar. Jumping about is very foolish, and even mad, but this is what Basil Davenport and other anthology salesmen of letters expect the reader to do.

Mr. Davenport, having all the charming, tumid faults of our "cultivated" age, claims that his selections are "in the best English translations," but as Henry Fielding might have said, there is nothing wrong with this assumption except that it is not true. As proof of his taste Mr. Davenport chooses Henry Wadsworth Longfellow's translation of Virgil in preference to the pre-Elizabethan Gavin Douglas's. Mr. Davenport would doubtless tell you that Gavin Douglas is hard to read, but earnest reading is a task for the higher faculties, and anyone who attempts to make a book simpler than it is at its best or in its original text is a puerile sophist. The simple truth is that all great poetry is difficult to understand; besides, there is the Virgil englished by Robert Andrew in the famous Baskerville edition of 1766.

When Mr. Davenport chooses a poet's rendering of Catullus,

it is no more than a single ode by Sir Philip Sidney. There are various fragments from Horace, but Christopher Smart, a poet of Samuel Johnson's time who did a lovely translation of the *Odes*, is absent. There is a piece of Livy here, but it is not done by Philemon Holland, the Elizabethan, who also did Suetonius. The ancients included in this volume perish under the rude, myrmidon hands of Andrew Lang whose *Iliad* has left us wasted and empty. As for Dryden's Plutarch, in which the blood and marrow have been extracted from the ancient body, just compare it with the Plutarch of the Elizabethan Sir Thomas North!

The anthologist has not hesitated to include Walter Pater's Apuleius. Pater himself is false wine and gimcrack pomegranates, and who can but wince at the thought of Apuleius being patered, for here we have two decadences rolled up into one.

Spare us, O Zeus, from easy reading. Man is by nature a stupid slattern who would rather read with his lower stomach, and he should not be indulged.

The Freeman, 1952

Robert Cantwell

WHITE-COLLAR NOOSE

Laugh and Lie Down, by Robert Cantwell

Usually a supine character is chosen by our novelists as a representative American. The hero of *An American Tragedy* is wholly spineless. Erskine Caldwell's pimps, butchers and millhands—William Faulkner's bootleggers and lynchers—all share in the same tired violence and explosive inertia.

Kenneth and William McArdle, the chief characters in Robert Cantwell's *Laugh and Lie Down,* belong to this willless class. (The title of the book is significant. Realism, in American literature today, has become the study of various kinds of fatigue.) Kenneth, the older brother, is a hardworking draftsman; William, who, like Kenneth, has white-collar nerves and sinews, is a factory hand on the night shift. Neither the drafting board nor the factory has given them any sort of handicraft satisfaction. Both brothers are in love with Berenice Adams, the daughter of a family supposed to have had money at one time and now anxious to keep up appearances. When he has to work around the house, Mr. Adams puts on a pair of overalls so as to look like a hired man. He is not anxious to have his daughter marry either of the McArdle boys; they have no money in the bank. She marries Kenneth and keeps it a secret.

William, for his part, has but one certitude: he doesn't want to work. He tries his hand at small-time bunco schemes. With Biddle, also a shoe-string opportunist, he opens up a sort of collecting agency. The two of them buy clothes and furniture on credit, then dun themselves on behalf of the business houses with which they dealt, and receive from the latter a commission of 33⅓ percent for their services. Finally, the two of them meet Benny, a hard-boiled crook who has succeeded where they have failed. He panders, bootlegs and commits bigamy for a living. Sometimes he "rolls" the drunken loggers for their paychecks.

William, Kenneth and Biddle all have minds of a sort, but they have minds that have been drugged by cowardice, by blurred plans and unrealized intentions. The class into which they have been born—the American white-collar class—is their nemesis. Kenneth sees only one way out—to go to another city and start anew. To William this seems futile; another town or city would be the same. In the end the two brothers and Berenice drive off in Kenneth's car. William has a bag containing some $4,000 stolen by Benny in the hold-up of a motion-picture theater where Biddle was the organist. The end of the book is consistent and well sustained. The car runs off the road and overturns. We leave Berenice and Kenneth lying underneath it in a complete coma—perhaps dead. Only William has any remnant of consciousness, and he prefers to close his eyes and get oblivion.

Robert Cantwell has written of a class. The city in which the characters live is somewhere in the state of Washington, but he does not definitely localize his scene, or make something special of it as Faulkner would have done, for the characters he has depicted so convincingly and with such naturalness are as typical of all America as is Socony or the A. & P. The style is simple and reportorial. Mr. Cantwell has chosen to write a sound first novel rather than an overambitious one, and I think that he has succeeded admirably.

New Republic, 1931

Erskine Caldwell

Tobacco Road, by Erskine Caldwell

Tobacco Road is the story of a family of Georgia crackers, their serfdom, slow starvation and economic and social stupefaction. Erskine Caldwell has caught with phonographic accuracy the illiterate and repetitive gibberish which reveals the seedy background, the scant hopes and the ineluctable vassalage of these poor whites. He is a much easier writer than William Faulkner or Elizabeth Madox Roberts. Without tortuous effort, he can chronicle simple statements of fact.

The Lesters live in a leaky, broken-down shack on a sandy, recalcitrant and neglected farm. Most of the day Jeeter Lester, the father, sits around meditatively mumbling over his hunger, his worthless blackjack wood and his prospects, hoping that when he dies he won't be buried in his overalls. His old woman, Ada, is always pining for a silk dress and some boxes of snuff. She wants the snuff to keep her mind off food, and the silk dress for her burial.

There have been seventeen Lester kids, at least one of whom is illegitimate, besides some other farm urchins in the vicinity which Jeeter claims must be his. Most of them have casually left home at different times, without ever bothering to tell Jeeter or Ada of their intentions or their destination. Besides the parents, Dude, who is sixteen and has never gone to school, and Ellie May, who has a harelip, still live there. The grandmother, Jeeter's mother, is also about the place, and they wish she were dead so that there would be more crackers and fatback for themselves. The land, like all the property around there, has passed into the hands of absentee landlords. However, still clinging to the soil, rooted to the barren farms by a superstitious fear of the industrial cities and mill towns, these American muzhiks wait and pray for succor and a year of pentecost which never comes.

The novel opens on a warm February day. Lov Benson, the son-in-law of Jeeter, is coming up Tobacco Road carrying a gunnysack of turnips. Almost a year ago Jeeter had traded in his twelve-year-old daughter, Pearl, to Lov for a week's wages, seven dollars, and some odds and ends. Lov complains that he hasn't been getting the benefits of a wife, for Pearl has slept on the pallet on the floor ever since their marriage. Jeeter, whose eyes have completely passed over into the gunnysack, promises to talk to Pearl if Lov will give him those bright gargantuan turnips. Failing to make him agree to this, Jeeter hits him over the head with a stick, and while the others hold Lov down, runs off to the woods with the bulging gunnysack.

There are incidents and passages in the book which evoke the grim cupidity and astringent humor of the peasants in *La Terre*. The marriage of Sister Bessie, a female preacher and Holy Roller, to sixteen-year-old Dude, has this same Zolaesque texture. And the episode in which Sister Bessie and Dude kneel down in prayer in a motorcar showroom before the automobile she has just purchased is Middletown in fantastic bas-relief.

In one of the Scandinavian countries or in Russia, I believe, *Tobacco Road* would be hailed as something of a literary event. Here the chances are that it will be quietly buried like *The Enormous Room* and other unclean documents. Not until Mr. Caldwell has learned to make poverty, hunger and sex something that can be nostalgically mistaken for art rather than truth will his writings be widely praised—at least that is one reader's guess.

New Republic, 1932

*

God's Little Acre, by Erskine Caldwell

Erskine Caldwell has been compared to Henry Fielding, and it is true that his books, *Tobacco Road,* a very original novel, and *God's Little Acre,* a much less gifted one, have something of the gamy flavor of that great eighteenth-century writer, though they have none of his structural ingenuity. *God's Little Acre,* like *Tobacco Road,* is a chronicle of Georgia crackers, of their economic vassalage, slow hunger, and supine lives anaesthetized by inutile hopes. Less a novel than an expanded short story, it has little to recommend it aside from a few highly amusing and picaresque touches and the deft portrait of Pluto Swint.

God's Little Acre evokes a half-dozen other "proletarian" novels; and to this whole group what George Saintsbury once wrote of *Tom Jones*—namely, that it lacked a certain height and depth—certainly applies. In the "proletarian" half of *God's Little Acre,* a wholly truncated section, the neglected plantation, firmly and irrevocably reproduced, is replaced by a mill town which is almost preternaturally sepulchral. The striking "lint-heads" are disincarnated specters moving in a quasi-Marxian haze ten thousand feet above Georgia and Carolina—and, for that matter, above all American humanity.

The frenetic desire of Will Thompson to open up the mill, turn on the power, and *make* cloth, which is in direct ratio to his wish to violate Griselda, tear every shred of manufactured garment from her body, sabotage her, as it were, is a strained emotional admixture of D. H. Lawrence and Sherwood Anderson. This apotheosis of dark sex and the humming machine recalls *Beyond Desire.* And *Beyond Desire,* which never transcends desire, and which is so writhing and inarticulate that it

210

makes painful reading, is a stale repercussion of the events of Gastonia and Mary Heaton Vorse's *Strike!* Grace Lumpkin's *To Make My Bread* (awarded the Gorki prize for proletarian literature), whose homespun narrative is inexorably slow from beginning to end, and Fielding Burke's *Call Home the Heart,* whose poetical came-the-dawn prose only succeeds in being coy, are reshufflings of the same material. One would suspect after a reading of these "proletarian" novels that it was a bourgeois fault to be able to write well.

The left bandwagonists, who encouraged the foregoing pogroms against literature, have also acclaimed John Dos Passos the white hope of the social revolutionary novel. However, he is not, as his psalm-singers have said, a more pliant and adept literary technician than either Dreiser or Sinclair Lewis. What characters has Mr. Dos Passos drawn that are as deeply recollected as Babbitt, Jennie Gerhardt, or even Eugene Witla? Compared with these how attenuated and slatternly composed are the fungous figures of J. Ward Moorehouse, Ben Compton, and Joe Williams! And three months after reading Dos Passos how many are able to distinguish Janey Stoddard from Eveline Hutchins?

Mr. Dos Passos's meretriciously naïve vernacular seems poor beside the prose of *Winesburg, Ohio.* Dismantle *42nd Parallel* or *1919* of its technical accoutrement—the blear-eyed camera eye, the newsreels, the superinduced biographical portraits—and what remains? Briefly, a sprawling, perforated narrative, dappled and dimpled with girlish Joycisms, which is as competent as the unheightened journalese of *Dodsworth,* one of Sinclair Lewis's worst novels.

For the Modern Library edition of *Three Soldiers* Mr. Dos Passos has recently done an introduction the rattling puerilities and gawkish perambulations of which beggar description. Expressing the dilemma of the modern writer in the following words: "Well, you're a novelist. What of it? What are you doing it for? What excuse have you got for not being ashamed of yourself?" Mr. Dos Passos then vouchsafes a new definition of the novel as well as a nostrum for the Doubting Thomases in the word racket: "A novel is a commodity that fulfils a certain need; people need to buy day dreams like they need to buy ice cream or aspirin or gin. . . . All you need to feel good about your work is to turn out the best commodity you can, play the luxury market, and to hell with doubt." The advice of this Marxist Lord Chesterfield to young authors seems much more like a sales letter addressed to what William James called the bitch goddess Success than a manifesto from a social-revolutionary novelist. Mr. Dos Passos and his left-wing backers ought to know that in a civilization in which novels are no more important than gin or ice cream there is little hope for a deeper culture and none for a revolution. But in literary matters the proletarian cheerleaders have always had the faculty of seeing everything but the obvious. However, it seems to be much more important to be on the bandwagon than to be either right or left.

The Nation, 1933

Lincoln Kirstein

THE FASTIDIOUS MOVEMENT

Flesh Is Heir, by Lincoln Kirstein

Mr. Lincoln Kirstein, the editor of *Hound and Horn,* may be grouped with a handful of young writers who represent the Fastidious Movement in American literature today. Though their achievements are still slender and tenuous, their aesthetic program is not to be dismissed. As a matter of fact, its importance has been far better exemplified in the provocative preface to Kenneth Burke's essayistic novel, *Towards a Better Life,* than in Mr. Kirstein's narrative, *Flesh Is Heir.* The publishers claim, speaking directly for their author, that the latter has written a novel without any traces of "naturalism" or "realism" in it. The entire statement is a humanistic pronouncement of sorts. Notwithstanding this, the only section of the book really worth reading strongly argues against the novelist's thesis, even disproves it.

The chapter titled "1922" is a closely knit chronicle of the institutional regimentation and life of a young boy in a preparatory school. This part of the novel is well detailed, and marked with incidents that bear a cogent resemblance to those unheightened occurrences and situations that clutter the pages of a Dreiser or a Sinclair Lewis. The prose, too, is amply sprinkled with slangy expressions and idiomatic turns that would seem out of place in a more formalized medium. The relationship between Roger Baum, an affluent Jew, explosively timorous, and Andy Stone, shiftless and sadistic, is compelling reading. Andy Stone, full of cruel, adolescent plans, and affecting a sub rosa knowledge of black magic, prognosticates that

213

Roger Baum will die soon. Roger Baum is doubtful but impressed. Aware of his power over Roger and wishing more, Andy Stone threatens to kill him on the night that there is a full moon. For Roger Baum the succeeding days thereafter are marked with illness, nightmares, repressions, and a poisonous reticence toward his schoolmates and masters. Andy Stone's presence, immediate and unseen, casts a hallucinatory aura over Roger Baum's waking and dream life, and not until Andy has left school does he manage to reintegrate himself.

The following chapter, "1924," dealing with the voluntary apprenticeship of Roger Baum in a stained-glass shop, is much slighter. And from then on the book dwindles into egregiously stereotyped conversations, unimportant peregrinations to London and Paris, and niggling autobiographical mementos. There are a few casual, hard-boiled episodes in the book: the seduction of a chorus girl by Andy Stone, her death, a shooting, an initiation, and a regurgitative frat scene—none of which is done in the eclectic and "unnaturalistic" manner.

Briefly, it seems that Mr. Kirstein has not been able to carry out his program because he has not yet sloughed off the influence that contemporary realistic readings have made upon him. And although in places he shows a talent for writing one can hardly recommend *Flesh Is Heir* either for its entertainment or its literary uniqueness.

The Nation, 1932

Down from the Ivory Tower

Harlan Miners Speak. The Report of the Dreiser Committee

The recent investigation of the Harlan miners' conditions by the writers' committee is significant not only because it has focused attention upon the misery of the coal diggers, heightened by the reign of terror and the lawlessness of Kentucky officials, but because it also marks a new era in American literature. This organized protest by contemporary literary men brings to an end a certain kind of old-fashioned bohemian aestheticism—the ballet poet living in his ivory tower ten thousand feet above politics.

This country, unlike France or Russia, has never been very arable soil for manifestos; whatever social and especially political coherence there has been among writers of the same period has been peripheral. There were "things in the air," historical currents, which did not so much unite these novelists as simultaneously impinge upon them. What better proof have we of this than the recent writings of Dreiser and Sherwood Anderson, their awakening in the late autumn of their careers to the need of group protest against injustice and oppression in the United States. For all their earnestness they are in a sense befuddled émigrés in their own land.

As a landmark in American prose and feeling, Sherwood Anderson's contribution to the present book is singularly arresting. In his essay, "I Want to Be Counted," an admixture of intuitive flashes and Midwestern cracker-box philosophizing about communism, he writes, and quite to the point: "We are, all of us, men and women living in one world while we think and feel, most of us, in an old and outworn world. We are living in one world, while we try to think and feel in another."

Concluding, he says that what is needed to assure Americans of their constitutional rights is fewer speakeasy citizens and more criminal syndicalists.

Aside from the chapters by Theodore Dreiser, John Dos Passos, Arnold Johnson, and others, the most interesting part of the book is that given over to the testimonies of the evasive Sheriff J. H. Blair and attorney William E. Brock of Harlan County. These Kentucky Socratic dialogues between Dreiser and the two officials have a cinema excitement about them, and are, besides, a commentary on the comedy of justice in that state's coal fields. The Dreyfus case seems like a political peccadillo compared with the high-handed and ruthless manner with which the Harlan law has dealt with the starving and persecuted miners.

A Washington hearing, which concludes the book, is a moving and disturbing account of the second expedition of the writers to Harlan, in which Waldo Frank and Allen Taub, an attorney for the International Labor Defense, were badly beaten by Kentucky merchants and reactionary zealots of the Ku Klux Klan variety.

Harlan Miners Speak is extremely important as an exposé of the cruel and harassing peonage which has been imposed upon our native pioneers. The Daughters of the American Revolution, so much absorbed in genealogy and taken up with pure blood, ought to raise a large fund for relief, so that these Kentucky miners, backwoodsmen of early Colonial stock, may not be completely wiped out by the coal operators and their henchmen. The book is significant, finally, as a symbol of a new tendency, an aesthetic, deeply tinctured by politics, which will leave its mark upon American letters and thinking.

The Nation, 1932

James T. Farrell

Young Lonigan, by James T. Farrell

Probably to avoid trouble with the Society for the Suppression of Vice, the publishers have chosen to issue *Young Lonigan* in a textbook format and to announce that it will be sold only to physicians, psychiatrists, teachers and social workers. In this way a grave injustice is done to the author. One gains the impression that the book is either a piece of sleazy erotica or a case history after the manner of Krafft-Ebing. It is neither one nor the other; it is in reality a novel, a very promising one, dealing with a Chicago gang in a spirit not dissimilar to that in which Michael Gold deals with the East Side in *Jews Without Money.*

The grown-up posturings of Studs Lonigan, his cigarette smoking and tobacco chewing, his adolescent hero-worship of boxers, his sexual daydreams, all stem from the hard-boiled Chicago street gang of which he is a part. The gang is the social unit. Its aspirations, its ethics, baseball and prize-fight slogans and tabloid ikons, when channeled into the world of business, racketeering and national politics, become our adult America. Briefly, our national pattern of life has its roots and source in the gang.

These South Side toughs steal milk bottles, raid candy stores and ice boxes, fight and stand on street corners watching broads go by, while making their estimates and decisions. Sex either softens them, makes them gushy and idealistic about women, or drives them into a predatory frenzy. For these adolescents it has all the secret fascination of lavatory inscriptions.

217

Much of the novel is written in the speech of Chicago's street arabs, the idiom of the tough guy, the monosyllables of the neighborhood idiot. In the hands of a lesser craftsman, these conversations would have been as irritating as talkie dialect. Farrell has rendered them with a convincing naturalness and hard integrity that give his book a place beside Erskine Caldwell and Robert Cantwell.

The background of the gang is the parochial school and Irish-American home life. The portrait of the family—old man Lonigan belching over the comic strips, Mrs. Lonigan exhorting Studs to pray and study that he may have a calling for the priesthood—are done with considerable deftness. The book ends with Studs adrift: having finished the eighth grade, he doesn't want to attend high school. Like Weary Reilley, who knows how to tell the old man and woman where to get off, he wants to have his own money, sleep with Lucy and be as scientific a puncher as Jim Corbett.

Young Lonigan, despite the manner of its publication, is not a study of the *psychopathia sexualis* of American boyhood. The emphasis, in reality, is on the texture of the language. Farrell's American idiom has a fresh pliancy and a kind of headlong vigor. With the development of these qualities he promises to go far as a writer.

New Republic, 1932

*

PORTRAIT OF THE GANGSTER

The Young Manhood of Studs Lonigan, by James T. Farrell

The cumulative effect of *Young Lonigan* (published 1932) and its sequel, *The Young Manhood of Studs Lonigan,* is exceedingly impressive. These two novels by James T. Farrell are the truest and most ruthless commentary upon street arab adolescence and manhood ever written in America. *Young Lonigan* is a study of a Chicago gang of boys from which our political life stems. Grown to maturity these drugstore cowboys, poolhall sharks, and killers on the make become ward heelers, racketeers and political leaders.

Since the characters belong somewhere in the upper brackets of the propertied classes, poverty is not the theme and the "mean streets" are not the milieu of either of these books. The special genre of brutal longings, the dehumanized, competitive desires, which characterize Studs Lonigan, the protagonist, belong to all America, and the sources from which they spring touch all shores and levels of society. The mind of the book, and not of the author, can be illustrated to some extent by the following: The reviewer, as a child, remembers looking into the window of a high-class cigar store and watching a thin, phthisical man, with a macabre, nicotine complexion, seated at a table, smoke one cigarette after another and drink milk and eat Hershey bars to sustain himself. This was in 1907 or 1908, and it was one of those horrendous endurance-contests to which the exacerbated wealthy as well as the shipping clerk go for their catharses.

Since then the American psyche has reaped the pentecost of new technological discoveries. There is the cartoon, with sound effects, out of which jump abstract ghouls, mice, ghosts, the dismembered imaginings of bad dreams; Walt Disney's confectionery fables for infantile minds. Then there were the Lloyd comedies of a few years back in which lovable, tortoise-shelled Harold invariably succeeded in whipping up the sadistic impulses of the "totalitarian" audience by precariously balancing himself on the ledge of a thirty-story window. This is the background without which we cannot understand the neuroses of Studs Lonigan, Weary Reilley, Paulie Haggerty, Davey Cohen, Barney Keefe and others.

These Chicago Attilas, when not attending the Catholic parochial school, raid candy stores, steal milk, and attempt to set in motion race riots in order to give their lives the dramatic atmosphere of Western pulp stories. Their sleazy pugilistic mores, their vandalistic and predatory habits of mind are harrowingly portrayed in a mimic war scene on a vacant lot. Standing in trenches which they have dug, these boys, protected by a Hooverville assortment of tin cans, boxes and barbed wire, hurl large rocks at one another. The raw, competitive motive of the American streets, which runs through our business, science, and art, is again made manifest in a football game in which the "home team" almost kills the fleet-footed Schwartz in order to win the game. And the same impulse of the street canaille is seen in a snapshot of Armistice Day on a Chicago El.

When the playmates of Studs Lonigan have flowered into manhood, "the Alky Squad of 58th Street," they become dipsomaniacs, contract venereal diseases, and die of tuberculosis. They are driven by the same kind of jungle appetites as compel Archibald MacLeish's Wall Street conquistadors to outstrip their competitors in power and prestige.

The one moment of relief and respite in the book comes when Studs, cowed by the death of Arnold Sheehan, decides to join a Y gymnasium so that he can trim down his alcoholic "aldermen" and live to be a centenarian. However, this feeling of penitence is fugitive, for at the close of the book Studs Lonigan is lying in the gutter, drunk and unconscious, after a New Year's rape party.

The two novels make a definite and original contribution to American literature. Unlike Jack Conroy's prose, which is the remnants of writing that has been done in the past five to seven years, Farrell's Americanese is enormously skilled and deeply fused.

Farrell's novels are the intransigent documents of a fellow-traveler, and doubtless will not please certain snipers in the ranks of the pseudo-Marxists—these sharpshooters, with one essay and one review in their belts, who have never made any deviations for the simple reason that they have never written one creative or critical line that will last. It is altogether regrettable that some of the more original and sensitive minds in the movement have not yet done a book on the Marxist approach to American literature and spared us some of the leftist hemorrhages.

It is true, there are no strikes or demonstrations in Farrell's novels. Besides that, there is scarcely a figure or a character that can be salvaged, and yet these books are highly serviceable to both workers and intellectuals.

If Mr. Farrell has taught us nothing more than how hooliganism arises, grows, and festers in this horrific America, and if he has shown us nothing else but where to look for the vandals, the Pelleys and Art Smiths, the American Storm Troopers, he has instructed us well and profoundly. Some day, in our future, classless society, readers will examine *The Young Manhood of Studs Lonigan,* and say, "Look what we were, and see what we have come through!"

New Masses, 1934

From Flushing to Calvary

I understand that one of the small, insurgent magazines has listed *Bottom Dogs* among the "defeatist" novels. Now for one thing, this seems to me to be a piece of egregiously sick leftism. Of course, it is true that all the bottom dog drifters and YMCA white collarites are ineluctably doomed at the outset of the novel. But no matter what one may charge this gelatinous mass of floating population with, it is certainly inaccurate to lay defeatism upon their backs also, because that implies a choice, which they have never had, simply because they never knew they had one. For one of the very few reasons that they don't take their hunger and social abasement singing the "Internationale" is that they have never heard of it. Never heard of communism. Words like *Bolshevism* either do not exist in their vocabulary at all, or are at best a kind of obscenity to be included in the national lavatory esoterica. And it is this American phenomenon which the *New Masses* and other intransigent organs of the left wing do not appear to be sensible of in their manifestos on "proletarian" literature.

In the same manner of political pique I have heard John Reeders and communists run down Soglow's drawings of starving, sullen and distraught workers. They object to their faces because they are not chirpy enough. Soglow's "pessimism" gets under their skins. They seem to expect emaciated strikers and miners doubled over with the "flux" (at least on canvases and on the printed page) to have that beatific and hollow smiling look of collegiate cheerleaders.

At the close of *Bottom Dogs* we leave Lorry, tortured and cowering, hoping that he may get the clap so that he can have the arctic white, clean sheets and the medical immaculateness of a venereal ward in a Los Angeles charity hospital. And in the final chapter of *From Flushing to Calvary* there is Lorry, starving and derelict, caught up in a communist riot at Union Square. An innocent bystander, he has been the victim of one of Grover Whalen's courteous cops. Lying on the pavement, the blood stingingly humming over the wound, he furtively lifts his head. A red flag is floppily streaming around the corner. It looks to him like one of those auctioneer's flags he has seen in front of furniture warehouses.

Through Washington Square and out of the book he walks, tightening his belt, the blood clotting over his head, and chanting a chapel hymn which he had sung when he was an inmate of an orphan asylum in Cleveland:

> 'neath its folds, defeat unknown,
> triumph, triumph, crowns our glorious way.

Now in order to please the communists I might have had Lorry at the end dash up to the *New Masses* offices or elsewhere and ask for membership in the Party. But then I would no longer be a novelist but a liar. For this would no more be possible for Lorry than for that other pathetic American protagonist in Dreiser's *An American Tragedy*.

Trotsky says, in *Literature and the World Revolution,* an extremely shrewd and provocative book of literary criticism, that it is not necessary to write about factories, munition plants or industrial strikes in order to create "proletarian" literature. And in the same manner of reasoning it is not essential to superimpose radicalism upon the American scene in order to indict or by implication present a bourgeois community from a revolutionary point of view. And implication literature can have just as deep a radical dye. Nor is it correct to inject communism into certain farming and agrarian sections of Missouri or Nebraska when those parts of the country have never really been penetrated by a Marxist ideology.

Perhaps something of the background and the narrative of *From Flushing to Calvary* should be indicated here. Incidentally, the two books can be read independently of one another.

It is no longer the scene so much, as in *Bottom Dogs,* which is the protagonist, as the kick-about figures who pass through it. And they only pass through it, for they never act but react upon their environment.

Lorry and his mother Lizzie live in Bensonhurst, a rheumy borough of New York, glutted with hardware dealers and delicatessen storekeepers. A former lady barber in Kansas City she tries her hand at beauty treatments of a sort so as to have some independence and be less burdensome to her son who is supporting her. She pares toenails and callouses, becomes something of a house-to-house canvasser for the violet ray. Her best prospects are ailing ones, for when she is unable to sell them, she usually manages to give them violet ray treatments for their lumbago or rheumatism.

Lizzie Lewis has all the hopes of the American nurtured on advertising slogans and fake nostrums for the poor derived from real estate ads and bill posters. Nothing ever quite downs her. She always believes her ship will yet come in. After these ventures have petered out, she decides to dabble and speculate in marriages. She puts advertisements in the matrimonial journals, borrowing noble sentiments and grammar from *Tom Jones* or *Manon Lescaut,* which Lorry has been reading. Believing in having a number of irons in the fire, she also takes up the profession of a quack abortionist. She has an Indian remedy which Cecile Henty, a Kansas City lady barber and part-time prostitute, had told her about years ago.

During the Christmas shopping season she is for a moment a cutpurse Moll Flanders. But as a shoplifter she barely escapes.

But both mother and son are doomed. Lorry, at first an assistant shipping clerk in a cigar factory and then a newsbutcher in the subway station, has nothing left but a homesickness for the orphan asylum, which is a kind of psychical umbilical cord he has never broken. Both have a nostalgia for the past, which is as horrific and harrowing as the present, but which appears less so, because it is the past, and because at least they have their roots there. She still regrets the day that she gave up her lady barber shop, and Lorry wants to and does run away from his mother to return to the orphanage in Cleveland. And only then does he discover that he is in no place and that no place is in him.

There is a long procession of other characters in the book. Lizzie's marital prospects, pregnant patients, their chronicle of opinions and schemes: and they are just as anxious to do her as she them.

Her one roomer, Willy Huppert, has come from Dusseldorf to earn some of the money to be had in Jack Dempsey's country. And according to the Americana pattern of success, when he is knocked out in the ring, he then takes singing lessons so that he can have a career as a radio broadcaster. At the end of two years in America he has succeeded in acquiring a secondhand suit of 14th Street clothes, an imitation leather bag, a going-out-of-business pair of shoes, a venereal disease and ulcers of the stomach.

And there is Jerry Calefonia, an Argentinian, who has a bicycle shop on 18th Avenue, Bensonhurst, who is seen in his cell for a crime of rape he didn't commit, weeping: "Cheap peoples live here!"

The inevitability of failure of the dollarless American trapped in a capitalistic society is one of the essential themes of the book.

What the author has tried to indicate here is not Lawrence's *Look! We Have Come Through,* but Look! What has come through us!

Contempo, 1932

Kenneth Fearing:
A Poet for Workers

Poems, by Kenneth Fearing

The evolution of the author of *Angel Arms* is amazing, and his place in American literature is not so easy to define as a glance at his book would immediately suggest. So close to America, he is actually more in the tradition of the French Symbolists. There is very much in his life, temperament and talents that recall Tristan Corbière. His fantastic patterns of slang and speech, "reasoned derangements of all the senses," his gargoylish diableries, are those of a Tristan Corbière, torn out of context and place, but a Corbière with Marxian insights. *Angel Arms,* published in 1929, was a slender but gifted volume of lean ironies, acid portraits of Woolworth shopgirls and New Yorkese cadences of doggerel lives.

In his *Poems* he has succeeded in inditing the sleazy cinema dreams, the five and dime loves and frustrations, the mystery pulp heroism and furnished room microcosm of the pulverized petty bourgeois. And this he has done with a novelist's technic; for besides being poems they are, in effect, short novels, with all the day-to-day thickness of incident, smell, dust, walls of the French nouvelles.

The poems have also the narrative development of the novel: at the beginning, there are close-ups of the bought magistrates, the disincarnated radio voice, the swivel-chair magnates, heard in private monologue and seen in "unrehearsed acts." The theme unscrolls and the "bargain heroes" stalk across the screen: the Will Hayses, the Gene Tunneys, the Al Capones—and "the ectoplasm" of the "profitable smile hovers inescapably everywhere about us."

By now the venal movie-cathedral mores have been established; the fatuity and "steam-heated grief" of the dividend-rulers, with their covert, nasty sense of guilt have been witnessed. The actual horror show then begins, but the most profoundly moving cinematographic horror show in contemporary poetry. Stephen Spender's "The city builds a horror in his brain," is an etiolated abstract statement the specific truth and specter of which is to be found in Kenneth Fearing's poems.

The tinfoil hopes, the thwarted aspirations and hollywood-esque ikons of the hopeless lower middle class are disclosed. It is a crushed procession of recumbent rooming house souls soaked in mazed, sanitarium dreams but forever being awakened by evictions and hunger. "You were decorated forty-six times in rapid succession by the King of Italy, took a Nobel Prize. Evicted again, you went downtown, slept at the movies." They listen to the obscenely unctuous Radio Voice, seeking "the rib of sirloin wrapped in papal documents."

The poet interweaves comments done with a newsreel eye but with inexorable Marxist interpretations: "All winter she came there begging for milk. So we had the shacks along the river burned by fire." "The child was nursed on Government bonds. Cut its teeth on a hand grenade. Grew fat on shrapnel. . . . Laughed at the bayonet through its heart." Here is the entire cycle of life and death today; and here are lines from a deeply imagined poem which make a perfect slogan.

Fearing is relentlessly tortured and for a moment it would seem as if despair were in the ascendancy. There is a funerary cry: "Something must be saved . . . from the rats and the fire on the city dumps; something for warmth through the long night of death." But in "Dénouement," a poem which, were it extended, would be a major piece of our times, the poet, looking beyond the horizon toward a socialist civilization, a Vita Nuova of the workers, sings out:

227

Sky be blue, and more than blue; wind, be flesh and blood, flesh
   and blood, be deathless;
walls, streets, be home;
desire, of millions, become more real than warmth and breath
   and strength and bread.

Kenneth Fearing's irony is very special, unique in the history
of American poetry. Were it not freighted with pity and a
gnarled, pulsating tenderness it would be a leer. But here is
one of the most perfect examples of satire in literature in its
truest light, that is, in its most tragic hue. It is as if Satire had
ironically disrobed herself.

His names, symbols, Beatrice Fairfax, Jesse James, Aimee
Semple McPherson, selected with uniform intention, are to
make use of his own words, Rialto Equations. Thus the aspos-
trophe to Beatrice Fairfax becomes clear: she is a reversed
Dantean Beatrice in a Paramount moving picture Vita Nuova.
And this is as near to Rimbaud's hell as any mortal would care
to approach.

Behind these equations, these "reasoned derangements,"
is satire turned upside down, that is, horror and revulsion.
Underneath the "death-ray smile," anguish and torture. The
reader must reverse every ironic comment and title to uncover
the true intention.

The poet's outlook, which in *Angel Arms* was like an elliptical
recollection of the laughing gas of rodents in a dismembered
dream, becomes something very positive in the *Poems.* Here
the intuitions and picture are an accusation and a foreshadow-
ing of the doom of the whole capitalistic society: "Maggots and
darkness will attend the alibi." And as the poems in their
chronological progression become more incisive and attain
Marxian lucidity, the caustic comments rise; expand into an
affirmative communist statement.

We should pause to sample the kind of telling irony in the
poems, as in "What if Jesse James Should Some Day Die?"

> Where will we ever again find food to eat, clothes to wear, a
> roof and a bed, now that the Wall Street plunger has gone to
> his hushed, exclusive, paid-up tomb?
> How can we get downtown today, with the traction king
> stretched flat on his back in the sand at Miami Beach?

Compare this with a passage in a somewhat similar vein out
of Cecil Day Lewis's *The Magnetic Mountain:*

> As for you, Bimbo, take off that false face!
> You've ceased to be funny, you're in disgrace.
> We can see the spy through the painted grin;
> You may talk patriotic but you can't take us in.

Lewis and Auden, gifted poets, Oxonians and sincere
communist sympathizers, are uneasy whenever they fall into
colloquialisms; their satire has a platitudinous glitter—rhythm
also becomes pedestrian. Their uncertainty and banality in
direct communication has a very definite class basis. In the use
of pasquinade and the speech of the masses in poetry Fearing is
not only at his best but has no peer either here or abroad.

Examine the texture of bitterness, and elegiac tenderness
for the oppressed, in "Lullaby," almost entirely wanting in the
bohemian poet of *Angel Arms:*

> are the trees that line the country estates, tall as the lynch trees,
> as straight, as black;
> is the moon that lights the mining towns; dim as the light upon
> tenement roofs, grey upon the hands at the bars of Moabit,
> cold as the bars of the Tombs.

Or in his "and let the paid-up rent become South Sea Music," a
song of the unemployed.

Doubtless, some of the cash-register columnists will utter:
"Mean streets and sordid lives in verse." For whenever a writer
has revealed what is ghastly true in present-day society they
have dismissed his book with this sort of cant headline. But the
poet here can reply: "Did I create these mean streets, this
hunger, this dollar sordidness?"

Kenneth Fearing's poems are never precious or esoteric. In essentials, they are close to the mood of the oppressed.

Kenneth Fearing is a poet for workers; his poems are deeply incarnadined in evictions, strikes, homelessness, protest; but his appeal is not restricted to his class. His poetry, for those who are still wavering, is one more piece of documented evidence of the horrible mutilation of human dreams and nobleness under capitalism. In very truth, such a fecund talent belongs especially to us.

New Masses, 1935

Robert Smith

CITY BIPEDS

One Winter in Boston, by Robert Smith

Dealing with the life and loves of a Boston shoe clerk, this novel is stereopticon American realism, with many previous examples upon which it is modeled. Robert Smith is quite as gifted at this sort of studied, pulseless naturalism, as most. What one cannot tell is how much experience such a writer is concealing. For he must expunge his esthetic sensibilities to achieve this artistic deception.

The young people in the shoe department of Ballard, Mason have the most wizened human limits. They are not minds; they are, as Mr. Smith indicates, strengthless mortal objects. One has "thin hair like wet feathers"; another is a "swarthy man in oversize clothes." The young Ballard esthete, son of the shoe merchant, is a "skinny, studious monster," and the rest of Boston humanity is a "clot of pedestrians."

The persons in this novel do not even have enough volition to leave their sick, swart rooms (which are the memorials of their inward malady) and go into the parks or to the river. Almost any regional bumpkin, who has the roots of hills, oaks, fields, in his nature, is a savant compared with these simian city bipeds. This reader, for one, closed Mr. Smith's novel refusing to believe that everyone on this economic and social level can be of such emasculated human texture.

New York Times Book Review, 1950

Giuseppe Berto

ARMS AND THE PEASANTS

The Works of God: And Other Stories,
by Giuseppe Berto (trans. Angus Davidson)

"The Works of God," the novelette in this volume by Giuseppe Berto, a gifted Italian author, is a tender pastoral. This chronicle of Italy's peasants is a clean, artless narrative of a wine-sodden old farmer, Mangano, his wife, a son and daughter, the daughter-in-law, a small grandson, a squealing pig, a few hens, a cow, and a two-wheeled wagon. It is also the record of the war which embittered and hurt the earth and dismembered peaceful rural families.

The military has told the peasants to leave the valley town; and as the family pack the bicycle, the mattress, the sewing machine into the cart, Mangano's sole anxiety is that the seven-month-old pig, with the powerful voice, should not be slaughtered out of season. Mangano's other demand is that the demijohn of wine be put into the two-wheeled cart. The family set out with the cart, to which the pig and the hens are tied. They walk on the asphalt road painted with moonlight and swollen with tangled metal masses of army trucks, the old woman stroking the head of her grandson, Filippo, and Mangano cursing his daughter-in-law, and talking to the pig, for whom he had a more intimate earth closeness than he felt for his cow or hens.

It is a mountain evening, pale with mist that softly lights up and garments the pebble-bed of the river. They trundle the cart until one of the massive army trucks strikes against its wheel. Some of the hens are killed, the squealing pig is thrown to the road, and the demijohn of rustic wine is spilt. This is the beginning of the demise of the family as a household group. Then Mangano steps on a mine, and two simple, warm-fleshed animals, the man and the pig, are blown to pieces.

The old woman moans about the inscrutable works of God. She covers her face with a black handkerchief, and weeps for the hens, the pig, the broken cart, for Mangano, who has been a gentle husband, laboring in the furrow, before he had been a soldier in a previous war.

There are three short stories besides this. Death is at the root of the other stories, as it is in all art and literature. In "Lull at Cassino" the soldiers draw lots to determine who shall risk his life on a scouting mission; in "The War Passed over Us" the soldier goes back to the place where his wife had died to rehearse in his piercing memory her final agony; and "The Need to Die" is about the last moments of a young partisan.

It is a sensitive little book, translated into plain nourishing words by Angus Davidson; and it is a good, healing remedy for people who have not the quiet and ease that rural images yield to the head, the nerves and the hands.

New York Times Book Review, 1950

Charles Baudelaire

THE POET WHO HATED NATURE

Baudelaire, by Jean-Paul Sartre (trans. Martin Turnell)

Though this little book by Jean-Paul Sartre was not written to increase the understanding of Baudelaire's verse, the reader will return to *The Flowers of Evil* and to the poet's letters with a wiser and more seasoned palate. Fortunately, the volume is not marred by the oddities of the existential language or the cruder and stale psychoanalytical vocabulary. There are some droll aspects of this study of the mental and nervous disorders of Charles Baudelaire, and after a while the catalogue of vices and maladies of the poet read like Lombroso's portrait of the genius as the insane and the epileptic. Besides, not all of Baudelaire's debauched habits are remarkable, as Sartre and some of the disciples of Satanism in literature believe.

Sartre himself asks what the relation is between poetry and evil, and whether verse is not impaired because the poet had ignoble and base traits. It seems to be an unnecessary interrogation, for the verse is the disgrace and the depravity in the man who created it, and certainly Baudelaire never took the trouble to hide his profligate nature, but rather sought to find novel and startling forms and symbols for it.

What can be said is that many of the poems are rather common and not surprising at all, because Baudelaire's vices were not so unusual, and are to a great extent just the general orthodoxies of present-day literary diabolism. It is also hard to believe that Baudelaire's sexual peculiarities any more than Aristotle's make either good or bad philosophy or literature. We are too often reminded that many people have all of

Baudelaire's abnormalities and are not artists but just hapless bores.

Pascal said that man is neither angel nor beast; he is rather the Baudelairean angelical brute that works and writes, and is terribly bored and lonely. Baudelaire, we know, wrote many bad lines, which are probably the result of some of his banal vices. However, if all of Baudelaire's turpitudes are not as brilliant as his disciples believe, one cannot disregard the prose poems on the sensual torpor of a stagnant pond, or those prolific clumps of trees and vegetation which he loathed because they reminded him of childbirth, or the onyx and jasper in the Garden of Lucifer, which are equivalents of bejeweled sins and precise thoughts.

Baudelaire wrote very little, because he hated nature, which was a symbol of abundance and parturition. Sartre writes: "A city is a perpetual creation; its buildings, smells, sounds and traffic belong to the human kingdom. Everything in it is poetry in the strict sense of the term. It is in this sense that the electrically operated advertisements, neon lights and cars which about the year 1920 roused the wonder of young people were profoundly Baudelairean." Baudelaire's ideal metaphysical city has no plant life, and thus his best poems are hard, flat, sterile minerals. Although he believed in the implacable rational lucidity of a poem, Baudelaire had a valiant detestation of determinism, and thought that man should exercise his freedom to create and objectify his identity.

It is easy to select the obvious paradoxes in Charles Baudelaire, but some of them provide us with gentle, ironic mirth. He made a cult of work, although he never wanted to undertake anything. He was a recluse who never went anywhere without a companion. Sartre says that he wanted a consecrated solitude with people in it. He suffered so from the sterile agitations of ennui that it took him six months to decide on a journey to a neighboring village.

235

This enfant terrible, who wanted to give the bourgeoisie the most bizarre affront, believed that if the French Academy accepted him, people would no longer suspect him. Poor Baudelaire, he was rejected by the gentlemen of the Academy because they regarded him as such a suspicious character!

This book is a speculative experience for anyone interested in the mysticism and mystery of evil. The fragments from Baudelaire's letters are as good as the prose poems.

New York Times Book Review, 1950

Algernon Blackwood

MOON-MADNESS

Tales of the Uncanny and Supernatural,
by Algernon Blackwood

These supernatural tales are not the usual Gothic ghost shudders. There is a good deal of personal mysticism rather than the preternatural in these mystery tone-poems. Some of the stories, like "The Touch of Pan," are social commentary veiled as legend. The hero of the tales is the reticent English character, who is not impervious at all, as Colonel Masters in "The Doll." The doll, the plaything of the Colonel's step-daughter, has malevolent and sexual magic. The gaunt-lipped protagonist in "The Touch of Pan," weary of profligacy, falls in love with a wood nymph and becomes a satyr.

The reserved Englishman in "Running Wolf" is fishing at Medicine Lake in the Canadian woods. An immobile timber wolf with human faculties watches him. The wolf is the spirit of a deceased Indian who had slain a wolf, totem animal of the tribe. The wolf maintains its vigil until the sportsman digs up the bones of the Indian and buries him.

In "The Little Beggar," a bachelor, living out his wan and punitive memories at his club and flat, goes into the streets each day to observe little boys and girls, his substitute children, at play. One of the boys calls him father and shows him an empty bag which contains the man's future. The boy and the vacant bag vanish, and the man with his desiccated memories returns to his flat.

"The South Wind" is a tale about a man in a high Alpine valley with emptied streets, a stone church, and metaphysical hotels. In the supernatural village is a deep bed of a killed stream, and the wind god or demon blows through the bare poplars on "viewless feet."

New York Times Book Review, 1950

Mary McCarthy

STALEMATED PEOPLE

Cast a Cold Eye, by Mary McCarthy

Cast a Cold Eye is a volume of short stories done in a fatigued, metronomic prose. The stories are essays on wedlock, and everybody is so bored in this book that it reminds one of Kant's definition of marriage as the exchange of sexual properties for economic convenience, except that the married couple in "Weeds," the first story, are so tired that it is very doubtful that there is any sort of exchange. "Weeds" is a garden narrative, as the opening line shows: "She would leave him, she thought, as soon as the petunias had bloomed." Which is a rotten time for a woman to leave a man. The parched young wife spends her days in her *psychopathia sexualis* garden of boredom, planting petunias, scabiosa, perennials, and other Freudian and Jungian flowers, because the husband has no ardor within himself and is too drained to compete with the seed catalogues.

"The Friend of the Family" is another story about a stalemated couple who are too exhausted and pithless to be cohesive or plainly disjunctive. This neuter relationship is somehow saved or simply prolonged by Francis Cleary, a bachelor who is neither quite male nor feminine; he hasn't enough lucid sexual identity to be clearly defined. Francis Cleary acts as a substitute husband, although he does not commit adultery; Francis does not commit anything. There is a piece of political doctrine oddly interpolated in this story. Miss McCarthy promises the reader that the world will have Francis Clearys so long as people refuse to accept Marx's "From each according to his capacities, to each according to his needs." This is droll dialectics and ought to make an impression even upon an anti-Marxian reader who would be willing to submit to any dogma to rid the American novel of Francis Cleary.

All the stories in this volume are stale, smart eroticism. One gets very weary of the up-to-date, tired sex in the fiction of the present-day street-gamin intelligentsia. There is so much of this *chic mademoiselle* pornography which parades as Marxism and great moral realism. Actually, it is just straight W. C. scatological novel-writing, and is altogether faked and very tired.

The Freeman, 1950

Sören Kierkegaard

Kierkegaard the Cripple, by Theodore Haecker
(trans. C. Van O. Bryn)

This monograph on Sören Kierkegaard by the late Theodore
Haecker is a remarkable study. Haecker was too sage and kind
to make foolish or rigid judgments about Kierkegaard's sickly
body. Though Kierkegaard referred to his crooked back as a
"hideous poultice," few of his disciples suspected that he was
a cripple. Haecker knew that pessimism is not the inevitable
result of poor health or penury. Schopenhauer had money and
considerable physical zest. However, Byron, Leopardi and
Richard III, whom Kierkegaard often mentioned, had that
malignant gloom which comes from a misshapen foot or back.
Kierkegaard, no less tormented than Richard, who commanded
his soldiers to blow the trumpets so that he would not hear his
mother's curses, could write in his diary, after he had been
rejected by a lady from Copenhagen: "She did not like my
handsome nose, my beautiful eyes, and my small feet. . . !"

Kierkegaard's critics have looked for the secrets of his nature
and works in the love affair with Regine Olson. Kierkegaard
had broken the engagement because he said that marriage was
not his vocation. A more simple explanation is that Kierkegaard
was bored. It does not matter that Regine was beautiful; what is
important is that Kierkegaard was disfigured, that men with
such defects are often arrogant with women. When Kierkegaard wrote about women he liked to see himself in the role of
the seducer, and it was no accident that he had said that one
can only persuade those whom one can seduce.

The evil genius in Kierkegaard was congenital ennui, which made him both simple-hearted and artful. For though he wrote about the lilies and the birds with the humility of the child, he also enjoyed listening to a repulsive man, just to watch the gemmed sweat roll down his cheeks.

Kierkegaard regarded himself as an apostle, though he hated pity, and, of course, could be pitiless. If he was not as good as he wanted to be, or as Haecker thought he should have been, the fault was in nature, and, perhaps, in that crooked back. Maybe only some of Kierkegaard's readers will care for Haecker's metaphysical speculations, but all will look at the drawings and the caricatures of Kierkegaard with a new interest that will make them consider once more the work and the life of the dialectical hunchback of Denmark.

New York Times Book Review, 1950

Fyodor Dostoevsky

GREAT PARABLE

Fyodor Dostoevsky, by René Fülöp-Miller
(trans. Richard and Clara Winston)

Although this is a critical book on Dostoevsky, the admirers of that epileptical saint of literature will learn much more from the life of the novelist than from Fülöp-Miller. However, it may be that the greatest novel and parable is Dostoevsky's life. Dostoevsky died, shortly after completing *The Brothers Karamazov,* reaching for a pen that had dropped. This exertion brought on a hemorrhage. However, Dostoevsky's pen was no more fatal or fantastic than his experiences. . . . At four o'clock in the morning a friend and the poet Nekrasov came to announce that the author of *Poor Folk,* Dostoevsky's first novel, was a genius. A few days later there was another knock on the door, and this time the gendarmes and some cossacks advised him that he was a conspirator and took him to the grim Peter and Paul Fortress. Dostoevsky had been seen talking to a group of young political enthusiasts about Fourier and Herzen.

The forced labor in Siberia, which was horrible enough, yielded less to the novelist than the fantastic comedy of misfortunes which were his after his release. The real steam-bath prison, as Dostoevsky said in a letter, was his first marriage. Just married, he was traveling with his wife in a coach behind which was her lover in a carriage. When Dostoevsky established himself and his wife in a Petersburg flat, he had to support her lover because he was unemployed. When his wife, who was a crazy consumptive, was dying, she insisted that he wind up clocks until the springs broke, and then demanded

243

that he put them together again.

Dostoevsky's poverty was also very bizarre and appears to belong more to literature than to life. He was not only fantastic with women because he was poor, he was perhaps a more ridiculous figure with them than Othello or foolish Lear. Dostoevsky fell in love with Polina, who is the heroine of the wittiest book he ever wrote, *The Gambler*. Few people have given Dostoevsky sufficient credit for being very clever. He could not hold Polina because he had no money, and so she fell in love with a rich Spaniard who quickly deserted her. However, Dostoevsky was no man to leave a woman who had cuckolded him. Raging with jealousy, he went at once to the casino to make a miraculous coup at the gambling tables to win back Polina. Dostoevsky had worked out a number system based on mystical intuition, arithmetic and chance, and won! But gambling so eased him of the chagrins of jealousy that he forgot all about Polina until he lost the greater part of what he had won. By the time he rejoined the deserted Polina, Dostoevsky had to pawn some of her luggage and clothes so that he could return to the green tables of chance.

There was nothing grubby about Dostoevsky's poverty, painful though it was. When Dostoevsky was in a gloomy room in one of those resort and bath towns in Germany, the proprietor of the hotel refused to give him meals on credit, although he did allow him hot tea twice a day. Dostoevsky, to avoid embarrassing the hotel guests as well as himself, rose an hour earlier so as not to pass the tables during meals and returned in the evenings after dinner, but found that his walks had increased his appetite enormously. Then, to forget food and his general wretchedness, he wrote novels and prepared notes for other books until the tallow candle burned down. When the hotelkeeper declined to give him another candle on credit, he sent out many letters to friends and publishers entreating them for money, and mailed them without stamps!

Then his beloved brother, Michael, died, and left a widow

and three children, and just enough roubles for his burial expenses. Dostoevsky supported them, and also took over the magazine, the *Epocha,* which Michael had founded, as well as its debts, something like 25,000 roubles. Dostoevsky was pursued by creditors, and had to accept a 3,000 rouble advance from an infamous publisher who demanded a lengthy novel to be finished on a certain day. This publisher also exacted of Dostoevsky all rights to his previous works should he fail to complete the book on time. Dostoevsky went to work on *Crime and Punishment,* but he also wanted to write about the gambling passion at the casinos, for with Dostoevsky his own droll agony was never very far behind the book. However, he did write *Crime and Punishment,* but was unable to deliver the manuscript to the publisher, who had left Petersburg to avoid receiving it so that he could claim Dostoevsky's novels. Fortunately, Dostoevsky's new young wife very cannily took the manuscript to the police station.

Epileptic fits were as useful to him as a novelist as his ridiculous gambling, the liaison with Polina, and his miserable but eccentric penury. Dostoevsky, like Mahomet, found his vision, his Prince Myshkin, through epileptic trances. Mr. Fülöp-Miller writes that after Oscar Wilde left Reading Gaol he was defunct as an artist, but Dostoevsky's mischances with women, the Siberian prison, and even the debts and the scurvy pawnbrokers to whom he had to go repeatedly, were not only no hindrances but provided him with the materials for the tales and the novels. Dostoevsky's life was itself de luxe genius, and as important as his astonishing books.

The Freeman, 1950

Colonial Writers

Time in New England. Photographs by Paul Strand,
text selected and edited by Nancy Newhall

The fragments from Colonial writers have been selected with taste by Nancy Newhall, and the remarkable photographs, by Paul Strand, of a tombstone or a stark church facade, are done with plain honesty, lacking any of the camera cant which sometimes makes the rude, pilgrim villages a sham Canaan.

There is the 1629 fragment, by Francis Thompson, chronicling the hopes of the voyagers who saw "yellow gilliflowers on the sea" and a Massachusetts shore that was a ripe, May meadow. But from the next piece, by James Pierpont, we see the tender, summery faith succeeded by January hardships, tears and prayers and long wilderness rains. Then there is Captain Edward Johnson's mention of early American artisans, the coopers, the glaziers, the nailors, the blacksmiths—men whose skills are almost as defunct today as some of the comely, but residual, epitaph towns like Ipswich, Salem and Concord, for which a megalopolitan, macadam American pines.

The text and the photographs make a clean and truthful American parable; one has, however, some niggling criticism to make. It is regrettable that the Anne Bradstreet poem has been included. Some university trade academic is always tormenting his students by getting out a book of some bad or negligible Colonial muse. Someone is always spuriously fattening our Parnassus, giving us the famine kine, the Anne Bradstreet poems, while neglecting the good, doughty writing of *The Simple Cobbler of Aggawam,* by Nathaniel Ward.

*

Bradford's History of Plymouth, edited by William T. Davis,
and Bradford's *Of Plymouth Plantation,* edited by
Samuel Eliot Morison

Here are two editions of the *History of Plymouth Plantation*
by Governor William Bradford. It is no easy choice to make
between them. The Knopf book [Morison's] is handsome, but
the Barnes and Noble volume is likely to fetch certain American
readers because it is done in the old Pilgrim spelling.

Much of the Plymouth chronicle and gospel is foul, dun
weather. As one reads of the marvelous desolations of the
Plymouth settlers, half of whom perished the first winter,
one cannot put out of his mind the word "plantation." The
Puritans from Leyden, clad in loathsome clothes, and setting
out with little butter, and no soles to mend their shoes, arrived
not in Canaan but, as one writer has said, in a "new-found
Golgotha." The settlers did not know how to sow English peas
and wheat in the new sands, or how to catch eels or to plant
maize. They had chosen the mean tidewater flats of Massachusetts as their seat; the soil was unfruitful and pitiless, and the
wintry pines and dunes were of a nature to diminish the soul.
The Plymouth settlers suffered even greater hardships than the
companions of Aeneas who ate their wooden trenchers when
they were hungry. Edward Winslow brought over the first
three heifers and a bull, but the Cape Cod and Plymouth
country is not good dairy country.

Besides hunger and exposure and the Cape Cod winds, the
most sorrowful fever of the Pilgrims was loneliness. A few
years before the settlers had come, Captain John Smith had

gone in a boat around the coast of Boston Bay, and had been amazed at the comeliness of the savages and the plenitude of corn, mulberries, grapes; but in so short a space of time had the entire race of Algonquin Indians died of the 1616-17 pestilence that "their souls and bones" were found in many places "lying still above ground."

The sight of a shallop coming from the Old World was a windfall from God to the lonely, stricken figures in the American wilderness. Often enough the captains were sharking traders who gave little for the beaver skins and clapboard of the Plymouth people; while the crews were knaves from the alleys of London. However, the colonists, weak from "short commons," were compelled to go with these rogues to Maine or to windy, sour Cape Cod seeking fish and a few hogsheads of beans and corn. The vessels foundered in the "dangerous shoulds and roring breakers," and on one occasion Bradford and Standish had to return on foot for fifty miles through the wild, biting snows until they arrived at the miserable huts of the settlement. The Plymouth community was just and orderly, but starvation was such an affliction that they furtively ate the green stalks or stole, "though many were well whipt for a few ears of corn, yet hunger made others to venture."

There was trouble, too, with the savage Narragansetts, who sent them new arrows encased in rattlesnake skin—a sign that they were ready for war. Some tribes had mutilated and enslaved mariners and explorers. Captain John Dermer, who went each season to the Maine fishing stations, had been duped and mortally wounded by Indians, and two vessels of French traders had been done away with. Though the Reverend Cotton Mather observed eighty years later the "woods were almost cleared of these pernicious creatures, to make room for a better growth," the savages received sufficient indignities from marauders who came to the American New Canaan for purposes that would be given more credit in a Liverpool alehouse than in a Puritan pew.

Much of the strength of Massachusetts lies in the annals of the Indian natives, with which Bradford's gospel and Captain John Smith's documents are filled. What is still extant in New England are the residual Indian names—for example, Patuxet, which means Plymouth, or the Squanton headlands. Squanto, the tutelary deity of Quincy, was the Indian friend of the Plymouth settlers. He showed them how to plant maize in the miserable Cape Cod soil, teaching them to set fish with the seed in the ground; he also told them of the beaver skins, and when the famished Pilgrims knew not where to look for manna, Squanto gave them fat eels.

These marvelous chronicles are dear memorials to our sick and corrupt modern commonwealth, and American poets are commencing to turn to them for a truer regard for honesty and vision than present-day experience furnishes. Besides Bradford's history, there is the vigorous *Three Episodes of Massachusetts History,* by the nineteenth-century annalist Charles Francis Adams, who made rich use of the records which William Bradford and John Winthrop have bequeathed to us. We must go to primeval American archives for myths to equal in truth and bravery the old account of Jason's expedition to Colchis for the golden fleece.

The Freeman, 1953

John Donne

Donne's Poetry and Modern Criticism, by Leonard Unger

These abstruse platonisms on John Donne do not tell the reader anything about his poetry, but are a clear revelation of a type of pompous criticism that is boring to the gods and to men. Mr. Unger, who is at least the peer of Allen Tate in syntax folly, tells us that Mr. Tate's language "is not near the denoting end of the line," and who would deny it, or affirm it?

Mr. Unger writes that metaphysical poetry is "the development of imagery by logical extension," which ought to mean that a poet develops his images rather reasonably. He may or may not do it, and no one will ever find out from Mr. Tate or Mr. Unger or from a poet that Socrates said could never explain his own work. After Mr. Unger has cited Mr. Tate and Mr. Ransom and Mr. Grierson, and again Mr. Tate (the list begins to sound like a merry-go-round), he assures us that metaphysical poetry is probably just wit. He quotes from John Crowe Ransom: "No one ought to remove the comparisons from their poems," because we are likely to "demolish . . . the poem." Such erudite gibberish is literary illiteracy; like legal English, it is a direct dagger attack against all English.

The Freeman, 1951

Ezra Pound

The Letters of Ezra Pound, 1907-1941, edited by D. D. Paige

These letters of Ezra Pound are for the quick and the cantankerous, and for poets, who, Horace said, belong to the most
irascible tribe of men. Pound's negations are the groundwork
for a whole poetry culture, and there is much sound advice in
the letters for the neophyte writer. Pound urged the novice to
study Catullus, Leopardi and Villon to prevent him from
"imitating the false classics." He had the scantiest regard for
the caitiff illiterates of the arts, demanding that a poet be a
vigorous reader. "Nacre and objets d'art" poesy was as repulsive to him as the rabble intellect, for he had just as little use for
the aesthete as he had for riffraff realism. Writing about aestheticism, he says, "Poetry must be as well written as prose."

In reading the letters one should never forget that Ezra
Pound was always the obsidian stylist. His detestation of a crepuscular language may have led him to his hatred of a Judaic-
Christian civilization. We may doubt that Matthew and the
adjectivial jeremiad are less good for writing than Aristotle's
Poetics, Longinus's *On the Sublime,* and Propertius; the Pound
index expurgatorius, on which are Virgil and the Elizabethans,
may be just as distasteful to us. But Pound's insistence that each
word have a bare, mineraled hardness is a credo for writers in
any century. An Objectivist, he points out that Imagism has
nothing in common with lawless vers libre. He has as small
patience with the fat, inert ear and the filmy, indigestive eye in
literature as the Prophets. Pound believes that the metaphor
and the adjective are generally nuisance stumbling blocks to
perception. It was Huysmans who said that the central force of
the sentence lies in the verb, and when the verb has this strong

male health in it, one can hope for good poems and a remarkable culture. A glance at Egyptian ideographs shows us that nouns are always acting, and so are free of the supine adjective.

Pound has never been a grammarian, and suggests no more than three or four canons for the Imagist poet to observe; he knows that one learns much more from great ancient examples than from principles. All of Pound's poetics could be contained in the smallest grammar of poetics; he had contempt for the Vedas, not because he was a Western thinker, but because the translations of Indian theogony are "mere theosophy" and are bad for poetry. His "Amurrican" spelling and street-urchin speech may be mistaken for parochialism; but actually he always despised U.S.A. verse, and all that despicable, pinchbeck regionalism which is the apotheosis of trash and ignorance.

Pound spent more than thirty-five years laboring for a covey of writers who may be as important as some of the Latins he respects; he employed diatribe, philippic, and pungent japes to get Joyce, Wyndham Lewis, H. D., Eliot into Harriet Monroe's poetry magazine and into the *Little Review*. Though he wanted to see his work on the printed page, he showed a pudic and almost blushing feeling about his own afflatus.

There are many baffling attitudes in Pound; his great regard for Dante, the Christian poet, is an enigma, if we do not remember that it is the austere language of the *Inferno* that the Imagist admired.

Let us bear in mind that Pound always had a conception of a poetry that must be quarried out of the austerest rock and driest mountain ravine words. In place of the sick Nazarene and what William Carlos Williams calls the "disordered imagery of Isaiah," he gave us the earthenware gods of Numa Pompilius and the poetry of Propertius. A hard, outside man, like Pound, cannot stomach the masochistic Golgotha pangs.

Some mention ought to be made of Ezra Pound's money theories which have brought him a direful fate. Pound felt that the canker in society and poetry is *usuria*. It is not at all unlikely that Pound's distaste for the surfeited epithet brought the poet to an Old Testament spleen about greed; but his attitude toward the Jew is as stylized as the Semitic Phoenician in *The Waste Land.* But no matter what we may think, Pound's poems no less than the verse of Juvenal, also anti-Semitic, are an important moiety of Christian, Jewish and Latin culture. Besides, the Jewish question can never be solved except by the art and literature question. It is not bizarre or just quaint that some of Ezra Pound's most fervent admirers are Jews. Ezra Pound has been the Socratic gadfly of poetry, sculpture, novels, waging a long war for Joyce's *Portrait of the Artist,* Wyndham Lewis's *Tarr,* for Eliot, and for Brancusi's stone figures.

Pound's faults now belong to History, which man has always interpreted as saying *mea culpa,* and so man exculpates himself of his sins, while he drives the good and virtuous into baleful apostasies. Dante, who would have cursed our *usuria* civilization as much as Jeremiah or Ezra Pound, would have placed Pound in the milder climes of Hell to be a companion of the poet Guido Cavalcanti, for Ezra Pound was never venal.

Tomorrow, 1951

Tradition of Opulence

Poets of the English Language,
edited by W. H. Auden and Norman Holmes Pearson

These are five small volumes of English and American poetry going from Langland's *Piers Plowman* up through Edwin Arlington Robinson. They are not the usual, stale anthologizing which so often contains the worst poems of the best poets. It was Herman Melville who said that it is the least part of genius that attracts the multitude. Mr. Auden, the poet, and Mr. Pearson have edited the books, and, for the most part, have shown a bias for the opulent, the orient pearl in verse, having in mind as their touchstones Marlowe's *Hero and Leander* and Ben Jonson's *The Alchemist.* What is usually so very vexsome about poetry anthologies is the inclusion of dead authors who would remain dead were it not for the business academics who are continually getting out fat, humbug textbooks of perfidious verse. As for the poet, Auden, it is hard to understand why he has imitated these academics by putting into an otherwise fine collection the amateur meters of Anne Bradstreet, Fitz-Greene Halleck and Philip Freneau.

The editors have given just attention to Christopher Smart, one of the four mad poets of England. Smart, grubbily neglected by his friend, Samuel Johnson, is not in Johnson's *Lives of the English Poets;* but all of Smart's *A Song of David,* that Ophir gold of poetry, and once so hard to obtain, is in this anthology. There are also two fragments from Christopher Smart's *Rejoice in the Lamb,* which the unfortunate poet wrote during his seven years in Bedlam. This remarkable piece of genius, which may well have been the model for Blake's visions, was almost unknown up to two or three years ago. However, it is greatly to

254

be feared that it will be the lesser Smart that will attract attention now. The cat-cult in *Rejoice in the Lamb* will be the main reason for awakened interest in him in certain affected circles.

One ought to mention Jones Very, a sort of small Christopher Smart of Salem, who was given to idiotic trances; Jones Very, as Robert Cantwell informs me, was a Salem contemporary of Hawthorne, and lived next door to the insane asylum; and whenever he had one of his godhead seizures, aggravated by a little drinking, his kind friends would take him over to the mental institution where he remained until he was lucid or crazy enough to write some more poems. However, there are no more than two examples of his verse in these volumes, and it is difficult to know whether or not he deserves less or more consideration than Bradstreet, Halleck and Freneau.

The editors have included some very good devotional poetry, a lovely, chanting plaint by George Herbert called "The Sacrifice," Donne's "Litanie," and Sidney Lanier's lengthy hymn to the marshes, always interesting for its sounds and syllables. George Chapman, famous for his translation of the *Iliad,* and Gavin Douglas, who did a beautiful pre-Elizabethan translation of the *Aeneid,* are represented in the books.

There are fifteen Herman Melville poems in these volumes; editors would have had to be quite daring to have put so much Melville into an anthology in the thirties. Ten years ago Richard Aldington had selected seventeen poems from Herman Melville for his Viking anthology, but he was told that so many Melville poems would not be good for library or college business. Maybe the theory that Melville had an amatory fixation on Hawthorne has made him a good anthology subject for a Freudian age.

In each of the five books there are some good and sensible words by the editors about the meaning of different poetry traditions. There is, for example, a short, lucid passage on Elizabethan punctuation. This passage has none of the gimcrack pedantry of the ordinary gibberish grammar which is

255

glutted with syntactically correct but quite trite and puerile sentences. Though the American anthology habit has contributed more to stupor than it has to whetting the appetite for great poets, these five books, with their many rare poems, will prove a great stimulation to the avid reader.

The Freeman, 1951

Paul Verlaine

WICKEDNESS AND PENANCE

Confessions of a Poet, by Paul Verlaine
(trans. Ruth Saltzman Wolf and Joanna Richardson)

These *Confessions,* written under the guidance of St. Augustine, whom Paul Verlaine selected to temper his wickedness, are debaucheries "scented with innocence." The volume, though seasoned with portentous historical occurrences, is a hymeneal remorse, penned when the poet was an aging reprobate, for his bride who had deserted him many years before because of her jealousy of Arthur Rimbaud, then sixteen and the boy paragon of French Parnassus.

No one with Philistine prudery should read these memoirs. One had better have nimble fingers in matters of ethics, and neither be too harsh nor too easy with this unbridled, penitential nature. Moreover, in every poet there is a deluxe fraud, but let no one be duped by the hoax either. It is easy to ask how such a man could have written so many maidenly raptures. Had not Verlaine nearly murdered his most steadfast friend, wounded Rimbaud, and in one of his tumid rages attempted to slay his mother? These, alas, are some of the small diableries of the virgin heart!

With the same kind of Christian, piquant penance he had purchased a farm for his mother to which he repaired with a nineteen-year-old boy. All that Paul Verlaine wrote was done on the lithe sandals of Mercury. The childhood at Metz, with the towers and turrets where the croaking ravens nested, the asperient questions of the child, "Father, what is the coup d'état?", and the puerile sensualisms of the boy at twelve have the charm of the Verlaine faun.

257

The *Confessions* are glutted with unpredictable, miscreant moods and acts. Following some oafish line like the "Jupiter of the low places" the reader falls upon a simple river or orchard song. Verlaine relished his role as a satyr with the vestal heart, and tells us with the mirth of the goat how he came across Baudelaire for the first time. He happened to espy a first edition of *Les Fleurs du Mal* lying on a seat, left there by an usher, and which he immediately confiscated.

After the *Confessions* one ought to go to Brutus or to Seneca for those cold November asperities; but then if one has too much midwinter, crabbed discontent in his soul, he ought as Plato advised a contemporary philosopher, to "pray to the Graces," or take up the *Confessions* of Paul Verlaine.

New York Times Book Review, 1951

Log Cabin Art

American Painting, by Virgil Barker, and
The Index of American Design, by Erwin O. Christensen

Virgil Barker's book is an annal of the development of Yankee art which shows it to have been cursed by trade and literalism. Pioneer lands have never been fecund earth for the artist; and the Colonial market-towns— Boston, Salem—were not places for Mediterranean affections or painting. Luther and John Calvin, who dominated the frontier mind, had a pernicious influence on art but were good for American household culture. A Shaker chair, settle, or sawbuck table are aphorisms in rectitude and a cleanly penury, and betoken a stable wedlock and family fervor. But neither John Calvin nor John Adams had the faculty for the image; and what is reckoned as American primitivism is often nativistic manual training art. Yankee painters did portraits and signs, and art was an occupation for women and girls, as one husband shows by giving notice that his "spouse mounts and paints fans." The Colonial artist was very likely as daft as his New England neighbors thought him, for one portraitist ornamented his shutters with the heads of sages.

The early Yankee was a log cabin esthete. One citizen, whose zeal for crude realism was very typical, wrote John Singleton Copley that one of his oils had people in it who were so natural that when his baby son was unable to shake hands with a man in the portrait, he "roared" and "shrieched."

John Adams, a busybody art connoisseur of the homespun indigenous school, wrote about portrait figures in much the same manner as the thwarted handshaking infant, saying, ". . . you can scarcely help discoursing with them, making questions and receiving answers." There are too few examples of early American oils in Mr. Barker's book, and though the reproduction of Eakins's *Max Schmitt in a Single Scull,* or Copley's *Mr. Watson and the Shark,* may provide a droll moment or two, they are of no benefit to the intellect.

Not unlike the volume on American painting is the book called *The Index of American Design,* by Erwin O. Christensen. The reader, recalling a populist America, with fine artisan towns and Wisconsin dairy country whose soil was kneaded like a good loaf of bread (which we no longer know how to bake), will examine with savory pleasure the pictures of a ladderback chair with a seat of twisted corn husks, or an Iowan seat table, or an eighteenth-century pine Bible-box, or a whale-oil lamp that Melville's Ahab might have held. But American history in this book quickly falls to pieces and becomes nostalgia, the contemporary national sickness. In place of remarkable examples of rural craftsmanship we have the pseudo-relics of the American junkyard iconography—a copper weathervane cock suitable as an emblem for a Broadway rathskeller, a zinc cast deer, and a fake "primitive" circus wagon, reminder of the most foolish of all the Muses, the calliope.

To sum up, Mr. Barker and Mr. Christensen both seem to prove that worship of primitivism in U. S. art is merely an excuse for esthetic inertia.

The Freeman, 1951

The Healing Word

Paracelsus: Selected Writings, trans. by Norbert Guterman, and Pascal's *Pensées,* trans. by H. F. Stewart

Some ages are better for thinkers than others, but all are bad. Paracelsus, whose contemporaries were Da Vinci, Michelangelo, Dürer, Holbein, and Erasmus, was as despised in Martin Luther's time as he would be now. There is some difference; Paracelsus was a great doctor, and also a noble writer, but today he would be a better doctor—and a boor. Some say that what we need are physicians and not culture, which is why we are so sick. We have medicines for dropsy, the gout, consumption, but what recipe is there for the reader of most contemporary reviews?

The life of Paracelsus is so typical that one is inclined to laugh rather than weep. He had almost every gift and nearly every tragedy. Paracelsus was the illegitimate son of a Swabian nobleman who was a physician, and a peasant woman of the Benedictine Abbey. The poor woman probably toiled in the sculleries; her famous son later worked in various cellars and alchemic kitchens where he searched for the philosopher's stone, the elixir, or a precious root or herb. He was a wild, Faustian nature, with a large, bald skull and furious eyes. He was also very irascible and deeply religious, particularly in his humble feeling for the poor and the hurt, always going to the hovel of a German or Swiss peasant just as Christ tarried at the pool of Bethesda to cure the leper and the blind.

Paracelsus detested the academic physicians of his day, and they abhorred him; he preferred a barber, a gypsy, or any plague to a textbook surgeon, whom he regarded as worse than the gallows. A patient in sixteenth-century Germany was generally a martyr to the blessed cause of Hippocrates and Galen.

For a very short space of time Paracelsus had fame; he had cured a renowned printer of an apoplectic stroke, and was appointed city physician of Salzburg. He lectured in the rough German Vulgate instead of Latin, held a public burning of a celebrated medical almanac which had destroyed more people than wars, disease and slander, and denounced the town fathers. He also had abundant sympathy for the German peasant revolt which Luther so fiercely quelled. After a year at Salzburg, Paracelsus had kindled the most exquisite antagonisms. A great traveler, he had celebrated foes in every part of Europe. In 1526 the Salzburg fathers issued a warrant for his arrest, and from that time on Paracelsus was a miserable itinerant and seldom spent two nights in the same bed. His swollen zeal for truth was taken for malice, and his hatred of fraud regarded as the grossest egotism. "Believe in the works, not in the words," was his creed and the pith of his life.

After his flight from Salzburg he went from one town to another, like some hunted Vulcan with medieval crucibles in a Ben Jonson or Goethe play; he was such a miserable waif that he did not know his father had died until four years after he was buried.

More gifted as a writer than the learned Erasmus, his fate was far worse than that of the Humanist, for he was without a patron and friendless. The writings of Paracelsus have nevertheless had a profound influence upon German mysticism; and the gifted prose of Marsden Hartley, the American painter, has in it some of the medievalism of Paracelsus, whom Hartley admired.

Paracelsus wrote treatises on open wounds, smallpox, paralysis, tumors, and also eleven tracts on consumption and dropsy; for him the art of medicine was in experience and in love. He had enormous faith in the "healing word," which when uttered by a sublime intelligence can be scripture.

Paracelsus was supposed to have been hurled from a cliff by envious physicians; it is also a legend that he was poisoned by the powder of diamonds. Another legend is that he kept always at his side some magical simple for the cure of the sick.

This Pantheon book has some fine reproductions of woodcuts from Dürer, Holbein and others; there is also talent in Norbert Guterman's translation, which is scriptural without being at all specious. The opening line of Paracelsus's "Credo" is defiant and droll: "I am different, let this not upset you." I, for one, am not disturbed, and I hope the good, discerning reader will feel the same way.

We have too many books, most of which represent our pride. Pascal, the enemy of pride, in a fit of asceticism sold his library, keeping only his Bible, St. Augustine, Montaigne, and very few others—to which should have been added Pascal's own *Pensées*.

Few realize or care to understand how pessimistic good Christian doctrine really is; there was no more loving or disenchanted man than Pascal. He had as chaste a nature as St. Francis's, and he was also as filled with fierce cosmic ennui as Dostoevsky. Pascal so feared pride, ambition and lust that he wore a belt of nails which he pressed against his skin every time he had a vain, spiteful or brutish thought. Anybody earnestly desiring to cure himself of malice, greed or ambition should read the maxims of Paracelsus and the undying *Pensées* of Pascal. Paracelsus had the old, large, planetary feeling about man, regarding him as a sun, a moon, the Milky Way; Pascal had the same spatial attitude toward human beings, even their sins. It is better to feel this way; otherwise, we fall into a terrible, wizened misanthropy. Our hatred of falsehood and hypocrisy should enlarge us no less than our love.

The Freeman, 1951

Four Harvests

Selected Poetry and Prose of Coleridge, edited by Donald A. Stauffer; *The Portable Melville,* edited by Jay Leyda; *Sartoris,* by William Faulkner

The republication of good books is now more essential than the writing of new ones. The latter too often inflame the palate rather than refresh the soul. Besides, most of the classics are out of print; it has become a hardship and a waste of shoe leather on Fourth Avenue to find an Herodotus in the famous Bohn Library, or a Terence in a Loeb edition.

What is of great benefit in Coleridge's *Biographia Literaria* is not the cumbersome, latinized prose, or the learning (which for its own time was no more than agreeable, wine-stuffed table talk), but Coleridge's affection, his ready access of love for people like Wordsworth and Southey. There is doubtless a number of living authors who write better than Coleridge, but there are desolately few whose diction is warm with human courtesy. As the ancient philosopher Empedocles held, "the thought of men is the blood around the heart." No doubt there is intellectual sickness in Coleridge, the sickness which he describes as the disease of slowed action. This has unusual meaning for us, since we too suffer from the plague of inertia. However, the difference between Coleridge and many of us is striking. Coleridge freely owned his faults, where the modern age hides or dissembles. It is said that Coleridge dropped to his knees twice each day, for he had an ample fear of his blemishes.

The asperities, too, in the *Biographia Literaria* are worth our attention. There are readers, surfeited with novelties in letters, who will peruse with pleasure Coleridge's invective against those who "sacrifice heart and head to point and drapers," or the plain assertion that the "mind is affected by thoughts, rather than by things."

Coleridge had a high moral temper and some real abilities as an oracle, and he earnestly ransacked a book to determine its didactic value, for he knew that not all gifted authors are inevitably wise or good or even moral. Callimachus, the ancient poet, was of the opinion that "a great book is a great evil." We think of the nineteenth century as a stable one. Compared with our own lunatic and bedlam time it was quiet. But, writing of the specious seers in his own day, Coleridge said that "in times of tumult they are . . . destined to come forth as the shaping spirit of Ruin."

Coleridge wrote a rough, thewy prose, and no one who peruses him quickly will understand what he is reading. But, then, it was Aesop's tortoise and not the fleet but feeble-minded coney which won the race.

There is now a Herman Melville society which is kindred to our earlier Robert Browning circles and the Tennyson groups which afforded such rare pleasure to widows and the remaining cousins and aunts and relatives of dead authors. But as Lao-tze said, "When the great Tao is obliterated . . . prudence and circumspection appear, and we have much hypocrisy."

Mr. Jay Leyda, the latest Melville authority, is supposed to be a remarkable bibliographer. But to speak without ambiguity, I do not like his portable Melville, nor does it please me to handle it.

There have been some very creditable editions of Melville. The Princeton University Press republished a book of Melville's essays which were bound and paginated with civil regard for the author. Besides, the essays were printed as wholes, and included "Hawthorne and His Mosses," which is speculation on the paschal lamb in the evil human heart. The Princeton University Press also reprinted *Timoleon,* poems which had no more than a boreal, metaphysical existence in Melville's own lifetime. Liveright brought out the shorter novels, including the famous "Encantadas," "Benito Cereno," the narrative monody, "Bartleby the Scrivener," and *Billy Budd.*

We little imagine the effect of modern life upon reading and writing, and do not realize that the very word "portable" is a sign of restive inattention and foolish locomotion. It is obvious that Mr. Leyda expects no one to be disciplined enough to remain more than a half-hour or so with any particular story. There is one chapter out of *The Confidence-Man* which is a most embittered outcry against American trade, but what can any one derive from less than a dozen pages out of a novel? There is also a puling amount of *Clarel,* the long Jerusalem poem, and a niggling few pages from *Mardi* and from the poem, "John Marr." There should be appended to each "portable" book an automatic factory whistle to blow the reader to his next assignment. There has been a great falling off in ordinary powers of attention, for reading is now reckoned an austere exercise of volition, where in former times it was thought to be an easy pastime. Montaigne's works were called the Breviary of Idlers.

Sartoris, first printed in 1929, is dedicated to Sherwood Anderson. But what was a chanting awareness of American place in Anderson is diseased distortion in Faulkner.

Faulkner's reputation is very stuffed at present. He has received the Nobel award. I confess that I hear so much about Faulkner as an apocalyptic writing beast that I return every few years to *Sanctuary, Mosquitoes, As I Lay Dying*—or, now, to *Sartoris*—expecting to be amply instructed in American decadence. I find, however, no rich, heady compost of vices, but poor-white-trash conversations of an amateurish, vaudeville texture. Example: "Old Louvinia drapped the bowl of peas and let out one squawk, but Cunnel shet her up and told her to run and git his boots and pistols and have 'em ready at the back do'."

266

In *Sartoris,* as in most of Faulkner's fiction, the corpse is the hero:

And the next day he was dead, whereupon, as though he had but waited for that to release him of the clumsy cluttering of bones and breath, by losing the frustration of his own flesh he could now stiffen and shape that which sprang from him into the fatal semblance of his dream . . .

It was a mournful folly to have published such arrant scribbling the first time, but it is total waste to reprint it when there are poets in America who can't get printed at all.

The Freeman, 1952

*

Lives of Donne, Wotton, Hooker, etc., by Izaak Walton; *The Life of George Crabbe,* by his son; *The Analects of Confucius,* trans. by W. E. Soothill; *Childhood, Boyhood and Youth,* by Leo Tolstoy; *Sesame and Lilies,* by John Ruskin; *Autobiography* of Edward Gibbon; *Essays,* by Ralph Waldo Emerson; *Selected Passages* of Plato; *Lives of the English Poets,* by Samuel Johnson; *Democracy in America,* by Alexis de Tocqueville

There are so many reasons for keeping young people out of college today that presently parents will have to return to the home university, the family library. Good house books, by which I mean Plutarch, Thoreau, Thucydides, Strabo and Izaak Walton, are little or no risk; contemporary college education, on the other hand, is what Ben Jonson would call hellebore, a bane or potion that produces idiocy. There are some good, rare and trustworthy books which are reprinted by the Oxford

University Press, Everyman's Library and the Loeb Classica. These volumes are far better for the exercise of character than the teaching in our universities. The new classics are a saturnalia in ennui; the old classics are moral teachers. Emerson once said that it is not possible to educate every lunkhead in these States, and Erasmus asserted that wherever there is popular education there is no higher learning. We are ailing from too much literacy and from too many universities whose aim is simian homogeneity.

These ten marvelous Oxford volumes give us true learning. For example, the life of George Crabbe, the English devotional poet, written by his son, is a work of humble, filial love. Though glutted with miseries, the lives of authors make sweet epitaphs. We read with the greatest quiet and benefit of the early afflictions of George Crabbe. Crabbe became an apprentice surgeon, for which he was so ill-suited that he passed many nights in quaking fits dreading that he might have to operate upon a patient. His flight to London was an adventure in penury and despair. With three pounds in his pocket, the youthful poet hoped for fame. By the time he was ready for the debtor's prison, George Crabbe had vainly solicited bread and patronage of various lords. Then, utterly desponding, he sent a piercing entreaty to the generous and cultivated Edmund Burke, who, without postponement, read the young man's verse, gave him lodging under his roof, and secured him publication and the friendship of Sir Joshua Reynolds and the grand pasha of literature, Dr. Samuel Johnson.

Here, too, in the World's Classics is that good angler, Izaak Walton, whose small biographies on Donne, Wotton, Hooker, George Herbert and others are as useful as Samuel Johnson's *Lives of the English Poets.* Every page of Walton's reinforces friendship and enlarges the affections. The good, grave Izaak is a learned bumpkin; his words are appropriately rural.

I would rather mourn with George Herbert than be intellectual with Ezra Pound. There is more comfort in Herbert's last words, cited by Walton, than in all Pound's *Cantos,* for they make us brothers: "My dear Friend, I am sorry I have nothing to present to my merciful God but sin and misery."

In Walton's life of Donne, he writes, "It hath been observed by wise and considering men that Wealth hath seldom been the Portion, and never the Mark to discover good People." We have witnessed the failure of wealth to produce virtue, but those who deeply care to see the Republic reinvigorated might look into Tocqueville's *Democracy in America.* Tocqueville wrote that America was a primeval Adam's garden of first fruits, minerals, rivers, livestock. But our Eden is gone, along with potatoes at Puritan prices.

To continue with our house education, let us read the *Analects,* or conversations, of Confucius. Any one who seriously reads the three masters—Izaak Walton, Tocqueville and Confucius —has already more knowledge and wisdom than the average American Ph.D. Says the *Analects:* "Only the virtuous are competent to love or to hate men," and "He who heard the truth in the morning might die content in the evening." "The man of honor," says Confucius, "thinks of his character, the inferior man of his position."

Let us go from Confucius to the *Autobiography* of the great Edward Gibbon, whose *Decline and Fall of the Roman Empire* is likely to be our own horoscope. It might be worth mentioning here that a graduate student in American History is permitted to write his doctorate dissertation without ever having read Gibbon, Livy or Polybius. But dissertations have little to do with culture. By the time our home university student has completed Leo Tolstoy's *Childhood, Boyhood and Youth* and perused Ruskin's *Sesame and Lilies,* he will have acquired more erudition than can be had in most graduate school regimens.

William Morris, the disciple and friend of Ruskin, believed that when women had the wheaten sheaves of a Titian madonna

269

we would have Utopia. One would not have to add much to this. Perhaps a good loaf of bread and ten or a dozen Oxford volumes, including Johnson, the life of George Crabbe, Plato, Homer and *The Clouds* of Aristophanes, all of which are to be found in the World's Classics Series.

The Freeman, 1952

*

The Letters of Anthony Trollope, edited by Bradford Allen Booth; *An Autobiography,* by Anthony Trollope; *North America,* by Anthony Trollope, edited by Donald Smalley and Bradford Allen Booth; *The Art of Sinking in Poetry,* by Martinus Scriblerus, edited by Edna Leake Steeves; *The Prologues and Epilogues of John Dryden,* by William Bradford Gardner; *The Best of Defoe's Reviews,* compiled and edited by William L. Payne; *The Great Digest: Unwobbling Pivot,* by Confucius, translation and commentary by Ezra Pound

Anthony Trollope wrote no great letters. The Trollope matter in Mr. Booth's book has a great deal of ledgerbook sense and strong, penny judgment, but it is not likely to raise either the spleen or the spirits. The epistles of famous authors are usually a property for the auction house rather than the heritage of a people.

Trollope wrote some spiritless notes to George Henry Lewes, who is better remembered for his relationship with George Eliot than for his Goethe book. Trollope advises the young Lewes that it is possible to remain alive and still be a writer, which is doubtful. Trollope expressed some misgivings about sending a young Englishman to the Continent to be educated because there he would falter in spelling and in ordinary English idioms.

270

There is one Trollope letter, offered a decade ago for sale in a Sotheby catalogue, which created much moral doubt in the minds of the owners. I cite the letter which Trollope obviously meant for a quip and some civil raillery:

My Dearest Miss Dorothea Sankey: My affectionate & most excellent wife is as you are aware, still living— and I am proud to say her health is good. Nevertheless it is always well to take time by the forelock and be prepared for all events. Should anything happen to her, will you supply her place— as soon as the proper period of decent mourning is over.

The best letters are written by men of a crabbed and soured temper; a line or two of Dean Swift humbles us, though it steals everything out of our souls and pockets; "I do not think life is of much value, but health is worth everything. . . . For my own part I labor for daily health as often and almost as many hours as a workman does for daily bread."

Trollope's *Autobiography* has a pedestrian gait, and his *North America* is not nearly as good as his mother's precise asperities in her scandalous nineteenth-century book on American customs. Trollope was not as incautious as his mother, and for that reason no better than an engaging dullard. The mother came to America in the Andrew Jackson era, and the son during the Civil War years. Their experience was very much the same. Both regarded Americans as braggarts, and the women as unruly and rude.

Despite my vast regard for Jonathan Swift, there is little to relish in Martinus Scriblerus, which was the pseudonym for Pope, Swift, Dr. Arbuthnot, Gay, and Parnell. The whole book is no more than the easy, slattern scribblings of men given to their ale; the wit has more ink and paper and library to it than tavern and gamin horseplay.

The Prologues and Epilogues of John Dryden are elegancies drawn from the head rather than the loins or the weak flesh. Nor is it plain what benefit any can have from reading a book

271

filled with such tedious and sauceless esprit. This is a typical kneel to Shakespeare:

> Shakespeare, who (taught by none) did first impart
> To Fletcher Wit, to labouring Johnson Art.

The Best of Defoe's Reviews is better, because the author had a plainer humor, though it is by no means worth a whole book. Defoe had small patience with bombastic jakes and asses, and regarded himself as a gentleman, which is a euphemism for the timorous, the poltroon and the passionless. Defoe's opposition to dueling was that it might kill him. This sounds more like Aristotle's logic than his view of the gentleman.

Though the editor has found it necessary to amend the punctuation of the author of *Moll Flanders,* some may care for the quick fooleries of Defoe. Defoe is almost as *bad* a writer as was Captain John Smith in his Virginia chronicles, which is full of marvelous misspellings and bizarre punctuations.

Ezra Pound has rendered Confucius in a disordered, mock vulgate. Despite its fossil, rabble patois, much is to be learned from this volume. Today, when people seek rush nostrums in more laws and in quacksalver politicians, it is good to go to the roots of acts. Confucius writes:

... wanting good government in their states, they first established order in their own families; wanting order in the home, they first disciplined themselves; desiring self-discipline, they rectified their own hearts; and wanting to rectify their hearts, they sought precise verbal definitions of their inarticulate thoughts.

If justice, morals, love, and friendship are to be no more than words in the dictionary, we cannot battle for them by lessening or increasing taxes, ushering out one churl to let in another, or changing laws and governments, but by making the greatest exactions upon our hearts whenever we salute a friend, bow to a mother, kiss a child, or make a promise.

The Freeman, 1952

*

Selected Prose, by Hugo von Hofmannsthal (trans. Mary Hottinger and Tania and James Stern); *The Western Gate: A San Francisco Reader,* edited by Joseph Henry Jackson; *1000 Years of Irish Prose,* edited by Vivian Mercier and David H. Greene

The first book listed above is the selected prose of Hugo von Hofmannsthal, the Austrian poet and philosopher of esthetics. Hofmannsthal had a kind of gifted lassitude, for his was not an active nature. The writings of many men of his rank have been printed in the last few years: there were Paul Valéry and the Dadaist, Guillaume Apollinaire—good men but not good enough to republish. Hofmannsthal, owes an abundant debt to the ancients, but whereas it is profitable to reprint Longinus, or even Demetrius, or Lessing, it is a waste to bring out an edition of Hofmannsthal. Commercial publishing has dropped so far down in dignity that it is almost wicked for the Bollingen Foundation to reprint such a sensitive mediocrity as Hofmannsthal at a time when it is almost impossible for talented Americans to be published. By this action the Bollingen people show themselves hostile to the native muse. They claim a great interest in religion and ritual; were this true they would make available to American readers Jane Harrison's *Prolegomena to the Study of Greek Religion,* Lord Kingsborough's *Mexican Antiquities,* Gavin Douglas's *Aeneid,* or Grote's learned books on Plato. I mention these books because they are remarkable and out of print, and also because Hofmannsthal is a debile Parnassian whose writings are the flimsiest copies of the *Bucolics* and *Georgics* of Virgil.

There is a lengthy introduction by the late Hermann Broch who also did a very long dithyrambic on Virgil which was no addition to the knowledge of Virgil. Hermann Broch writes that Hofmannsthal was influenced by the philosophers of India

273

and by Heraclitus, which is very good except that I would rather read the Rig Veda or reread the cryptic fragments of the thinker of Ephesus. All styles are good save those one cannot understand. Be plain, Falstaff advises Pistol. What the esthetes so copiously lack is sense, which Horace said was the origin of a good style.

The first of the selected writings in Hofmannsthal's volume is a long short story called "Andreas" which contains a plethora of wind, stars, rustic goats and swains. The moral scenery is beneficial, and I have no fault to find with neatherds on the slopes of the Tyrol. Besides, Austrian scenery quiets the modern, restive reader. However, Andreas is a species of Kafka sensitive. Andreas is an Austrian Galahad who hates cats and dogs, regarding them as figures of the vilest sensualism. As a child he had broken the back of a cat and the spine of a dog, which is what a boy of weak and febrile nerves might do. There might be a modern excuse for such cruelty, for cats and dogs are taking the place of children, and we are making so much progress as a civilized people that soon we shall be a national feline and dog pound without any children to break their vertebrae. In the Hofmannsthal book there is also an apocryphal letter written by Lord Chandos, a novitiate in esthetics, to Lord Francis Bacon. There are some nice, dolorous aphorisms of Hippocrates, and the writing all around is sonorous, if emasculate. Lord Chandos is a young, delicate Lord Alfred Douglas who writes:

When in my hunting lodge I drank the warm foaming milk which an unkempt wench had drained into a wooden pail from the udder of a beautiful gentle-eyed cow, the sensation was no different from that which I experienced when, seated on a bench, built into the window of my study, my mind absorbed the sweet and foaming nourishment from a book.

This is nard and honey which I can take or leave without harm or advantage. There is also a random revulsion of Lord Chandos which is likely to spoil any man's dinner without sharpening his faculties: "I had given the order for a copious supply of rat-poison to be scattered in the milk-cellars of one of my dairy-farms."

Do American Foundations always have to be wrong? Are they being forced to support the blind, the halt and the lepers of Hippocrene? Can they not make one single mistake for the good—and for literature—by helping some American Seneca or Hercules of letters instead of nourishing the academic booby?

Of the two other books listed above one is a manual on San Francisco, the other an Irish prose anthology. Both are rapid transit college survey courses. The first is clogged with poor, shaggy annals on Spanish missions and the misery of the Indians under Spanish Catholicism along with a bit of Bret Harte and Rudyard Kipling doggerel. The Irish volume is a crazy mélange of Yeats, Synge, Lady Gregory, Joyce, Liam O'Flaherty, Sean O'Casey, with at least twenty-five other Gaelic authors of the last seventy years. The editors propose to cover 930 years of Gael and Saxon prose in a second volume. A millenium is a long time for that most feeble and reedy faculty, human memory. The oak, the elephant and the whale live scores of years longer than human beings, yet they read nothing, whereas man reads all the time but has not the sense of the fungus to know that it is folly to cast a thousand years at the brain in one bundle.

The Freeman, 1952

William Carlos Williams

THE ART OF CONCEALMENT

The Autobiography of William Carlos Williams

Autobiography is the art of telling almost everything: had Shakespeare violated this canon neither his identity nor his plays would be a riddle. It is the ideal lie, for it is as much as a man dare confess without being repulsive to himself in his own soul. St. Paul could not force to his lips the lusts in his great nature; Dostoevsky, a Pauline novelist, writes that crimes are hierarchic, some worse than others.

At the age of sixty-eight, William Carlos Williams has published his autobiography. He is old enough to write wise memoirs, and he has been a figure in American literature, so that we might reasonably hope to go to his book looking for maxims and parables of benefit to our lives. But Williams is an enormous deceiver, not because he tells almost everything, but because he reveals nothing of fundamental importance to the spirit. A man ought not to do a book merely to relive his past, for if he does, he is asking Circe to translate him into a pig.

The first part of the volume is devoted to the rubble memorabilia of Williams's lost youth. There were Ezra Pound, modern satyr of Attica, and Hilda Doolittle, Sappho of the Imagists, his classmates at the University of Pennsylvania. Charles Demuth, painter and friend of Alfred Stieglitz, Mosaic lawgiver of the camera, was also his companion. There are the obstetrical reminiscences at the old French hospital. There was Baroness Elsa von Freytag, a Dada Venus who wore a coal scuttle mounted with moons and postage stamps for a hat. She was delirious for the young Williams. Unable to wring from him more than a few

276

kisses, which spiced her appetite without relieving it, she knocked him down with one Prussian fist.

The past that Williams divulges is a New York and Paris Sodom of the arts. There are fugitive references to the *Dial* and to Richard Johns, founder of the little magazine *Pagany.* There is the George Antheil musical debacle. Antheil, like Sherwood Anderson, wore his hair in bangs in the Gertrude Stein fashion. The Antheil concert given at Carnegie Hall in 1926 or '27 was a Bacchic insult to the bourgeoisie. There were fourteen grand pianos, a fog horn, an electric alarm on the stage. Antheil's *Ballet Méchanique* was a front page scandal in the New York papers, with no defenders save for Williams and the gaga zoot suiters of the seven arts.

The bizarre Imagists, Vorticists, Objectivists and activists who were Williams's friends opposed the university and the Augean stable of newspaper culture, and they derided both commercial and academic books. But they themselves spawned verse, essays and novels more subhuman and cold than anything that has ever come off the campus or out of the commercial publishing world. Take a fleeting glance at a few of those enthusiastic, Dada natures. There was Emanuel Carnevali, the nineteen-year-old Chicago Rimbaud; there was Ernest Walsh, a tubercular Irish-American poet who starved with six wardrobe trunks at the Paris Ritz. There was Ethel Moorhead, militant Gaelic feminist, who had marched on 10 Downing Street for the three freedoms: free sex, free verse, and the woman's ballot. She founded the little volcanic magazine, *This Quarter,* so that Ernest Walsh could publish his Chaucerian Americanese. In *This Quarter* appeared the early Joyce, Carnevali, the first Hemingway short story, Pound, Kay Boyle's verse, Joseph Vogel, Robert McAlmon—and Edward Dahlberg.

What has happened to these exuberant children of the arts, living or deceased—Carnevali, Walsh, Kay Boyle, Lincoln Gillespie (who came from an aristocratic Philadelphia family and who talked as Joyce wrote), Robert McAlmon, John Hermann (selling Venetian blinds in New Orleans when I last saw him a decade ago), Nathan Asch, and Dr. Williams himself? Originally they had fled from trade and congealed academic stupidity to be free, deracinated writers in Paris. Then they returned to America crying out, "God is dead! Long live grammar."

Williams writes that he always has been a liar, and always will be. But a man at sixty-eight is too old to lie. Williams not only hides people who are not successful, but he altogether conceals his own gifts. He has lost his true memory and has become a weathervane admirer. His feelings for the gifts of Josephine Herbst and Louis Zukofsky are very ardent in private, and yet in this book he does little more than prattle about Josephine Herbst, and is not even gallant enough in his hasty mention of Louis Zukofsky to assert that he started the Objectivist movement to which Williams himself belonged. He has become mellow, which is another word for moldering.

The Freeman, 1952

D. H. Lawrence

D. H. Lawrence: Portrait of a Genius But..., by Richard Aldington, and *Journey with Genius*, by Witter Bynner

Aldington's book, done with a carping heart, is entertaining spite. It is not so much a portrait of Lawrence as a confession of Aldington's. Aldington writes as though D. H. Lawrence had pilfered his destiny; the truth is that Aldington's own life is a study in contemporary compromise. It may be that no one really compromises, but that everybody just fathoms his nature. This, however, is a very risky doctrine to accept. One has moral obligations to heaven, friends, nature, and to one's vestal fires, and a man might bend fate a little if he will only try.

I am almost totally at odds with Aldington's and Bynner's portraits of Lawrence. These two bickering, gadfly books were written out of envy. Few can bear their own faults in others, and Aldington detests Lawrence's errors because his own have never been the leaven for a Quixote trauma. Lawrence is almost everything that Aldington and Bynner say he was, but in their two books we have the world talking about the spirit. Aldington detests Lawrence because he regarded himself as a savior and a messiah. Suppose Lawrence was wrong? There are those who say Christ was wrong. But who would relinquish the parables even if it could be proved that Jesus were an imposter?

Lawrence had a broken pottery-jug face, rusty robin hair, and a wild potato nose. The wild desert seer or Cenobite in him was what neither Aldington nor Bynner could bear. Aldington relates how the young provincial Lawrence, just out

279

of a coal digger's house at Derbyshire, attended his first party given by Ford Madox Ford and Violet Hunt. The youth had never had roast beef, brussels sprouts, plum pudding with champagne, and he thought that if such a repast were the guerdon of a few poems which Ford had accepted, imagine what he would receive as a famous author—why, a thousand pounds a year! Then the poet met Frieda, wife of an unamorous professor and mother of three children, and with five pounds they left England for the Continent.

Here Aldington pauses to disclose that Lawrence, who had deprived a professor with an impecunious psyche of a wife with Vesuvian blood, was always prating about wedlock as though he were virginal. But Aldington should know that the greatest prudes were hotfleshed men, like Augustine, and Paul in the seventh chapter of Romans, or Tolstoy. When carnal men cease being prudes, civilization will disappear.

Aldington writes that almost all of Lawrence's friends went away from him, that he caricatured them. His friends were his sitters in the various novels, and if they had not the wit and learning and character of Sir Thomas Browne or Giordano Bruno, was that Lawrence's fault? Witter Bynner tells us that in Mexico City Lawrence suddenly turned upon Fred Leighton and told him to go away, because he was no good for him. Well, people sap us of our truths, and had we the prescience to tell persons who break the fluid of our spirit and harm our best ends to leave us, we might spare ourselves many disgraces. Still, Lawrence was a froward man; it is a terrible disease and is fast ruining the modern character. We have become a nation of liars, not alone for profit but because it is a kind of profligacy, like reading a newspaper, or being busy. But Richard Aldington is more froward than Lawrence because he tells the truth less often.

Aldington also declares that Lawrence had a frugal, pocketbook heart, and that he lied about the money he really had to avoid giving it to the needy. According to Aldington, Messiah

Lawrence was really a moneychanger in the temple of literature. It may be true that Lawrence did not tell everybody that he had, at times, a few hundred pounds in the bank. He was so vulnerable to the needs of writing waifs that he had to conceal his means. Oddly enough, Aldington rails at the gullible Lawrence for giving money to low, humble people. But a man who cannot be duped is a rascal, and though Lawrence did not show Maurice Magnus his bank book, he did help him. Magnus was some sort of impresario of the ballet, a third-rate artist and a first-class sponger, but Lawrence did not know how to tell him to go. Lawrence got Maurice Magnus's book published, which Aldington rightly says is of no worth, and wrote his famous hundred-page preface to the volume. It is a remarkable piece of Italian landscape and it shows a conscience which we have lost.

Lawrence was a literary scold; he used to write me bullying, didactic letters when I was living in diggings in Chelsea, London. But when he suspected that I was not eating very often, he sent me a five-pound note.

Most men hate what is not average, and there is a great deal of the ordinary in Richard Aldington's gifts. Richard Aldington has written a bitter book in which he blames D. H. Lawrence for being testy! It is a Judas book, for there is hardly a human trait in Lawrence that Aldington does not flay. Doubtless D. H. Lawrence had every fault Aldington says he had, but who is Aldington to cast a first stone?

The Freeman, 1952

*

Studies in Classic American Literature, by D. H. Lawrence

It has become common to regard D. H. Lawrence's work as the tiger with the flaming colors of Joseph's Coat, but to cast the man in the ditch. When I was in diggings in London, sleeping until mid-afternoon so that I could sustain myself by one meal a day at a pub or from the tuppenny meat-wagons, he sent me five pounds. He wrote me didactic, bullying letters which were accompanied by the two gudgeons and the barley loaves. I had not met the celebrated man, or given him any hint of those blighted London days. But hunger is an angel, and though I regret many other torments in my life, I do not cast out indigence, my dearest teacher. We are eunuchs because we believe in money which can beget nothing. The epitaph of Thomas Churchyard is "Poetry and Poverty this tomb doth inclose."

I saw D. H. Lawrence for the first time at Sylvia Beach's bookshop in Paris; he had already written a preface for my first novel *Bottom Dogs,* receiving a pelting guerdon for his valiant work. I watched this lissome man talking to Sylvia Beach, because, for me, he embodied the wild, rioting Muses. He had a goatish jaw with beard, russet, earthed hair, and a potato nose. He looked like a Mayan idol, with beans for eyes and squash seeds for teeth—to use his own phrase, he was a crucified faun.

Some days later when we walked across the Boulevard Raspail I realized that the man was dying in his clothes. I had to help this spirited forty-two-year-old nature, for he was that rather than a writer, to his room at the Hotel Grand Versailles.

He was the most moral man of his age, and he never ceased advising me to be the bony Spartan. He urged me not to let publishers cozen me of my lentils, and I never have because they never gave me any. He also counseled me not to be unlucky and always write with a great bitterness. I have heeded his advice as best I could, for I have been a bitter stylist, and I have always been luckless. For all his fame, which he thought a disgrace, he replied to my letters at once. Being a genius he was alone, needing even my callow epistles without sun, wheat, grapes, and rain. He quoted La Bruyère who said that all our miseries come from not being able to be alone.

It was I who left off writing to him because I was ashamed of the empty, Cana words I sent to him. Of his person I can say what Lord Bolingbroke asserted of Bacon, "He was so great a man that I do not recollect whether he had any faults or not." Idol-breaking is seeing what we did not perceive in our purblind youth; unchanging yea-saying is stagnant water, for those who do not continually reject their former ikons and idols are always boys. Though I have altered my thoughts regarding his gifts, let it be my portion when I retire to Erebus to have as companions the disembodied dust of Hesiod, Homer, Musaeus, Apollo, and D. H. Lawrence. "Eat and carouse with Bacchus," Lawrence says, "or munch dry bread with Jesus, but don't sit down without one of the gods."

Poetry, 1954

Leo Tolstoy

What Is Art?, by Leo Tolstoy (trans. Aylmer Maude)

The Oxford University Press has reprinted the remarkable polemic, *What Is Art?,* translated by Aylmer Maude, whose study of Tolstoy published in 1910 is as valuable as Gilchrist's famous book on William Blake. *What Is Art?* is a moral tract on the evil of the arts. It is a superficial folly to set aside this book because Tolstoy said that Shakespeare and Beethoven were decadent. Tolstoy is right in distrusting the artist, for genius is a lawless angel over which few have prevailed. Christ went to the wilderness to overcome temptation, but the poet seeks wilderness solitude to cultivate it.

Tolstoy attacked Baudelaire, Mallarmé, Verlaine, all of whom were artistic hermits of special sins. In *What Is Art?* Tolstoy assails the decadence of "The Gallant Marksman," a prose-poem by Baudelaire. In this poem the poet, the religious dandy of literary abstractions, goes to the forest in a carriage and stops at a shooting gallery. The poet takes a rifle and aims at one of the decoy dolls, a scene which presents the agony of the esthete in quest of *le mot juste.* The poet missing several times, his "delicious, execrable" wife mocks him. Taking aim again, he imagines that the doll he decapitates is his wife as well as time, "the monster."

The disciples of the shooting-gallery school of esthetics are Pound, Eliot, Auden, Isherwood, Williams, Tate and Ransom. What unites all these people is intellectual perversity, the cult of solitude and *le mot juste* which results in a private, lonely alphabet. The old literature is founded on the Mosaic family laws, the parents, filial obedience, and marriage. One will look in vain for the conjugal table and the household hearth in

284

modern letters. As Baudelaire says in "The Stranger," also quoted by Tolstoy: "I have neither father nor mother, no sister, brother."

The Solomons of literature, Isaiah, Euripides, Donne, Tolstoy, lament loneliness, barrenness and the passing away of the summer fruits, but the modern cult abominates women— and masculine force. "Only the brute is really potent," wrote Baudelaire. Baudelaire took from Poe, his teacher, the mountain tarns and the miasmas and employed them as symbols of impotence, sterility and absolute extinction. Whatever grew, ripened or bloomed was for Baudelaire a horror. In the Poe short stories the women are almost invariably murdered.

Behind the cult of "originality" is the sanctified platitude. The idols, Wilde, Gide, Eliot, Williams, Pound and Cummings, have devoured more people than Moloch, but who dares question their tyrant screeds? What is the value of such doggerel as Eliot's ". . . the women come and go / Talking of Michelangelo." If one says that "I grow old . . . I grow old . . . I shall wear the bottoms of my trousers rolled" is Yahoo nursery verse, he is churlishly told that such banality is the poet's literary intention. No one troubles to add that this does not make the result any less trite.

Reputation in the arts is mass hypnotism. The greatest frauds are accepted with comatose welcome. The composer is as violently perverse as the painter, for what is important is intentionally to do violence to sounds, objects, reality. Fire department sirens and whistles, as in the pulp opuses of Edgar Varèse, are regarded as titanism in sensibility. Now we are told that Aaron Copeland may make an opera out of the libidinous illiteracies of *Studs Lonigan,* by James T. Farrell. These are the Satans of carnage who are taking their revenge against reality and man. It was for this reason that Plato and Tolstoy feared that music would enslave the will.

We go to the great masters with humility. We reread Tolstoy with the same reverence that Liu Tsung Yuan said he had for the poetry of his friend, Han Yu, never opening his books without first washing his hands. We turn to the Bible to escape the torpor of the heart. But we go to new poetry for novelty and the image, which does not increase compassion but coldness.

A hypersensitive and often subhuman art is the result of the beauty-cult which Tolstoy hated. Tolstoy pointed out that Plato, Socrates and Aristotle did not think that goodness and beauty always coincide.

The perverse is the touchstone of the modern man of taste, and we see a sybaritic use of a Biblical reference in Gide's *If It Die*, taken from John the Evangelist. By *If It Die* Gide referred to Wilde and his disciples, who have had the most noxious effects upon the American arts, the ballet, the stage, the movies, music and painting. These arts that prey upon the nervous system swindle man of his morals and of his affections.

Many sophists regarded Gibbon as a philister for saying that the decline of the family brought about the fall of Rome. The difference between a virtuous, republican Cato and a Heliogabalus lies in the disappearance of Roman household virtues: marriage, progeny and filial respect. By the time of Catullus, Martial, Horace, the Roman vestal virgin had given way to the lewd idol.

In all of Tolstoy's writings he particularly impugns any kind of violence. The whole contemporary art-cult is based upon an art of shock which results in the deliberate disorder of language, sounds, objects and sex. It is this kind of intentional devilism which has given us surrealism and existentialism. Tolstoy had an unusual conscience, and we can open *What Is Art?* with the same assurance that we have when we turn to the five books of Moses or the Sermon on the Mount.

The Freeman, 1952

Lewis Mumford

OUR MACHINE CULTURE

Art and Technics, by Lewis Mumford

A good book is a Buddha, a teacher, and Lewis Mumford's little volume has real didactic value. Mumford is one of the exiles of the arts who stayed at home and viewed the decline of the national character. He refused to imitate the cultists of the word, the gaga sensualists who went to Paris only to return as station-wagon littérateurs or academy he-dowagers of letters.

One must first be a humble pupil, or one will always be the most groping journeyman. Mumford's most important mentor and friend was Joel Elias Spingarn, who had said there was nothing under the sun that is new in art. Spingarn, deriving his wisdom from Solomon rather than Ezra Pound, had remarked, "If Eliot is the greatest poet of our times, Poor Times!" The new has been the flag of the arts, and very few modern writers besides Mumford have realized that this is a doomsday banner.

Mumford is no opponent of the machine, although he is greatly troubled by the nihilism of the mechanical age. The Luddites, English workingmen and women, broke the machines with their hands because they desired to return to handicrafts. We, however, have let the machines destroy our hands, the result of which has been a malignant, touchless culture. One of the ten commandments of present-day art and civilization is thou shalt not touch. The aim of the nihilist is to have nothing to touch.

What Kropotkin, Marx, the socialists and communists have not considered is that machines can be dispiriting agents that enfeeble the will. The effect of the machine upon love, friendship, marriage, volition, amusements has been most baleful. Mumford despairs of our sick arts which are the expression of the self-love and perversity that rages in the American soul. He has a horror of the froward artist who does not heed Lao-tze's admonition "Let your yea be yea, and your nay be nay, for whatsoever is more than this cometh of evil." The poet today is Narcissus, declares Mumford. Our "originals" have invented an auto-alphabet, which is writing for one's self.

Mumford does not want to abandon the machine, though his logic leads him to the point of view of William Morris, who said, "Apart from the desire to produce beautiful things, the leading passion of my life has been and is hatred of modern civilization." Man is first *homo sapiens* rather than a tool-using animal, writes Mumford. What he means is that contemplation is much more important than artifacts. This is ancient wisdom, for in the old Hebraic world the artisan came long after the sage, the meditative shepherd, and the harper; and the rude potter worked remote from holy places.

The evil genius of mechanical pastimes is very apparent. The American entertainments are no longer rustic or communal, a river picnic, the buggy ride, or Sunday in the park, but tend to be of a solitary character. Modern man gets his recreation from the electric devil-boxes, the radio, television, and the movies. What a mournful people are the Americans, said Maxim Gorki, who have to get their entertainment out of mechanical amusements.

We are so bored we cannot sit. Our screed is going. Mumford tells us that Abbé Gratry, the great logician of the last century, suggested that each one retire every day for a half hour to be still! Mumford also relates that a psychologist has recently discovered that weaving is a healing work. Modern people are always discovering what was known to the Amorites in 4500 B.C.

It is plain that Mumford has grave doubts regarding new technics, but he says it is futile to attempt to limit them.

Presently Lewis Mumford, one of the very few sane thinkers in the land today, must become more emphatic in denouncing our mechanical culture. Our inventions and entertainments come from the same nihilism and boredom that is so characteristic of our crepuscular torpid arts. The machines raise up such ennui that, as Solomon said, the eye can never be satisfied with seeing nor the ear filled with hearing.

The Freeman, 1952

Henry James

The Golden Bowl, by Henry James, and
The Good Soldier, by Ford Madox Ford

Ford Madox Ford, whose novels are being republished by
Knopf, liked and respected Henry James, whom he called "the
master." Ford was the loving turtle-dove of Ecclesiastes; talent
for him was April rain and the first green things. His memoirs
—*Portraits from Life,* for example—seem to me more worthy
of reissue than his novels. James had done the young Ford in a
novel, Morton Densher in *The Wings of the Dove,* piling up
those panicky, precautionary, and altogether mediocre adjectives in the lorn hope that one of them would catch the man.
James said that every epithet should be a paying piece, but
described Ford as a longish, leanish, fairish gentleman. The
Ford I knew was feeble, wise, old, with a puffy gait. I used to
meet him as he shuffled slowly up Eighth Street. His speech
was no less muffled than his walk, and I found it very hard to
understand him because I was arrogant and self-loving. I could
not imagine that such a Caliban could contain genius. He
always stopped to give me an obese, asthmatic greeting, and
pudgily asked me to bring him my novels. He lived at 10 Fifth
Avenue where he had a pair of poor little rooms, with no more
than six pieces of furniture.

He used to give Thursday teas with Sutter cookies. In the
beginning I said little to him. Then I began to revalue the heavy,
sluggish tortoise of letters. He was already a public figure,
much admired and not read, and he was reputed to be a
marvelous liar. It was Sherwood Anderson, who began his
apprenticeship as a writer by feigning madness, who told me
how much Ford lied. Anderson later gave up the pretense to

madness, and went sane. Ford was another sort of deceiver; he belonged to that most lonely of tribes, the crazy, windmill sect of Don Quixote, who could not endure solitude and the ordinary limits of human experience. What Ford did not have to give he simply invented. It was not enough that he had helped D. H. Lawrence, Ezra Pound, William Carlos Williams, Allen Tate, Nathan Asch, and I don't know how many others. James had said that Ford had too much sense to be in art, and too little to be out of it. True, neither Ford nor James was disfigured by passion. They were men of taste, which, without poetic fire, is prudential, congealed genius. But let us return to Henry James.

James, Joseph Conrad, Stephen Crane and Ford lived within walking or buggy distance from each other in rural England. James, at Rye, kept a fine house and lawn with a butler, upper and lower housemaid, cook, knife-boy and gardener. A devotee of style, he wrote superannuated, panting sentences with a dull metronomic beat. He accumulated his circumlocutions for design, for he cared more for propriety than he did for the universe.

James studied decorum so mercilessly that he knew whether the florid face of a hostess and her carpet jarred, or whether her dress went with the Dresden *objet d'art*. He believed in the moral properties of appointments; milieu was his passion. Everything he did was for taste, and it was impossible for him to be clear because he wanted to be tactful. He fussed over his sentences, putting in long, enervating parentheses, and then tortured the poor, tired sentence all over again to make a positively arid and mediocre observation. He created a specious rhetoric loaded with many syntactical faults which have since been taken up as literary metaphysics by the Jamesian acolytes. What was important with James was not to show any fault barbarously. He never could forgive Gustave Flaubert for receiving him in Paris in a soiled smock.

James loathed poverty and frumpish materials. He wrote: "The worst horror was the acres of varnish." When Ford brought a guest who the old man at Rye thought was of low origin, he refused to receive him. The poor could never be put in right relation to intrigue.

The sole Jamesian principle is taste, not energy. The matriarch in *The Golden Bowl,* though in middling circumstances, is accustomed to objects of genteel breeding, and is suitable to be the mentor of virgins and wan young men. Mrs. Touchett (*Portrait of a Lady*) takes Isabel Archer away from vulgar Albany and sets her where she may by the finest shadings move from maidenhood to gentle, fiscal bridehood. In *The Golden Bowl* it is the elderly Fanny Assingham upon whom the Prince leans. Her husband is a doltish colonel who helps her provide a gelded marriage in which two people occupy space at different intervals. The Prince is dull, or as James writes in one of his countless, high-born platitudes, "innocent, beautiful, vague."

James was the canniest male peeper that ever observed feminine habits. In his lengthy, busybody sentences he is not behind the arras watching a woman; he is much too near the subject-matter for that. In *The Golden Bowl,* when Charlotte Stant comes into the room and sees her hostess with a man she is not prepared for, she comes in altogether composed—which is just what a woman would do, and exactly what a man cannot do without being exorbitantly clumsy. Such trifling details are only valued by the feminine. James comprehends the female urgency to delay, and knows that patience is a tactic; it is his knowledge of decorum that enables him to guess an adulterous act in *The Portrait of a Lady.* When Isabel Archer notices her husband seated while he is talking to Madame Merle, who is standing, she knows that the relaxed, intimate familiarity between them is illicit.

James had so little masculine force that he had to take up the lady trades of the ruse, the advantage and the investment. He offers the refined and superannuated *scandale,* untainted by impropriety or the rank misdemeanors of the blood.

The Freeman, 1952

George Ross Ridge

Preface to *The Black Beatitudes,* by George Ross Ridge

I have read *The Black Beatitudes* several times and always with passion. It is a little American song of Zarathustra written by the poet, George Ross Ridge, when he was seventeen. Usually we produce men who are boys, and almost never wise children, like Chatterton, Hart Crane, Rimbaud, or Ridge.

Ridge assails what Nietzsche calls the "ass festival" of the old, shrewd morals. Has not virtue, preempted by the respectable people, become more fell than vice?

The cenobite of poetry no longer flees to the desert or to remote, darkling mountains to fashion his parables; he eats his cactus and drinks his "bloodparched lips," according to Ridge, in a city apartment, that "viscera of dark grottoes," and "locks himself in the market-place." Eating himself piecemeal, because there is no woman with stout, country loins to ease him, and no friend or adversary to placate his eagle faculties, he "counts the hours with centipede's legs."

Most persons live dead, or are stillborn; when they die, they only absent themselves, as Thoreau said. George Ross Ridge writes: "There was a time I thought autumn melancholy, but soon I learned spring to be even sadder; your birth was a greater agony than your death will be."

These are black, rapturous maxims composed in a no-saying, nihilistic century. But far better the brave, black beatitudes than the worm-eaten sunsets and moons of the venal bourgeoisie and the honest folk whom Baudelaire despised.

1963

III

Fiction

The Dream Life of Mary Moody

The fire in the wood stove was burning low. Mrs. Moody, the wife of the man who was lying in the coffin, stared mutely at the glowing embers. She felt cold, mentally numb, and indifferent. Two junk peddlers were glancing furtively at one another, while a Catholic priest intoned a funereal hymn. His fat fingers, which he used as an indicator, moved haltingly from one word to the other. The undertaker, an intimate friend of the deceased one, looked speculatively at the long, thin head of the dead man and then at his child-like body. His carefully brushed suit seemed to lie about him like swaddling clothes. The peculiar light cast over his waxen face by the flickering candle gave one the impression of a grotesque Chinese mask. While Willie, the undertaker's assistant, officiously retouched a crease in the still man's trousers, the two junk peddlers, with caps in their hands, were gingerly moving towards the door.

Mrs. Moody went towards the window. There she stood and contemplated the rows of bottles which were piled pyramidally upon one another. Patches of January snow had gathered about and between them, and the wintry sunlight sportively played through their colored glass. As she gazed at the elongated necks of these bottles she suddenly thought of her husband, and then she realized that she had not been thinking of him. She had been musing upon bottles all morning and all the week, and since the day that she had married Mr. Moody. She stared at the wood stove and wondered why he had not built a kiln and been a bottle manufacturer instead of a bottle picker.

As she stood at the window and took inventory of the rows of bottles that lay in the backyard she spoke to him as she had always spoken to him: she carried on long soliloquies which were always addressed to him; she would remonstrate with

297

him, rebuke him, irk him; but when he would come home late in the evenings for his supper she could say nothing. His voice, become hoarse and cracked through his calling, stifled her. He was always weary, absolutely fatigued; it oppressed her, crushed her completely. Silently he would eat his meal and then rekindle the fire in the stove with newspapers and the wood of orange boxes. Following this he would light his pipe and sprawl his aching feet upon the stove.

Always at nine she heard his heavy shuffle creaking against the boards of the floor. She would call to him: "Jim, how many bottles today?" When she heard his sullen muttering she would pass her greasy fingers through her thin, nondescript hair, feel herself deteriorating, and lament the futile, passing years. Then she would throw herself into a violent temper, swear, and scatter pans and utensils about which she knew would never break. As he would slip out of his suspenders and seat himself on the edge of the iron bed, he would answer: "Oh, let me alone. Where's Mary?"

At this point Mrs. Moody frowned and covertly glanced about the room. The hymns were done. Mary Moody was sitting on a box in the corner quite still. Her immobility fretted her mother. Mrs. Moody turned away and looked again at the bottles. There were four hundred of them, the entire estate that Mr. Moody had left her. The cleric offered his condolences, while the two junk peddlers hurriedly stammered out some terse speech and said they would be missing Bottler Moody. The undertaker quietly went out through the door, while Willie dexterously relit a candle that had become extinguished. Then he left. Mary, who was still huddled together on the box, stared blankly before her. Her mother, with set determination, went out into the backyard to recount the bottles.

Mary was alone with the dead man. She stirred and moved towards the wood stove, where she warmed herself. She looked at her father for one long minute and wept in a muffled voice. Then she sat down on the floor and opened the door of the stove. The flames crackled and illumined her delicate face and created a curious halo about her pale flaxen hair. She was so tired and weak and wanted to sleep, but could not. She felt hungry and wanted to munch on a crust of dry bread that was lying on the kitchen table, but when she saw the wooden box in the middle of the room and looked at the sickly yellow flame which came from the waxen tapers she felt ill and faint.

Suddenly she heard in the distance the discordant rumbling of the elevated train. She trembled. She ran towards the window and pressed her dumpy nose against the pane. She blew her breath against it and peered through the clear space. It came nearer. Its maddening rhythm evoked other rhythms, other sounds and movements. Her whole body quivered with motion. Bits of pictures, ephemeral images, fragments of her own sensuous and visual experiences came back to her: a lumber yard, a thin drizzle, the odors of wet wood, the dank earth, dead autumnal leaves, the silken petticoat and carmine lips of Margaret O'Rourke, a strip of Belgian lace in a shop window, the street lamp at night, the gas-lit office of the undertaker where Mr. Moody was wont to spend his Saturday evenings. She could hear her father sharply cutting the cards with his long, bony fingers. Mary remembered how nicely and quietly he did it, and with what nervous expectancy she awaited his turn to cut and shuffle the pack. She would watch Willie, whose intentness hypnotized her. The dull light from the gas jet hurt her eyes. He would become blurred and assume the shapes, faces of the king of hearts and jack of diamonds. She also recalled that when the playing cards had become thumb-marked and had lost their original stiffness Willie would become inattentive and doze off for awhile. Afterwards he would slowly rise from his chair, lazily stretch his arms, and, addressing his employer, the undertaker, would say: "Shall I be washin' the new gent upstairs now." This casual remark always oppressed Mary and made her think of such lurid thoughts. She would promise herself faithfully and with tears in her eyes that she would never go to the undertaker's office again. She would want to run home, but she was afraid to go into the dark streets alone. She feared the stillness of the night, the intermittent rumbling of the elevated train. She would begin to timidly tug at her father's coat and implore him to come home. At night she would wrap herself closely in her blanket. She would turn her back to the window, as she was afraid to look into the back-yard. Sometimes big tom cats from the alley would slink over the green and blue bottles and cast eerie shadows on the ground, which appeared like corpses to her.

Mary, too, would lose interest in the old cards, which no longer gave off the sharp, rhythmic sound that so delighted her ear. She would no longer accompany her father on Saturday evenings until Willie would meet and tell her: "Well, Mary, we're havin' a brand new deck this even'. Ye mustn't miss it." Mary also liked to contemplate with naïve speculation the cigarette whorls that rose to the gray ceiling of the under-taker's office. She thought at times that the players' faces and eyes became so unreal and imaginary when they were veiled underneath circles of smoke. On days when she was walking through the park in the Battery her eyes would curiously wander after the smoke that issued from the boats which plied up and down the Hudson. She tried to detect its flight, and believed that the stars received their milky body from the smoke and their light from the sparks which the horseshoes gave off as they struck against the cobblestones. At times, when she could find no way of amusing herself, she would draw in the air invisible spirals and bizarre figures with her white, bloodless fingers.

At school she was stupid and dazed. Her teacher thought she was slow, lazy, and lethargic. She had no friends: the children looked askance at her, because she seemed dull and eccentric; they did not play with her, although she often watched them with longing. She was too timid to ask them to let her play. Her peculiarities, her coarse underwear, which could be seen below her thin, cotton dress, and through her torn stockings, embarrassed them and made them titter. They behaved towards her like grown-ups who have been surprised by a certain candid turn of speech from a vaudeville actor in a theater.

Jim Moody, the bottle picker, was buried. His widow no longer found it necessary to think either evil or good of him; his existence in her mind, which had always been rather vague and blurred, had no further reason for being; since he did not come to the house any more, nor mutter, "Where's Mary?" nor throw his heavy, muddy boots in the corner before falling into bed. Mary scarcely ever saw her mother, who now spent her days and nights in the alleys and streets picking bottles. The widow secretly hid her savings in the ground in the backyard underneath a pile of broken bottles. She knew Mary would never play there. She hoped in a few months to leave—to leave the moist ashes, coffins, mist, and glass of the city and till her own earth, see grass, farm fences, smell alfalfa, clover, take in her dry hands the rich, crude earth, and live in a sunny valley in Southern California. Meanwhile she plied her trade indefatigably; she picked them in order that she might run away from them. She hated bottles, because they were taciturn and immobile like her late husband.

In the morning, when Mary awoke, she either found on the kitchen table food for the day or ten cents for rolls and coffee. Mary ate little: her pallid face became more ethereal. Sometimes she wept: she did not know why; she never blamed anyone for her misery. She felt in a sort of vague way that it was as it should be. Mournfully she would gaze at the cold stars and attribute to them the cause of her father's death.

One night she was hurrying home. It was bitterly cold and desolate, and she was anxious to creep into her little bed. The stars looked like the icy points of stalactites, and the snowy clouds seemed to be huddled together like bleating lambs. As she was about to turn the corner into a side street she heard a familiar voice calling after her. Mary looked back and saw the

301

face of the undertaker. Willie, with a long cob pipe in his mouth, was at her side. "Mary, we're not seein' ye any more these here days," said the undertaker quietly. Mary turned away, gazed vacantly at the fragile streak of light which the gas lamp stained on the sidewalk, and shivered with cold. "No," she finally said, in almost a whisper. "Yes," said Willie, taking his pipe out of his mouth with deliberation, "the cards don't cut so well, Mary, since yer away." The undertaker laid his long, thin hand gently on her head and said cautiously to the child: "I've been thinkin' much of ye—thinkin', perhaps, maybe I could be adoptin' ye fer my own little girl." Mary's eyes appeared troubled. She looked uneasy, and stammered, as she went into the by-street: "But I have a mother!" The undertaker gazed sadly after the little figure, which had already become enveloped in cheerless darkness. Willie put his cob pipe back into his mouth, and he and the undertaker silently walked along the street.

As she neared the wooden frame house she saw a light in the kitchen. The oil lamp was lit. She saw her mother, as she opened the back door. Mrs. Moody was in excellent spirits. She fried an egg for Mary, gave her a letter, and placed in her little palm a fifty-cent piece. She told Mary that she was going away for a while, but that Mary would get the right care while she was gone. Mary put the letter and the half-dollar in her overcoat pocket and mechanically moved towards her bed. "How about yer egg?" asked her mother kindly. Mary sat down at the table and nibbled at the egg without appetite. She rose again and started to untie her shoelaces. "Aren't ye washin' yer dirty face?" laughed Mrs. Moody, jestingly, underneath which there lurked a touch of hysteria. Mary sprinkled a little of the ice-cold water that came from the faucet on her face, dried herself, and crept into bed. She felt feverish and depressed by a fitful cough. Her mother came near the bed and solicitously wrapped her in a long overcoat which she took off; she stood there and lightly stroked her hair. Mrs. Moody felt sad and uncomfortable. She studied Mary's face, as if through this she hoped to quiet her own thoughts. She looked critically into Mary's glassy eyes, which accentuated the transparent texture of her skin. They seemed to start from her head and to dance in space like hollow eyes of two steel pistols directed at her. "His eyes!" she thought, recovering herself. There before her she saw the same small, taciturn mouth—his mouth, the same careless, almost indifferent pout about the lips, which delicately parted. She turned away and suddenly glanced at the alarm clock. It was nine. She expected to hear his monotonous muttering from the bedroom and to feel pounding against her thin temples the thud of his muddy boots falling one after the other.

That night Mary could not sleep. She coughed, and turned from one side to the other. Through the windowpane she saw a weird and familiar figure bent over the earth. As she gazed at the bottles near by, upon which the moon cast its icy gleams, she saw its shadow, twisted like a dipper, heaping up dirt. Fascinated by what frightened her, she glanced at it out of the corners of her eyes. She then closed her eyes tightly and tried to sleep.

The morning was clear. Cold currents of air crept through the crannies and cracks of the windows. Mary rose. She felt strangely calm and light of body. She drank her coffee hurriedly and hastily bit into a piece of roll. She could hardly wait to feel her little feet against the gray pavement. The sun rose and warmed the city. Mary walked with rapid steps, and thought of all the things she would do. With fifty cents in her pocket she experienced the buoyant security of one accustomed to penury. She wanted to ride in the elevated train, see everything in passing—rows and rows of red-brick tenement houses moving before her like one motion-picture scene after another, throngs of people like dots below her, vendors' carts piled with oranges, apples, deep yellow bananas.

The noonday was blessed. The sun was soft and limpid and streaked the cobblestones and bare, gray trees with its golden gleam. Everything was astir. The surface cars struck their own

303

rhythms against the steel tracks, mixing them with the staccato cries of the peddlers in the streets. The elevated train, with its intermittent noise—a noise whose nervous, jerky, rapid movement was like that of a jazz orchestra—completed the metropolitan chorus. Mary halted before a fruit stand and contemplated with sensuous pleasure the round, red and yellow tangerines which were piled upon one another like an Egyptian pyramid. She tremblingly touched one with her fingers, the skin of which was delicately tinted with the blood that ran through them like that of the red juice of the tangerine, which seemed to give color to its own thin peel. The man in the white apron gave her a shopkeeper's glance. She felt in her pocket for her money, courageously picking up the tangerine in her hand. Behind her she heard the loud rumbling of a wagon and the startled cries of a few passersby. As she started to turn around she was struck and fell on the sunny sidewalk. An automobile had collided with a milk wagon and sent it through the window. The milk flowed over the pavement and mingled with the blood that trickled from her head. Someone picked her up. The tangerine was still in her hand. A policeman came and searched in her pockets and took from them the half-dollar and a letter addressed to the undertaker. Crowds pressed about and sought with a hungry look the automobile driver, who had escaped.

Before they reached the undertaker's establishment, which was a few blocks distant, Mary Moody was dead. They entered the undertaker's office. It was empty. The policeman looked about. The room was desolately vacant. On the dull, wood table lay a cob pipe and a deck of cards. The officer called. The undertaker appeared at the head of the stairway and came down. "Will ya take her?" asked the officer, handing him the letter. "Otherwise they'll have to lay her away in Potter's Field." He took the child, removed the pipe and the cards, and laid her gently on the cold table. Then he read a note which was scrawled on a piece of paper: "I'm leavin' Mary with you.

She's his'n, not mine, and he was always yer friend. Yu and Mary are suited, and both so quite like."

"Shall I be washin' Mary?" asked Willie that evening. "No," answered the undertaker, "I'll do it. But I wish you'd go to that notion store and ask them to give you the silk dress and the ribbons I ordered."

This Quarter, 1929

Graphophone
Nickelodeon Days

'it looks like a big
like a big night tonight
a big night tonight . . .'

And yet it all came back, the taste of it, the tang and brine of it,
like the windy crispy newspaper afternoon air over the san
francisco wharves. All that he was and could never completely
unknow   all those down-and-out days went carouselling
through his brain   ragtiming through his head the alley-
nights in back of the 8th street lady barber shop, a broken
spiderweb, the barefooted nigger evenings in fall, *run-sheep-*
run, the tough hot bakery independence avenue julys, wading
in khaki mudpuddles sunk in vacant lots   locust, cherry,
maple, walnut, wyandotte, the smelly leaves, the roots, the
branches, the gutters of the streets, the water from the fire-
pump swobbing them—he could never erase them.

   Still slides, *love me and the world is mine,* graphophone
nickelodeons, slot machine phonographs

                              it looks like a big
                              like a big night tonight
                              a big night tonight

a hot time
in the old town
tonight
   one cent muscle machine: how many lamps can you light,
can you ring the bell,
you ring the bell: penny arcade moving pictures:

                                        ladies night in
                                        a turkish bath

What the book
agent saw
punching bag, muscle builder, fortune teller, penny arcade
postcard proverbs:
                        a rolling stone
                        gathers no moss
                        (but who in the hell)
                        wants to gather moss)

   george washington public school on independence avenue:
                        there's some one tapping
                        on the maple tree
                        jackie frost, jackie frost
                        came in the night
                        who killed cock robin
                        it was i with my little hatchet
                        ring around a rosie
                        a hot time in the old
                        town tonight

   get a peep at *venus* through the telescope for only a nickel!
cheap at half the price but why through a telescope   it's a
word beginning with f, strawberry pimples on her cheeks,
drawers were always falling, *honey boy i hate to see you leave
me,* kimonoes, garters, corsets, hairpins, perfume behind her
ears, emma, loosely kimonoed, her thighs, a dream out of
beverly of graustark, her talcum-powdered lotion-creamed
breasts—a long moving picture soul kiss   hot tossing
nights, her thighs whorling like an electric barber pole: the
penny arcade automatic piano jangling away in spasms...

                        call me up some rainy afternoon
                        and we'll have a quiet little spoon

                                307

and we'll talk about the weather
i'll see that my mother takes a walk
mum's the word, baby dear . . .

when he grew up he'd eat thirty lemon pies all at once . . . *oh,
oh, oh don't be afraid*

dago bread, cheney watermelon hucksters, lyric moving picture house, open air tents, lawdie lawdie tabernacle sermons,
halley's comet, the end of the world, bad rodent dreams in the
8th street flat, bohunk nightmares, blackhand barky trees,
pimpish gaslight joints, the midnight ride of a can of beer, *ach
du lieber augustin*

   the kansas city west bottoms, a wiry and rusty rat trap, the
bluffs, stale, gone-looking boxcar smoke in the back of his
throat, red caboose bonfires, corn-stalk smoking, m.k.t.,
chicago & alton blakean alfalfa field midnights, *casy jones got
another papa,* roundhouse cindery toe-stubbing noons, adobe
main street 11 o'clock mornings, armour & swift packinghouse summers, dusty hoofbeaten heifer clouds, kansas city
stockyards, biting cement feedbag dust 4th of julys, dog-lolling
street bum days, cool strawy bins, hosstrough waterpail stalls
in stedna's liverystables, hoss swopping piddling saturdays,
pony boy, pony boy, won't you be my tony boy, manurish
heeled oklahoma stockmen, good tippers, got a haircut, egg
shampoo, a shave, a massage, and a manicure, took the whole
works in his mother's barber shop: street car conductors,
cheap skates: stingier than a close shave, awful mashers,
twenty three skidoo for you kid   the flatiron salesman was
an old rounder

   Bananas and cream kellogg's cornflakes sundays, dragging,
ant-like bath sundays, grand pa's tar soap, dutch cleanser, gold
dust twins, whiskbroom, scoured kitchen sink, carpet dusting

308

—he had to shoo the furniture polish rag over the postcard views of swope park, the old shanty union depot, his mother said he was more trouble than his measly help was worth: he was good riddance

the grand opera house, tige and buster brown, the funnies, in my old kentucky home, *massa's in the cold cold ground,* cecile was the orneriest chippy in the star lady barber shop, had ten men on the string, you couldn't trust her from here to there

Mary was a still-water, never ate meat on good fridays, wore high top-boots, lace shirtwaists which concealed her flatiron breasts: her legs were lost in the amusement park grotto of her shroud-black clothskirt: she never cut up with the trade: when she quit lizzie's shop the saloonkeeper next door set her up in diamonds and lighthousekeeping and bought her all kinds of fancy cutglass: cecile said, you could take it from her, they never took out a license

the question girl, a week's run at the grand opera, the spokey bohunk umbrella factory across the way: he played around the wooden boxcar cases with ghizella who was too smart for her age but what could you expect, her mother always slept with another codger every night, her paw was a cranky round-shouldered old screw who ran a barber's itch college down on the lower commissionhouse main street, near the cowboy and indian gillis theater and the city carrot peas asparagus cream cheese vegetable and meat market, but lorry thought she was a regular peach: her watercolor hair, curly papershavings, was prettier than the coca cola girl on the owl drugstore anniversary sale calendar: when he was going on nine, with tantalizing mesmerizing *school days* in the back wings of his head, he hummed:—

oh gee, be sweet to me kid
i'm awfully fond of you
i'm blue when you're cross to me
come treat me square kid
i love you for fair—for
i'm crazy kid, crazy for you
love me the way you did—
fill me with joy, my honey boy
oh gee, be sweet to me kid . . .

. . . because she wouldn't kiss him   one saturday afternoon
when his mother was shaving and haircutting and joshing in
the star lady barber shop ghizella helped him carry the provi-
sion basket up the steep hill to the 8th street flat: they were in
the lacecurtained cutglass parlor sitting on the piano-stool: don
harney, the peroxide blonde, with the troublesome appendix,
who was kept by drew, a reporter on the k.c. journal, was in the
next room hotwaterbottling her right side: lorry was dead gone
on ghizella who told him how she and leslie had played house
together: then how leslie and his sister had done it: and how
she and leslie's sister had played taking turns doing the house-
keeping and putting the sofapillow in its proper place and
folding back the sunday bedspread   ghizella played

i like coffee
i like tea
i like lorry
and lorry likes me

on the bass upright piano so that don harney in the next room
couldn't hear her   ghizella said it was good, so good, much
better than cracker jacks or taffy and lorry wanted to ask for it
but he was tongue-tied and couldn't get a word out of his
mouth   then there was eight year old mabel who he knew
when they lived up on shady forest avenue who told him how

it was done but he was afraid   when mabel was seventeen she
left her husband and two kids in joplin and ran off with her
uncle   the last he heard about ghizella she was streethustling
in windy chi.: rundown at the heels, saving u.s. cigar coupons
for a set of roger's silverware and working in a turdy whore-
house: she had gone clean nuts, that's what bud taylor said before
he knocked up buella claire   when ghizella was eleven a black
stovepipe nigger dragged her into a vacant lot. bud heard his
maw talking about it to mr. coffee, the flatiron salesman

The oblong pasteboard pictures inside *sweet caporal* and
hassan turkish cigarettesboxes of john l. sullivan, stanley
ketchel (shot by accident), william mc kinley, joe gans (kicked
off with t.b.), golden goldfilling smiling heavyweight champion
jack johnson (railroaded out of country for white-slaving), ad
wolgast (the chicago stockyard boy), abe attel (flashiest light-
weight in ring), 3-fingered mordecai brown (greatest spitball
pitcher of all times), second baseman larry lajoie, casey at the
bat discus-throwers, polevaulters, olympic players, roald
amundsen, arctic pole missouri dairy refrigerators, teddy
roosevelt, big game hunters, rough riders, *remember the
maine,* commodore perry, don't shoot boys, the kansas city
paseo, the spanish-american war, the u.s. armory, teddy
roosevelt days, wide-open pretzel limburger cheese saloon
times

> oh bring back those eggs
> at ten a dozen,
> bring back those wonderful
> days

bock, swiss, porterhouse charlie steak, hot tamale, chili con
carne mexican greasers, the schottishe, 12*th street blues,* the
millionaire tramp, the candy kid . . .

all that was his boyhood louvre . . . phineas's dad's three gilded balled pawnshop on walnut street (that's the way to ball the jack: some day phineas would grow up and have three balls like his father had and be as strong as samson): phineas was rich and used toney words: *booty,* willis woods theater, country club district, fairmount park airs: he wore swell knickers and a button on his coatlapel with printing on back: *to hell with the maine* . . .

Peck's quick lunch, nickel lemon creamy suns, buttered oyster cracker packing lard tincan noontimes, two bits chicken dinners, chili beans, parchment yellow spuds, high yellow oleomargarine, the greasy crisco moon, upstairs, back, over tischa's licensed house: clean as a pin: all the switchmen and railroad johnnies went there for a piece of tail: 12th street was classier then   tischa had delicatessen winnie wurst sores in an anthill mound on her cheeks and beer-stained hair and ran around with a silk jazzshirted, lislesocked dopefiend with a brilliantine advertising pompadour: he had toney mint's breath: lorry chewed wrigley's spearmint: he wanted a sweet hightone hotel baltimore breath   he wanted to be the candy kid and a willis woods theater dude: . . .

> you've got me going going kid
> you are my little merry wid
> you are just the candy kid
> you've got me going going some . . .

*   *   *   *   *   *

> *'tickle me here*
> *tickle me dear*
> *tickle me love*
> *in these lonesome ribs'*
>   james whitcomb riley

Automatic pianola clinking rain, clinking clinking champagne alaskan eugene field ice, edgar guest shooting gallery verse

Lew Dockstader's minstrels, blackfaced coon nights, black stovepipe nigger alleys, ghizella, poor dear, ringling bros. circus, barnum & bailey, a sucker born every minute, and now that we have stop-watches, dockstader's minstrels better than sis hopkins:

> if a body meets a body
> comin' through the rye

people were buying tickets to beat the band, a packed house every night, bigger event than the priest of pallas parade, or the arrival of the millionaire tramp

A colored jokebook drop curtain: blackfaces in purity squad whitegloves, marching up and down the stage

> keep time
> keep time

An orchestration of seventy chairs; two comedians start in with a hick's barndance jig, turkey in the hay

> turkey in the straw

Programs are still rustling. The lowney chocolates, hersey and bon bons candy-butcher has just died down. The minstrel joshing gets under way. It's still a horse on the audience.

say nigger, where wuz you born?

in virginia.

well, what part?

all of me, nigger, all of me.

The audience titters. Thin potato chip titters crackle in the theater *sweet caporal* dust.

so, you all comes of noble blood.

yes sah.

well, what kind of blood do you all come from?

i done told you, nigger, i comes of high blood

lookee, here, coon, the only high blood you got in you is high blood pressure.

The programs whiskbroom the hot air again.
A darky tenors

> mr brown, went around
> all around,
> with his violin,
> lawdy, how he played it,
> made it moan
> so beautiful
> fiddle up, fiddle up

then another jokester interrupts:
why don't you try an operatic air?
operatic air, what kinda air is that?
try madame butterfly.
you try her.

A fat man in the audience boo-hoos into his handkerchief, makes round circular liquid yodels, and gurgles up and down his galli curci coloratura stairs. The rest of the orchestra take him up.

A fellow in the niggerheaven gallery whistles through his fingers. The crowd is pulsing and motorthrobbing with the actors. The jokester waits and then goes on:
all right, i'll try her.
what you waitin' for, go on and try her.

all right. the next song, to please the ladies in the box, is entitled, madame butterfly, to her frigid husband: some day, he'll come.

Cattle stampeding stampeding of feet everywhere. Thick yellow spudblocks of laughter jam the air. The audience brings down the house. Then the jokester, like a referee in the center of the ring, holds up his hands for quiet, and continues.

now for the benefit of the reading-loving public in the theater, i'll recite:

> 'lilies are both pure and fair
>   growing midst the roses there—
> roses, too, both red and pink,

are quite beautiful, i think.'
but—
another runner-up interrupts:
roses, red, violets blue,
i can row, can-oe, can-oe.

A skinny toothpick cigarmanufacturer wipes the blobs of carousel tears whorling on his spectacles. Then he adjusts his chair in the box. He tries to remove the part that he knows is his from the adhesive tailormade cloth.

The minstrel ringleader makes a stab at another. The clinking clinking eugene field ice hoarfrosts the theater air.

the years had dragged a weary pace
since last those joys i tasted,

The fellow in the gallery sirens through his fingers. And then: drag him out!

Lew Dockstader enters. Lew Dockstader who shook the country like the russian revolution of 1905.

*   *   *   *   *   *

*'layers and layers of sensation
and no heart in it.'*

peer gynt.

And now thousands and hundreds of lady barbershop female smells flooded him: witch hazel, bay rum, facecreams, hairtonics, talcumpowdered breasts, Emma, loosely kimonoed, her body damp and smelling of his thick bedroom imaginings —all that flooded in upon him, but he was not there. And all the neuter odors of shoeleather, sprinkled streets, tar, lumber piles, stirred in his nose, but he was not in it. For he had not yet emerged from them, could not.

And from the american minstrel troubadour trouvere days: a bit of blank cartridge verse:

315

'the years had dragged a weary pace
   since last those joys i tasted
and i have grown so wan of face
   and oh, so slender-waisted!'
'o saw ye bonny lesley
   as she gaed o'er the border?
she's gane, like alexander,
   to spread her conquests farther.'

punching bag, guess your weight fortune teller lines:
'so now, in the prime of my manhood, i polish
     this lyric gem'
     'or shall i wear the bottoms of my trousers rolled?'
'of the clink of the ice in the pitcher the boy brings up
    the hall'
up the hall up the hall of the memory-membrane tissues of
the nose, clinking, clinking against metaphysical corridors and
stirring up the museum—desolation in his blood—'o metaphysical head.'

      *   *   *   *   *   *

*   'ist das nicht das weisenhaus,*
*   ya wohl, das ist das weisenhaus . . .'*

   The cleveland orphanage, the old mother's home down the
block, the green dollar bill blades of grass out on the front
lawn, *es ist verboten,* fifty demerits for stubbing one's toes
against them, the waterfountain mute as a stillborn child in
soured and dried shrubbery february: ratty wet wooden chicken
coop march: mick and gullyside januarys   the slit of sky seen
through the orphan asylum dormitory window, an enameled
mush tinplate—snowblue enamel   in summer the fountain
played on 1st and 2nd picnics *ist das nicht das weisenhaus,*
down the hill, the mill on the floss, snoring silas marner after-

noons in the schoolhouse, around the bend over the diphtheria pond, becker's stalecakes, becker's heavy neckboils, herman mush tate's dictionary of sure-fire words earthier than the bible, woodland avenue pushcart boulevard, goulashy every-other-wednesday sausages, christine's drawer's, mick and gullyside january days, hospital pruney sundays, *ist das nicht das weisenhaus, ya wohl, das ist das weisenhaus, we the people of the united states, i pledge allegiance, one nation, indivisible, with liberty and justice for all, ya wohl, das ist das weisenhaus, o wie schön es, o wie schön es, o tennenbaum, o tennenbaum, und die kuchen schmekt so gut,* every-other-wednesday sausages, gray pruney graham cracker sundays, we the people of the united states

The goddam potsdam court, unter den linden, milwaukee lager, schlager beer, donner und blitzen, *hail, hail the gang's all here,* conf. 1917, his first skylark blueserge long pants, virgin mary white immaculate american carnation confirmation day, *good bye j.o.a., i say good bye to you, without the least regret* . . . out in the city, a former inmate, out in the big wide world, the american playboy of the western world, raymond hitchcock—*hitchy koo—oh, oh, oh, it's the cutest little thing,* lake erie air, free free euclid avenue air, high tone air, vaudeville air, rockefeller park, wade park, Keith's Circuit 1917 . . . *if i only had your disposition, i'd be lovin' you all the time, if you're crazy about the women, you're not crazy at all, you're so pretty, oh, so pretty, you're some pretty doll,* that's the way life was out in the big city, The keith's circuit vaudeville slapstick war: *i may be gone for a long long time, over there, over there,* khaki forever, three cheers for, social criticism: *i didn't raise my boy to be a soldier, then what are you doing over here,* you goddam son of bitchin' bolsheviks, the big parades, the war, The War, THE FATHER, SON, AND THE HOLY GHOST: THE WAR: *all ye millions i embrace thee,* the redlight districts were shut down, puberty skyscraper erections, tallest building in the world, bigger and better wars, *all*

ye millions i embrace thee, you goddam son of bitchin' bolsheviks, *then what are you doing over here, over there, over there*
    The yanks are coming . . . the yanks are coming, puberty
skyscraper erections, the vaginal walls of jericho are falling

*   *   *   *   *   *

> 'And upon her forehead was a name
> written, MYSTERY, BABYLON
> THE GREAT, THE MOTHER OF
> HARLOTS AND ABOMINATIONS
> OF THE EARTH.'
>   the revelation

NEW YORK, the syphilitic body of god, its jaundiced electric
lights diseasing the night, welfare island, a cancerous blurred
negative, the stippled waters of the east river, over the queens-
boro bridge, faster, faster, faster, *eveready flashlight batteries,*
adams black jack, And upon her forehead was a name
written, SOCONY, SOCONY, MYSTERY, chiclets, dentyne,
brisbane steel frame cottages, *BABYLON THE GREAT, SO-*
CONY, THE MOTHER OF HARLOTS, queens boulevard,
welcome to long island city, *AND ABOMINATIONS OF THE*
EARTH, faster, faster, *batter my heart, batter my heart*
    MAIN st. FLUSHING to CALVARY, saul's *dead march,* the
theater moon, *pomp and circumstance,* the stars strung tele-
graph-wise across a logarithm table in the back of a text book,
coney island calvary cemetery nights, *and his son isaac and*
ishmael buried him in the cave of machpelah in the field of
ephron, mardi gras confetti seaside bathing saturday evenings,
oyster house seaside brine, secondhand seaweed, the ritzy
calvary cemetery leaves swing over the daily graphic slabs: the
dream surrealistic theater leaves . . . the theater moon, an
open can of armour & swift packinghouse lard, *batter my*
heart . . .

318

It went carouselling through his brain. . . . He took the evening in the palm of his hands and rubbed his eyelids across it.

Pagany, 1931

Samuel Beckett's Wake

Today I'm going to die, and bless your heart, on the Assumption. Ah me, it's daybreak, the clouds a herd of fleecy lambs, and the sun brazen as Menelaus' house. But I feel simply awful, down at the mouth, and full of the most dreadful revulsions, as if I had just stepped upon human ordure.

Jesus and Holy Mother Mary, I'm dying, or dead as all my friends, a whole cemetery of my enemies and their relations, and their foes and their bloody friends; may every blessed one of them burn in ice and freeze in fire.

I can see my palsied mother at the window of our cottage, hanging out my father's drawers. Never mind that; it's all one and the same; for what's bad is sure to be worse were it not evil in the beginning.

The crocuses are peeping up above the turf. It's late afternoon, as if that mattered, and my stale uncle is Bible reading and hawking up saffron phlegm. Curse the old concupiscent devil, and his luskish uncle, and all of them pewing every Sunday. Damn the whole pewing lot: my mother's mother, and her pewing gammer, and my father's father's excrement, and my priggish grand-aunt's stinking shift, wormy, mind you, as her crafty lusts, and what of her halfpenny ancestors, and all my distant cousins which our mother earth has transubstantiated into maggots. Yes, they are snug and quiet many feet deep in the ground which is no better than a jakes. Forget I said that. They were good as worthless folk can be, and not a whit better.

Still I'm dying, always dying, and nature making ready to receive my worn-out body. What a bloody affair is the body. But let that be. Let the postman whistle while I'm lying on my pallet. Maybe it's St. John the Baptist's Day, when the roses of Picardy are blooming, and there are the birds, winged angels, and their droppings, and the turds of pigeons white as the sepulchre, bless you, but rotten within. And consider the fowls in the air dunging and copulating, as if living and dying were anything else. Consider the ducks, the widgeon and the teal, spawning simply to shit upon the whole race.

What's the point of it? The rain's falling and falling and dying upon the bogs, and the skies are black and bellowing. I'm talking to myself; know it, and I don't know it. Why should I bother with anyone, though it's a stiff vigil to be speaking to oneself.

Jesus, I'm shrivelled. My nerves are boiling in the wind. And now, now, all those years dying too, and clean gone. But I must go on, stumbling, and being and not being, and realizing, mind you, the night lies snug in my socks that my mother smelled as I was approaching the door. She said she knew me by the smell of the buttons on my jacket. My old sunken mother, Brigit, I always called her, and my father sucking his pipe or his nether lip, or removing his spermal trousers, and his mind somewhere else, in Galway or Donegal, whilst he wandered and sucked the buttons on his pants.

That brings me back to my wrinkled, aged story about those long glowing walks on the shingle. There I sauntered plucking up pebbles, and counting them, or weren't they stones or shells, and putting them in my dying gray coat, or into my dead pockets. And I'd suck the stones, come to think of it, as if one could come to anything. I can hear the shingle ringing against the shore, and I was sucking up stones, like the saints suck their slabs.

What's it all come to, Holy Mother Mary save me, but sucking and counting stones till the Last Judgment. Mind you, the beginning is the same as the conclusion, the Alpha and the Omega, just sucking and counting pebbles like Ariadne strolling alone on the beach and feeding the swallows.

Isn't the dawn, the noon, and evensong solely various colors on my shoes? I walk in the dusk, a bit more extinguished, mind you; but that's the predicament; people wondering why my gray coat grew thin and weak and good-for-nothing.

But let's get on with the story, and have done with the bloody lonely business: love, friendship, and graving one more useless relative, whilst a dog pauses to urine upon a neighboring headstone. O Lord, who'll listen to my story, the tale of sucking up stones shrunk by the dark, thick rains upon the bogs that suck up the water. I shall keep my eyes shut, and let the twilight come between my legs, and creep into the dead pockets of my gray coat.

I must go on. I've only come to the prologue of my story. It's All Souls' Day; but suppose I had sucked sixteen stones instead of four. Jesus, Mary and Joseph, those stones were sons to me. But as the accursed human race is cruel in all latitudes, I gulped them down my craw, every bloody one of them, just as Saturn swallowed a stone that Rhea swaddled so that the father would think he'd eaten up all his issue.

Well, where's the salvation? I cannot find the solution. I still have a particular odor of my own, like my old man's trousers, and his father's rotten breeches, and his mother's mother's moldy shawl, and her mother's stays stained with a thousand years of smoldering sweat on them. Brigit needed a man, for the old man was already sighing beneath the turf.

I walked thinking on, and I saw the sea and the stones I had sucked before the Flood. It's all over with, the inglorious story; but I'll speak calmly, and let the ground curse my soul.

My mother never refused to see me, though her memory was about clean dead. When I was a foetus in her uterus, she was a thin, sinking faggot. Why was she always saying goodbye; what was good about it? The poor, dear dam was coughing up her lungs, and you could see by her coffin-shaped face that she was preparing for the priest and extreme unction; and her apron as fetid as a new grave in Connemara, bless her. And once more I say farewell to the turdy race.

But the story has not yet ended, although everything from the start was finished.

It was a fine day; but was it; has it ever been? We are one and none.

But I must get on with the story. I've already bid goodbye to my mother's mother's mother, and her father's father, and all of them, mind you, sucking up stones in graveyards.

It was the Purification, and the lass in the neighboring yard, with a plump bottom sleek as a slip; and I was padding it with my nervous, seminal fingers. That was long ago; but is it ever? I was a virile lad, quiet and fast at hard knowledge, and with quick sperm.

Now, and now, mind you, vespers has come and gone; and I've come to no conclusion. But I tell you, I hate Abraham, Isaac and Jacob, and James the Just, and Aaron's rod and the Ephesian sod.

And if all this snivelling be titled the discourse of Plato and the Seraphim, I know I'm an auld windy ballocks, cat-winded, mind you, but nevertheless, I detest all of you, and may every bone and flesh of you expire of Herod's worms or the cat's flux.

Goodnight, God bless, God damn, and peace to my sod, and my lost and gone cod.

Prose, 1973

Index

Abelard, Peter, 54
Acosta, José de, 193, 195
Adams, Henry, 72
Adams, Charles Francis, 249
Adams, John, 259-60
Adams, Samuel Francis, 101
Addison, Joseph, 106
Aiken, Conrad, 84-92
Alcott, Chauncey, 153
Aldington, Richard, 58, 61, 255, 279-81
Alvarado, Pedro de, 182, 186
Amiel, Henri Frédéric, 50
Anacreon, 86
Anaxagoras, 54
Anaximenes, 54
Anderson, Sherwood, 6, 7, 22, 56-58, 71, 72-73, 131, 139, 159, 170,
    172-73, 175, 210-11, 215-16, 266, 277, 290-91
Andrew, Robert, 204
Antheil, George, 277
Antisthenes, 89, 95, 100, 130, 134
Apollinaire, Guillaume, 273
Apuleius, Lucius, 205
Ariel, 5, 130
Aristippus, 100, 168
Aristophanes, 190, 270
Aristotle, 103, 126, 165, 189, 195, 234, 251, 272, 286
Arnold, Matthew, 48
Artaxerxes, 87
Arvin, Newton, 77-83
Asch, Nathan, 278-291
Aspasia, 87-88
Auden, W. H., 229, 254, 284
Augustine, Saint, 195, 257, 263, 280
Azuela, Mariano, 69

Backstairs (film), 4
Bacon, Francis, 274, 283
Balboa, Vasco Núñez de, 184

Bale, John, bishop of Ossory, 161
Balfour, Arthur, 43
Bandelier, Adolph, 101
Bandelier, Fanny, 101
Barbusse, Henri, 36
Barcia, Andrés de, 101
Barker, Virgil, 259-60
Barnes, Djuna, 63, 145-46
Barrie, Sir J. M., 156
Bartram, John, 101
Bates, Henry W., 105
Baudelaire, Charles, 3, 8, 70, 95, 130, 135, 163, 164, 172, 234-36, 258, 284-85, 293
Beach, Sylvia, 282
Beard, Charles, 53
Beaumont, Francis, and John Fletcher, 160
Becher, Johannes, 42
Beethoven, Ludwig van, 172, 284
Bennett, Arnold, 135
Bergson, Henri, 4, 8, 163
Berto, Giuseppe, 232-33
Beverly of Graustark (film), 153, 307
Bhagavad Gita, 103
Blackwood, Algernon, 237-38
Blake, William, 49, 66, 254
Blue Shirts (novel), 40
Boehme, Jacob, 100
Bolingbroke, Lord, 283
Bourne, Randolph, 44-55, 104, 172
Boyle, Kay, 122, 134, 137-39, 175, 277
Bradford, William, 101, 247-49
Bradstreet, Anne, 246, 254, 255
Brancusi, Constantin, 4, 58, 253
Brande, Dorothea, 42
Brecht, Bertolt, 42
Breton, Nicholas, 88
Brinton, Daniel, 100
Britton, Coburn, 160, 164, 169
Broch, Hermann, 273
Brooks, Van Wyck, 7, 29, 49, 51, 53, 135
Brown, Charles Brockden, 51, 78

Browne, Sir Thomas, 58, 105, 106, 280
Browning, Robert, 60, 265
Brüning, Heinrich, 21
Bruno, Giordano, 136, 280
Buddha, 156, 166, 287
Buffon, Georges de, 105
Burchfield, Charles, 154
Burke, Edmund, 268
Burke, Fielding, 211
Burke, Kenneth, 213
Burne-Jones, Edward, 85
Burns, Robert, 316
Burnshaw, Stanley, 127
Bury, Richard de, 160
Butler, Nicholas Murray, 49
Butler, Samuel, 32-33, 71
Bynner, Witter, 279-81
Byron, Lord, 104-5, 241

Cabeza de Vaca, Álvar Núñez, 100, 166
Caesar, Julius, 204
Caillaux, Joseph, 38, 45
Caldwell, Erskine, 33, 67, 69, 70, 206, 208-10, 218
Caliban, 5, 135, 290
Callahan, Judge, 28
Callimachus, 161, 265
Calvin, John, 259
Cantwell, Robert, 206-7, 218, 255
Carlyle, Thomas, 60
Carnevali, Emanuel, 134, 135, 139-43, 175, 277
Cato the Elder, 286
Cato the Younger, 169
Catullus, Gaius Valerius, 201-5, 251, 286
Cavalcanti, Guido, 253
Cézanne, Paul, 169
Chambers, Ann, 155
Champlain, Samuel de, 185-86
Chandos, Lord, 274-75
Chang Yen-yuan, 164
Chapayev (film), 46
Chaplin, Charles, 125

Chapman, George, 161, 255
Chatterton, Thomas, 293
Chaucer, Geoffrey, 74, 102, 137, 168
Chesterfield, Lord, 212
Chesterton, G. K., 135
Chilam Balam of Chumayel, The Book of, 100
Chopin, Frédéric, 111
Christensen, Erwin O., 260
Chrysostom, Saint John, 88
Churchyard, Thomas, 282
Cicero, 88, 162
Claudel, Paul, 37
Clemenceau, Georges, 35
Cocteau, Jean, 89
Coleridge, Samuel Taylor, 59, 106, 131, 161, 264-65
Collins, Seward, 27
Columbus, Christopher, 116, 181, 183-84, 193, 194, 195
Columella, Lucius, 165
Confucius, 269, 272
Congreve, William, 102
Conrad, Joseph, 60, 61, 66, 291
Conroy, Jack, 33, 220
Cook, A. B., 103, 168
Copeland, Aaron, 285
Copley, John Singleton, 259-60
Corbett, Jim, 218
Corbière, Tristan, 95, 226
Coronado, Francisco Vásquez de, 101
Cortés, Hernando, 182
Coughlin, Father, 38, 42
Cowley, Abraham, 35
Cowley, Malcolm, 35
Crabbe, George, 268, 270
Crane, Hart, 73, 85, 122-33, 138, 139, 293
Crane, Stephen, 51, 60, 66, 291
Crates, 168
Croce, Benedetto, 7, 36, 140
Croly, Herbert, 45
Cropper, Harvey, 164
Crosby, Harry and Caresse, 122, 123-24, 139
Cummings, E. E., 35, 36, 65, 209, 285

328

Curtius, Julius, 21

Daedalus, 86
Dahlberg, Edward, other works: *Because I Was Flesh,* 172; *Bottom Dogs,* 123, 136, 140, 222, 224, 282; *Can/Do These Bones Live,* 65, 76; *From Flushing to Calvary,* 222-25
Daniel, Samuel, 106
D'Annunzio, Gabriele, 36
Dante, 75, 144, 227-28, 252, 253
Darwin, Charles, 105
Davenport, Basil, 204-5
Defoe, Daniel, 272
Degas, Edgar, 169
Dekker, Thomas, 106, 141, 161, 177
De la Mare, Walter, 95
Demetrius, 86, 273
Democritus, 87, 88, 163
Dempsey, Jack, 225
Demuth, Charles, 276
Dennis, Lawrence, 27
Derain, André, 169
Descartes, René, 47
De Soto, Hernando, 182, 195
Deterding, Sir Henri, 35
Dewey, John, 45-48, 52
Dickens, Charles, 91
Dickinson, Emily, 75, 78, 79, 91, 127
Dimitrov, Georgi, 39
Diodorus Siculus, 195
Diogenes, 168
Diogenes Laërtius, 168
Dionysius, 90
Dioscorides, Pedanius, 161, 184, 193
D'Israeli, Isaac, 167
Dockstader, Lew, 313-15
Domitian, 130
Donne, John, 31, 96, 102, 130, 162, 250, 255, 268, 269, 285, 318
Doolittle, Hilda, 252, 276
Dos Passos, John, 33, 35, 36, 87, 211-12, 216
Dostoevsky, Fyodor, 69, 125, 163, 243-45, 263, 276
Douglas, Gavin, 62, 204, 255, 273

Douglas, Lord Alfred, 274
Douglas, Norman, 61, 165
Dove, Arthur G., 45
Drayton, Michael, 130
Dreiser, Theodore, 7, 21, 33, 37, 52, 59, 71, 73, 139, 148, 154, 156, 169, 170-72, 206, 211, 213, 215-16, 223
Dryden, John, 106, 162, 205, 271-72
Dudley, Donald R., 168
Duncan, Raymond, 139
Dunlap, William, 51, 78
Duns Scotus, John, 130
Dürer, Albrecht, 261, 263
Dutt, R. Palme, 37

Eakins, Thomas, 260
Eddy, Mary Baker, 150
Eggleston, Edward, 171
Eliot, George, 270, 316
Eliot, T. S., 36, 42, 85, 87, 88, 105, 144, 252, 253, 284, 285, 287, 316
Ellis, Havelock, 110
Emerson, Ralph Waldo, 51, 91, 268
Empedocles, 57, 103, 186, 197, 264
Epictetus, 134
Epicurus, 87
Epimenides, 91
Erasmus, Desiderius, 54, 172, 179, 261, 262, 268
Eratosthenes, 195
Euripides, 86-87, 103, 105, 285
Evans, Donald, 46

Falstaff, 56, 274
Farquhar, George, 55
Farrell, James T., 32, 71, 217-21, 285
Faulkner, William, 67-68, 70-71, 206, 207, 208, 266-67
Faust (film), 4
Fearing, Kenneth, 226-30
Feuchtwanger, Lion, 41
Field, Eugene, 313, 315
Fielding, Henry, 204, 210, 224
Fitton, Mary, 95
Fitts, Dudley, 104

Flaubert, Gustave, 3, 5, 41, 62, 63, 172, 291
Fletcher, John, 128, 160
Ford, Ford Madox, 56-66, 144, 280, 290-92
Fourier, Charles, 243
Fowler, Henry Watson, 106
France, Anatole, 35, 41
Francis, Saint, 189, 263
Frank, Waldo, 29-34, 37, 44, 48, 73, 129, 130-31, 132-33, 135, 216
Fraser, James Earle, 45
Freneau, Philip, 51-52, 78, 254, 255
Freytag, Baroness Elsa von, 276-77
Fuller, Henry B., 171

Gabo, Naum, 96
Galsworthy, John, 60
Gandhi, Mahatma, 38
Garcilaso de la Vega, 100
Garland, Hamlin, 98, 171
Garnett family, 60, 61, 67
Gauguin, Paul, 67
Gentile, Giovanni, 36
Gibbon, Edward, 269, 286
Gide, André, 74, 285, 286
Gigli, Beniamino, 27
Gilchrist, Alexander, 66, 71, 161, 284
Gilchrist, Mrs., 71-72, 161
Gilgamesh, 189
Gill, Eric, 95, 164
Gillespie, Lincoln, 144, 277-78
Gissing, George, 52
Goebbels, Joseph, 25-26, 38
Goethe, Johann Wolfgang von, 262, 270
Gold, Michael, 217
Golding, Arthur, 105
Goldsmith, Oliver, 59
Gompers, Samuel, 46
Gomperz, Theodore, 104
Goncharov, Ivan, 103
Göring, Hermann, 27, 40
Gorki, Maxim, 35, 57, 67, 168-69, 288
Goya, Francisco de, 70, 78

Gratry, Abbé, 288
Graves, Robert, 168
Greco, El, 149
Greene, Robert, 167
Gregory, Horace, 201-3
Gregory, Lady Augusta, 275
Grierson, Sir Herbert, 250
Grote, George, 104, 167, 273
Guest, Edgar, 313
Guevara y de Noroña, Antonio de, 140

Hackett, Byrne, 76
Haecker, Theodore, 241-42
Halleck, Fitz-Greene, 254, 255
Hamlet, 72, 95, 98, 138
Handel, George Frederick, 318
Han Yu, 286
Hardy, Thomas, 7, 48, 61
Harrison, Jane, 103, 184, 186, 187, 273
Harte, Bret, 275
Hartley, Marsden, 58, 262
Hauptmann, Gerhardt, 35, 36
Hawthorne, Nathaniel, 72, 255, 265
Hazlitt, William, 103, 106, 167
Hecataeus, 88
Heine, Heinrich, 18, 64, 125, 175
Held, Anna, 154
Heliogabalus, 286
Hemingway, Ernest, 35, 36, 63, 69-70, 71, 134, 135, 277
Henry the Eighth (film), 4
Heraclitus, 47, 84, 89, 93-94, 274
Herbert, George, 60, 93, 255, 268-69
Herbst, Josephine, 37, 65, 69, 101, 134-35, 137, 147, 278
Hermann, John, 134, 278
Herodotus, 87, 101, 179, 264
Herzen, Aleksandr, 70, 243
Hesiod, 100, 101, 104, 283
Heywood, Thomas, 161
Hindenburg, Paul von, 22, 41
Hippocrates, 274
Hitchcock, Raymond, 317

Hitler, Adolf, 16-22, 23, 27-28, 35, 37, 38, 40, 41
Hobbes, Thomas, 87
Hofmannsthal, Hugo von, 273-75
Holbein, Hans, 261, 263
Hölderlin, Friedrich, 104, 175
Holland, Philemon, 205
Holofernes, 163
Homer, 54, 84, 85, 87, 89, 93, 100, 109, 150, 166, 184, 185, 186,
    194, 205, 270, 283
Hooker, Richard, 268
Hoover, Herbert, 37, 201
Horace, 100, 104, 178, 205, 251, 274, 286
Horton, Philip, 130
Hudson, W. H., 60
Hugenberg, Alfred, 17, 22
Humboldt, Baron Alexander von, 85, 105, 195, 196
Hunt, Holman, 60
Hunt, Violet, 280
Huntington, Constant, 123
Huysmans, Joris Karl, 73, 251

Iago, 180
Ibsen, Henrik, 33, 315
Isaiah, 56, 252, 285
Isherwood, Christopher, 284

Jackson, Holbrook, 161
Jacobson, Eddie, 154-55
James, Alice, 90
James, Henry, 29, 35, 60, 62, 63, 75, 84-85, 87, 88, 90-91, 290-92
James, William, 54, 90-91, 95, 212
Jastrow, Morris, 103
Jerome, Saint, 193
John, Saint, 56
Johns, Richard, 277
Johnson, Arnold, 216
Johnson, Captain Edward, 246
Johnson, Samuel, 59, 205, 254, 268, 270
Johst, Hanns, 38
Jolas, Eugene, 122
Jonson, Ben, 60, 62, 88, 100, 127, 160, 165, 167, 176, 254, 262, 267

Josephus, Flavius, 105
Joyce, James, 5-6, 7, 63, 85, 86, 88, 134, 144, 145, 211, 252, 253, 275, 277, 278
Judith, 163
Jung, Carl Gustav, 33
Juvenal, 253

Kafka, Franz, 274
Kahn, Otto H., 123-24
Kant, Immanuel, 239
Keats, John, 103, 129, 130, 131
Kerrigan, Anthony, 101
Khruschev, Nikita, 123
Kierkegaard, Sören, 52, 71, 95, 241-42
Kingsborough, Lord, 273
Kipling, Rudyard, 35, 36, 275
Kirstein, Lincoln, 213-14
Klee, Paul, 95, 96
Kling, Joseph, 131
Krafft-Ebing, Richard von, 217, 239
Kropotkin, Prince Pyotr, 97-98, 287
Krupp family, 35, 38
Kunitz, Joshua, 42
Kuro Hsi, 164

La Bruyère, Jean de, 95, 104, 168, 283
La Fontaine, Jean de, 105
Lamb, Charles, 160, 161
Landor, Walter Savage, 59, 100
Lang, Andrew, 205
Langdon, Harry, 4
Langland, William, 64, 168, 254
Lanier, Sidney, 255
Lao-tze, 265, 288
La Rochefoucauld, duc de, 124
Las Casas, Bartolomé de, 182, 183
Lautréamont, le Comte de, 122, 139
Lavater, Johann, 179
Lawrence, D. H., 31, 57, 61, 65, 73, 74, 76, 83, 89, 108, 123, 132, 139, 141, 146-47, 210, 225, 279-83, 291
Lee, Ivy, 27

Leighton, Fred, 280
Leland, John, 161
Lenin, Nikolai, 25, 32, 42, 176
Leopardi, Giacomo, 133, 241, 251
Le Sage, Alain René, 173
Lessing, Gotthold Ephraim, 203, 273
Leucippus, 87
Lewes, George Henry, 270
Lewis, Cecil Day, 229
Lewis, Sinclair, 21, 32, 33, 211, 213
Lewis, Wyndham, 41, 61, 71, 72, 124, 126, 145, 252, 253
Lewisohn, Ludwig, 42
Leyda, Jay, 75, 265-66
Liebknecht, Karl, 35
Lippman, Walter, 45
Liu Tsung Yuan, 285-86
Livy, 159, 204, 205, 269
Lloyd, Harold, 219
Lombroso, Cesare, 234
Long, Haniel, 100, 166
Long, Huey, 42
Longfellow, Henry Wadsworth, 204
Longinus, Cassius, 251, 273
Lowell, Amy, 53
Lowell, Robert, 65, 104
Lucian, 100
Lucretius, 102, 204
Lumpkin, Grace, 211
Luther, Martin, 259, 261, 262
Lyell, Sir Charles, 105

Mackail, John, 104
MacLeish, Archibald, 132, 220
Macrobius, 88, 162
MacShane, Frank, 59-66, 101
Macy, John, 76
Magnus, Maurice, 281
Maillol, Aristide, 164
Male and Female (film), 156
Mallarmé, Stéphane, 284
Manetho, 192

Mann, Heinrich, 42
Mann, Klaus, 41
Marchbanks (Shaw's *Candida*), 32
Marchwitza, Hans, 42
Margrie, William, 40
Marie Antoinette, 3
Marlowe, Christopher, 124, 127, 130, 131, 132, 160, 254
Marinetti, Emilio, 36
Martial, 104, 204, 286
Martindale, Elsa, 60
Marx, Karl, 78, 131, 239-40, 287
Massey, Gerald, 168
Massinger, Philip, 160
Mather, Cotton, 248
McAlmon, Robert, 122, 134, 139, 141, 142, 143-46, 277
McCarthy, Mary, 239-40
McCormack, Anna O'Hara, 37
McCown, Eugene, 123
Meighan, Thomas, 156
Melville, Herman, 49, 71-73, 75-83, 129, 169, 170-71, 254, 255, 260,
    265-66
Mencken, H. L., 48
Mephistopheles, 4, 71, 95
Meynell family, 61
Michelangelo, 261
Miller, Henry, 120
Milton, John, 100, 105, 144, 159, 160, 179
Minnegerode, Meade, 76
Molina, Christoval de, 190
Monet, Claude, 169
Monroe, Harriet, 130, 139, 252
Montaigne, Michel de, 105, 263, 266
Montezuma, 123
Moore, Marianne, 130
Moorhead, Ethel, 134-36, 141, 143, 146, 277
Morris, William, 97, 269-70, 288
Mosley, Sir Osward, 41, 42
Motolinia, Fr. Toribio, 182, 188-89, 192
Mühsam, Erich, 42
Mumford, Lewis, 53, 76, 79, 287-89
Münchausen, Börries von, 18

Munson, Gorham, 135
Murray, Gilbert, 105
Musaeus, 55, 283
Mussolini, Benito, 36, 37
Myers, Gustavus, 172

Nashe, Thomas, 167
Nerval, Gérard de, 173
Neukrantz, Klaus, 36, 42
Newman, Cardinal, 50
Nicholson, Meredith, 48
Nietzsche, Friedrich, 29, 47, 70, 103, 293
Norris, Frank, 68-70, 156
North, Sir Thomas, 205
Numa Pompilius, 252

O'Casey, Sean, 275
O'Flaherty, Liam, 275
Olson, Charles, 73, 76-83
Olson, Regine, 241
O'Neill, Eugene, 131
Oppenheim, James, 44
Orellana, Francisco de, 185
Ovid, 100, 105, 162, 165, 188, 189, 191

Paracelsus, Philippus Aureolus, 100, 261-63
Parkman, Francis, 78
Parmenides, 89
Parrington, Louis Vernon, 29, 33
Pascal, Blaise, 108, 235, 263
Pater, Walter, 74, 205
Pattee, Fred Lewis, 76
Paul, Saint, 78, 126, 276, 280
Pausanias, 104, 189
Peabody sister, 78
Pearce, Charles A., 166
Péguy, Charles, 38
Pelley, William Dudley, 23-25, 27-28, 221
Pendergast, Tom, 154
Pericles, 87
Peter Martyr, 193

Petrarch, 75
Philostratus, 105, 130
Picasso, Pablo, 95
Pierpont, James, 246
Pilsudski, Józef, 37
Pindar, 166, 195
Pizarro, Gonzalo, 182
Plato, 97, 102, 163, 258, 270, 273, 285, 286, 323
Plautus, 134
Plekhanov, Georgi, 41-42, 176
Plievier, Theodor, 36, 42
Pliny the Elder, 85, 109, 181, 194, 197
Plotinus, 102, 132, 134
Plutarch, 205, 267
Poe, Edgar Allan, 6, 70, 71, 73, 75, 77, 78, 91, 285
Polybius, 269
Pope, Alexander, 52, 63, 271
Porphyry, 93, 130, 165-66, 186
Porten, Henny, 4
Pound, Ezra, 57, 61-62, 64, 73, 87, 88, 103, 105, 134, 135, 138, 251-
    53, 268-69, 272, 276, 277, 284, 285, 287, 291
Prescott, William, 100-101
Prévost, Abbé, 224
Proclus, 134
Propertius, 93, 104, 251, 252
Protesilaus, 103
Proust, Marcel, 36, 41, 125
Ptolemy, 194
Pythagoras, 184

Question Girl, The (musical), 153, 309
Quetzalcoatl, 187, 190
Quevedo, Francisco Gómez de, 104, 122, 129, 168
Quixote, Don, and/or Sancho Panza, 4-5, 56, 57, 59, 78, 113, 125,
    148, 196, 279, 291

Rabelais, François, 85, 100, 104, 156, 171
Radek, Karl, 176
Raleigh, Sir Walter, 103
Ransom, John Crowe, 250, 284
Rascoe, Burton, 31

Rasputin, Grigori, 67
Read, Sir Herbert, 63, 65, 74, 93-99, 101-2
Remarque, Erich, 17
Renan, Joseph, 37
Renn, Ludwig, 36
Reynolds, Sir Joshua, 268
Richard III, 241
Ridge, George Ross, 293
Rig Veda, 103, 130, 161, 274
Riley, James Whitcomb, 312
Rilke, Rainer Maria, 104
Rimbaud, Arthur, 228, 257, 277, 293
Roberts, Elizabeth Madox, 208
Robinson, Edward Arlington, 254
Röhm, Ernst, 27
Rolland, Romain, 35, 45
Romulus, 188
Rosenberg, Alfred, 27
Rosenfeld, Paul, 6-7, 73
Rossetti, Christina, 60, 130
Rossetti, Dante Gabriel, 60, 85
Rousseau, Jean Jacques, 3
Rozanov, Vasily, 163
Ruskin, John, 59, 60, 97, 98, 101, 136, 269
Russell, Bertrand, 35, 38
Rycaut, Sir Paul, 100

Sahagún, Bernardino de, 101, 187
Saintsbury, George, 210
Sallust, 161
Sand, George, 111
Sartre, Jean-Paul, 234-35
Saturnin, Saint, 189
Saul, 163
Savonarola, Girolamo, 56
Schiller, Johann von, 58, 175
Schopenhauer, Arthur, 241
Schultz, Sigmund, 19
Seltzer, Thomas, 131
Seneca, 87, 105, 162, 258, 275

Shakespeare, William, 57, 62, 64, 78, 83, 95-96, 108, 171, 173, 272, 276, 284
Shaw, George Bernard, 35, 41
Sherman, Stuart, 48
Sidney, Sir Philip, 106, 205
Simons, A. M., 46
Sitwell, Edith, 175
Skeat, W. W., 64, 106
Smart, Christopher, 106, 205, 254-55
Smith, Art, 23, 26-28, 221
Smith, Captain John, 247-49, 272
Smith, Robert, 231
Smith, William, 104, 168
Snow, Wilbert, 76
Socrates, 86, 87-88, 104, 120, 134, 167, 190, 250, 286
Soglow, Otto, 222
Solomon, 89, 285, 288, 289
Sophocles, 95
Southey, Robert, 264
Spargo, John, 46
Sparhawk-Jones, Elizabeth, 58
Spender, Stephen, 227
Spengler, Oswald, 38-39
Spenser, Edmund, 52, 95
Spingarn, Joel E., 7, 140, 287
Spinoza, Baruch, 102
Spirit of the Brush, The, 164
Squanto, 249
Stalin, Joseph, 176
Standish, Myles, 248
Statius, 87, 134
Steele, Sir Richard, 106
Stein, Gertrude, 35, 63, 71, 124, 144, 277
Stein, Leo, 144
Stendhal, 65
Stieglitz, Alfred, 44, 56, 76, 169, 276
Strabo, 88, 109, 194, 267
Suetonius, 204, 205
Swanson, Gloria, 156
Swift, Jonathan, 68, 100, 106, 178, 271
Swinburne, Algernon, 104, 167

340

Synge, John Millington, 275, 317

Tacitus, 64
Tagore, Rabindranath, 23
Talmud, 165
Tanguay, Eva, 154
Tate, Allen, 61, 65, 100, 104, 129, 131, 138, 250, 284, 291
Taub, Allen, 216
Taylor, Edward, 106
Temple, Shirley, 131
Tennyson, Alfred, Lord, 61, 265
Terence, 204, 264
Teresa, Saint, 163
Thales, 93, 101
Themistocles, 85
Theognis, 100
Theophrastus, 165, 168
Thompson, Francis, 246
Thoreau, Henry David, 51, 68-69, 94, 97, 101, 174, 175, 267, 293
Thucydides, 100, 267
Thyssen, Fritz, 26, 38
Tillers of the Soil (film), 4
Titus, Edward R., 146-47
Tocqueville, Alexis de, 269
Tolstoy, Leo, 48, 52, 71, 97, 98, 168-69, 269, 280, 284-86
Torquemada, Juan de, 191
Toulouse-Lautrec, Henri de, 95
Tourneur, Cyril, 128
Traherne, Thomas, 93, 106
Trollope, Anthony, 270-71
Trollope, Frances, 271
Trotsky, Leon, 223
Truman, Harry S., 154-55
Tucker, Sophie, 124
Turati, Filippo, 42
Turgenev, Ivan, 48
Twain, Mark, 15

Unamuno, Miguel de, 39

Valencia, Martin de, 188

Valéry, Paul, 63, 136, 273
Vanbrugh, Sir John, 55
Varèse, Edgar, 285
Verlaine, Paul, 95, 257-58, 284
Very, Jones, 255
Vico, Giovanni Battista, 140
Villon, François, 251
Vinci, Leonardo da, 261
Virgil, 64, 84-85, 93, 162, 179, 204, 251, 255, 273
Vogel, Joseph, 277
Vorse, Mary Heaton, 211

Walsh, Ernest, 134-38, 141, 142, 277
Walton, Izaak, 58, 64, 161, 267-69
Ward, Nathaniel, 246
Weaver, Raymond, 76, 83
Webster, John, 62, 130, 174
Wells, H. G., 35, 36, 41, 60, 61
West, Mae, 125
West, Nathanael, 73, 147
Whistler, James McNeill, 135
Whiston, William, 105
White, Gilbert, 64, 105
White, Stanford, 155-56
Whitman, Walt, 51, 71-72, 75, 79, 91, 131-32
Wilde, Oscar, 3, 66, 67, 74, 89, 245, 285, 286
Williams, William Carlos, 58, 63, 65, 73, 100-101, 139, 252, 276-78, 284, 285, 291
Wilson, Edmund, 29, 35, 36, 125
Wilson, Woodrow, 35, 46
Winslow, Edward, 247
Winthrop, John, 249
Wolfe, Humbert, 136
Wolfe, Thomas, 31
Woodberry, George, 76
Wordsworth, William, 93, 95, 96, 264
Wotton, Sir Henry, 268

Xenophon, 104, 167

Yeats, William Butler, 275

Yupanqui Pachacutec, 196

Zarathustra, 293
Zeno, 168
Zola, Emile, 5, 41, 67, 209
Zukofsky, Louis, 73, 75, 278